There
is
a
Fountain

There is a fountain filled with blood
Drawn from Immanuel's veins
And sinners plunged beneath that flood
Lose all their guilty stains.

The dying thief rejoiced to see
That fountain in his day
And there may I, though vile as he
Wash all my sins away.

—OLD PROTESTANT HYMN

There
is
a
Fountain

THE AUTOBIOGRAPHY OF A CIVIL RIGHTS LAWYER

BY

CONRAD LYNN

LAWRENCE HILL & COMPANY

Westport, Connecticut

Copyright © 1979 by Conrad J. Lynn

Library of Congress Catalog Card Number: 78-19854

ISBN 0-88208-098-9

First Edition: April 1979

1 2 3 4 5 6 7 8 9 10

Lawrence Hill & Company, Publishers, Inc.

Manufactured in the United States of America

Library of Congress C I P Data

Lynn, Conrad J
   There is a fountain.

   Includes index.
   1. Lynn, Conrad J.   2. Lawyers--United States--
Biography. I. Title.
KF373.L96A35   342'.73'085 [B]   78-19854
ISBN 0-88208-098-9

This book was produced for the publisher by
Ray Freiman & Company, Stamford, Connecticut.

In
Memory
of
Winfred Lynn

Acknowledgements

A book may be drafted in isolation but it attains publication only after major collective effort. Experiences over half a century in sensitive areas of the society, makes it difficult for the author to select those instances which may have significance for the general public.

Many cases have seemed to me as important as anything within the covers of this volume, but I must give particular acknowledgement and thanks to William Hoffman for his forthright accomplishment in bringing this recital within tolerable limits.

I wish to express my gratitude also to the publisher, Lawrence Hill, who brought long years of editorial skill into play to give some coherence to this work.

Table of Contents

AUTHOR'S FOREWORD   xi

CHAPTER 1
The Harlem Six   3

CHAPTER 2
Early Years   34

CHAPTER 3
Political Growth in College   45

CHAPTER 4
Teething at the Bar and the WPA   52

CHAPTER 5
*Political Differences
and the Spanish Civil War*   65

CHAPTER 6
On My Own   73

CHAPTER 7
Pilgrimage to Washington for Jobs   84

CHAPTER 8
*The Case Against Segregation
in the Army*   92

CHAPTER 9
*The War Ends and
We Stage the First Freedom Ride*   103

Contents

CHAPTER 10
The Fight Against McCarthyism   115

CHAPTER 11
*Albizu Campos
and the Puerto Rican Dream*   123

CHAPTER 12
The Kissing Case   141

CHAPTER 13
*Williams, the NAACP
and the Klan*   158

CHAPTER 14
A Visit to Cuba   167

CHAPTER 15
Confrontation with HUAC   177

CHAPTER 16
*Malcolm X and
the Fight Against the War*   187

CHAPTER 17
To the War Zone   196

CHAPTER 18
The Black Panthers   208

CHAPTER 19
The ZANU Guerillas   221

EPILOGUE   231

INDEX   233

Foreword

Of what value is the story of a person's life? The autobiographical exercise is a typical expression of the ego. A diary aids a mature person in recalling the joys and agonies of childhood and adolescence. But how does the experience of the individual justify publication?

The appeal of the exercise, I suppose, lies in the opportunity given to the reader to compare feelings, thoughts, and struggles with those of the auto-biographer. In the relatively placid atmosphere of middle-class, late nineteenth-century England or France such stories could be mainly appreci-ated for their evocations of pleasant family life. But the twentieth century has witnessed the collapse of most of the traditional standards of Western civilization. Anyone whose life has spanned most of this century and who has been impelled by circumstances to participate in some of its turmoil and strife may be entitled to feel that his problems, his doubts, his hesitations, and his decisions may throw some light on why events proceeded in one way and not another. Perhaps, experience may afford some clue to the pos-sibilities of the future. The disappointments of early life, if convincingly recounted, may aid a new generation in avoiding the pitfalls which bedeviled their elders and diverted them from their goals.

It is probably true that most little children in our society are suffused with ideals. They are born into homes where religious values such as love, compassion, fair dealing, patriotism, honesty, and respect for others are taught. If the family is not religious, quite often the parents are even more likely to explicitly teach the offspring the basic concepts that they are convinced hold the society together. This custom is practiced by the poor as well as the rich. Most parents hope that their children will be born into a more propitious world, a world less trouble prone, than that which they have experienced. Life has caused them to betray many of the ideals they had been taught as children, but the hope "springs eternal" that their children will grow up in an environment which will enable them to realize these ideals.

My mother and father were examples of this type. Before their marriage, both worked in the home of a wealthy Northern family, accustomed to spending its winters in a popular watering place, Augusta, Georgia. They were married in the Baptist faith. They were both encouraged to believe that if they worked hard and feared God, they could make a future for their offspring. They never wavered in that conviction.

They had formed their points of view around the turn of the century. Their employer and patron was a multimillionaire Republican. When the family moved north to Newport, Rhode Island, and then to Rockville Centre, Long Island, it remained under the benevolent eyes of the white upper class. Joseph Lynn even had the thrill, on one occasion, of meeting his idol, Teddy Roosevelt. Small wonder it was then that when my father discovered I had been converted to communism, he had the impulse to kill me. His entire emotional investment in me had gone up in the red fire of revolution. 1929 was not 1900. I sensed that the world in which I would have to make my way would be marked by the decay of the established structures in which my father had placed his faith.

Certainly, I had no idea that capitalism through one device or another would hang on so tenaciously in America. Nor did I realize that the communism I had embraced would go through the drastic changes that have characterized its development in the twentieth century. Innumerable obstacles beset the path of anyone trying to understand the course of human events. No single person has been able to comprehend all the factors that influence history. It would be hard to deny, however, that the basic ideas of Karl Marx have afforded a key to understanding the fundamental factors about which the world has been in conflict for the last one hundred and fifty years. His followers have been in conflict with each other about the meaning and application of these concepts. And his enemies, by a careful study of his predictions, have gained valuable insights on how to ward off or forestall the inevitable.

When I was a tot, the first flag I waved contained forty-six stars. Manifest Destiny was the prevailing American dogma. Hegel had conceived of History as the March of God through the World. McKinley and Theodore Roosevelt took to heart Rudyard Kipling's admonitions:

> Take up the White Man's burden—
>   Send forth the best ye breed—
> Go bind your sons to exile
>   To serve your captives' need;
> To wait in heavy harness,

On fluttered folk and wild—
Your new-caught, sullen peoples,
Half-devil and half-child.

. . . .

Take up the White Man's burden—
And reap his old reward:
The blame of those ye better,
The hate of those ye guard—
The cry of hosts ye humor
(Ah, slowly!) toward the light:—
"Why brought ye us from bondage,
Our loved Egyptian night?"

The American ruling class had no doubt that the God of Hegel stood at the head of its hosts. Its role in World War I confirmed it in this conviction. True, the beastly Bolsheviki had seized control of a backward Eurasian nation, but far less attention was paid in America to the significance of that development than in Europe and the vast colonialized regions of the earth.

It was not until 1929 that doubts began to affect our ruling plutocracy. It was only a year before this that I had begun to cast aside some of the illusions with which I entered college in 1926 as a dedicated Republican, bent on becoming a preacher of the Gospel. My motives, at the time, in switching to a prelaw major were not altogether clear to me, but my persistence in finishing law school was certainly not to be ascribed to my new friends in the Communist party.

In 1931, while I was a member of the Young Communist League, the local Party bureaucrats tried night after night to persuade me to drop out of law school and become an organizer for the Party. They tried to convince me that capitalism was on the verge of collapse and there was no future, even in a capitalist sense, for me in that profession.

But the privations of a lifetime had taught me to be very hardheaded in making judgments about my future. I listened patiently to their arguments and turned them down. The electrifying writings of Victor Serge, Friedrich Engels, Leon Trotsky, and, later, Thornstein Veblen, C. L. R. James, and Charles A. Beard, although thrilling in their ecumenical grasp and their literary pyrotechnics, seldom caused me to make a judgment that my actual situation in the world made unrealistic. One of the earliest Marxist works that I read, R. Palme Dutt's *Fascism and Social Revolution*, had convinced me that there was no inevitability about the triumph of social justice. Indeed, the totalitarian night loomed up ahead. And George Orwell had convinced me that that night could come by way of the left as well as by the right.

Yet the dream of the New Society would not down. Humankind has the capacity to overcome the cruel, greedy, and selfish interests which would imprison it in a permanent enslavement. Differing in one particular or another with most of my associates, I came ultimately to feel that my value lay in teaching the necessities for the best course of action for the inarticulate peoples with whom I was identified through the example of law cases. Those I have described here are a few of many.

Having finished law school as a revolutionary, I had no illusions that my services would be sought by the owners of property. I was able to obtain a job on WPA in order to weather the depression, and by the outset of World War II I had gained enough recognition from the forces of the left as well as among the inhabitants of the ghetto to sustain myself financially.

I depended on my individual practice and was thus able to resist the blandishments of the Establishment as well as those of the liberal and left bureaucracies. But the path I followed was not undeviating. There were times when I remained "straight" in my beliefs because an opportunity to join the Establishment was snatched away from me. Rivalries and jealousies of my left associates acted as a barrier to my becoming a member of their Establishments.

In reading of my associates and friends over the years, observers may be tempted to conclude that my friendships were, on the whole, neither deep nor longlasting. That would be a surface judgment. It would be more nearly accurate to say that the fidelity of many of my companions to our common goal was fleeting, and we parted when they listened to another siren. Bayard Rustin belonged to the Young Communist League in the 1930s. In the Socialist party convention in 1972 he helped defeat the resolution deploring the bombing of Hanoi. He has become far closer to Jack Brennan, the hardhats, and Nixon than to his erstwhile associates among the pacifists. Others who have had a similar journey are discussed in these pages. The aim is not to villify or muckrake but to show how difficult it is to pursue the North Star.

As I complete my forty-sixth year of practice, I am thrilled by the beginning of a new wave of black pride in the inner cities. The prisons, where so many of our children are receiving their basic political education, have become the source of demands that black victims of the system be represented by militant lawyers. It is refreshing to know that they do not regard me as a has-been.

Millions of words are printed each month on the doings of high society, the devious machinations of politicians, the cultural concerns of the middle class and on their sports heroes. Seldom is an attempt made to give voice to the longings, the anguish, and the desperation of the deprived. Perhaps, the preoccupation in making a livelihood among and delivering a message to these brothers and sisters may qualify me to convey something of their thoughts.

Conrad Lynn
April 1979

There
is
a
Fountain

CHAPTER 1

The Harlem Six

"How can I make you believe this?" asked author Truman Nelson in his book *The Torture of Mothers,* which was a nonfiction account of the incredible case of the Harlem Six. "This is what is blocking the long outcry in my throat," Truman Nelson continued, "impacting the anger and frustration until I become too dumb and sick with the gorge and glut of my own indigestible fury. Even keeping my voice down, even speaking to you in a whisper, my breath staggers and halts under the weight of this monstrous wrong."

Truman Nelson was right: the problem the author encounters in telling the story of the Harlem Six is precisely that it is so shocking and unbelievable. And worse. It is a story most people do not want to believe could happen.

Six black youngsters became entangled with police in the early spring of 1964. Their story is, unfortunately, not completed, since one of them is still in jail. Nevertheless, the case is valuable because it shows the measures that judicial authority will take to repress dissent and to cover its own tracks. The Harlem Six was perhaps the most complicated case of legal repression ever tried in New York City.

On April 17, 1964, some black children were on their way home from school at about 3:30 in the afternoon. At the corner of 128th Street and Lenox Avenue, a twelve-year-old girl brushed against a crate of grapefruit at the DeLuca fruit stand. Some of the fruit fell to the pavement and the children began throwing it around like baseballs.

Edward DeLuca, the proprietor, blew his whistle to attract the attention of the policeman on the beat. But unknown to Mr. DeLuca, Mayor Wagner had quietly placed his tactical-patrol police in the basements of the public buildings in the neighborhood, in anticipation of a long, hot summer. These were not policemen who walked a beat, but heavily armed specialist in riot control. A policeman had to be at least six feet tall even to be considered for the tactical patrol.

The tactical-patrol police responded to Edward DeLuca's whistle. They beat the youngsters with clubs and blackjacks, and the terrified screams of the children—all of them were twelve or younger—attracted a crowd.

The incident probably would have been ignored had it not been for two separate acts of intervention. First, a black hosiery salesman, Frank Stafford, age thirty-one and the father of two children, came out of a restaurant. "They had this kid in between the cops" Frank Stafford later testified. "So I spoke up and asked them, 'Why are you beating him like that? You all going to take him on to jail. You don't have to beat him like that.' Police jump up and start swinging on me. He put the gun on me and said, 'Get over there.' I said, 'What for?' Then one hit me on the back of the head from behind."

Frank Stafford was beaten unconscious. Then an officer took his billy club and gouged out one of Stafford's eyes.

Fecundo Acion, a forty-seven-year-old Puerto Rican seaman, tried to pull the policeman away from Frank Stafford. The policeman wheeled around and swung his billy with both hands and it caught Acion on the bridge of his nose, shattering the bone.

A cook named Herbert Paine described what he saw:

> The cops were running behind a couple of kids. They snatched at one of the kids and reached and grabbed at another. So the kids were trying to find out what was going on. So the cops asked why they went and bothered this man's fruit stand. So the kid said, "Listen, I don't know nothing about it." Then they start shaking the kid around, smashing him around. The kid said, "Wait a minute, listen, don't shake me like this. I don't know nothing about it." So the kid got mad and drop his books. Then the kid try to get away from the cop. The cop keep pulling him and smashing him around. So he hit him a couple of times with his stick. So the kid say, "Wait a minute, why are you hitting me? So listen, I'll fight you, I'll fight for my rights," he said. "I didn't do anything." All of a sudden here come more cops. And the rest of the kids they are just standing around. And the cops start smashing every kid that they see. So the kids just put up a fight, start fighting with their fists. Then this boy, this particular boy, they hit him on the head a couple times. And he got mad. He start fighting and kicking the cop and hitting with his fist. So three cops teamed up on this particular kid and just beat him down. Till he couldn't take it any more. All he could do was give in. He couldn't throw another lick. So they messed up his eyes. They were all bloody, his nose, mouth, head. And he couldn't move. Here come the rest of the kids. They were throwing garbage pails, and the

cops just pull out their sticks and keep hitting, hitting, hitting everybody they see standing in the street. So they smashed four or five kids and put them in the car. Now here come an old man walking out a stoop, and asked one cop, "Say, listen sir, what's going on out here?" The cop turn around and smash him a couple times in the head. So that were about it.

Edward DeLuca, the owner of the fruit stand, said if he had known "the cops were going to go crazy," he would never have blown his whistle. "I've been here thirty-five years," DeLuca stated, "and nothing like this ever happened."

Another businessman spoke at greater length:

In the first place, I don't have anything against a person running a business and using police to protect his property. But what really hurt me to see with my own eyes was when a policeman don't know exactly who it was who did the damage and just runs smashing anybody. It could have been me. I just got through doing a little work for a friend of mine and I was walking through the block and I saw the police just smashing anybody, just smashing anybody he thought did it. And just smashing them around and hammering them like that. My goodness, anybody with common sense could just explain himself and express himself in a way to make the police understand. Because everybody's got a sense of humor. They got to have a good sense of humor to call themselves a police and work for the state or for the city. And this police come and ask me, "Say, did you have anything to do with this fruit and vegetable stand?" And I didn't. All I would say is "No sir, I don't know anything about it." He should let me go, let me alone. But not come and hit me across the head and with his stick, busting my nose and eyes and everything, when I know nothing about it. My goodness, that's too much.

In the middle of the melee came the second intervention, from teenage members of a club, who had been training themselves in karate. They interposed themselves between the police and the children and began exhorting the crowd to fight back. Faced with an angry crowd, the police took Stafford and Acion and one of the karate students, Wallace Baker to the station house.

Frank Stafford described what happened at the station house:

About thirty-five I'd say came into the room and started beating, punching us in the jaw, in the stomach, in the chest, beating us with a padded club. It's not a blackjack but it's got leather on it and it's got big stitches on the side and it's about twelve inches long. They just beat us across the back, pull us on the floor, spit on us, call us "niggers, dogs, animals. You got what you deserve," these are the things they said to us. They call us dogs and animals when I don't see why. They call us "cop-fighters," that was the name that they used. "Cop-fighters." And every cop that come in, they holler, "Oh, you are the cop-fighters." And punch me in the chest, in the jaw, in the stomach. When they first start beating us they rest up for a little while, like went out and rested and started all over again. They took off their coats and put on their sweat sweaters and come in like they were going to a gymnasium or something to have a sparring match. There was this old man they were beating back in the street. He said his age was forty-seven years old when we got back into the station. Like they beat me they beat the elderly fellow. They throw him almost through one of the radiators. Two of them pick him up and throw him into the wall. I thought he was dead over there. And being I wouldn't fall on the floor, they grabbed me and pulled a little piece out of my neck. And all the time we were handcuffed behind our backs. They beat us up in this room a good while and an aide came from Harlem Hospital. He said to me why had they called him in 'cause there was nothing he could do. He put a bandage 'cross my eye. And then they started beating us again. But the pains I suffered I couldn't suffer any more 'cause I was already hurt. And when they started beating on me the second time I was telling them they might as well kill me.

It was nineteen hours before Stafford was taken to the hospital, and by that time it was too late to save his eye. "I have quite a few police look at me pretty hard," Stafford later testified. "But I don't have nothing to say. I keep walking down the street like I don't even see them. My lawyer he axe me to keep somebody with me at all times 'cause the police may try to mess with me again."

Wallace Baker was beaten for almost ten hours at the station house, and by the next morning he was in Harlem Hospital, unconscious, suffering from multiple skull fractures. His wrists were burned where the police had handcuffed him to a radiator, and his legs were so swollen that hospital attendants had to cut his pants off in order to remove them. The "torture of mothers" began with a phone call to Mrs. Baker: "I had to sign for Wally because they thought they had broke his neck," she said. "So I had to go to the hospital to sign for X-rays for Wallace. His neck was over one-sided. He has a patch across his lip, his face was swollen. I went in and I asked the colored cop there could I see him? He said 'Yes, go in.' The white one told me to get out, I couldn't talk to him."

The incident became known in the newspapers as "the Little Fruit Stand Riot." It would probably have been quickly forgotten had it not been for an event that took place twelve days later, on April 29, 1964. In the late afternoon of that day, Frank and Margit Sugar, Hungarian Jewish refugees who were proprietors of a secondhand clothing store on the corner of 125th Street and Fifth Avenue, were brutally attacked in their store. Mrs. Sugar was killed, the victim of thirteen knife wounds. Fortunately, her husband was saved by a team of surgeons at Harlem Hospital.

Within hours, four of the six karate club members whom the police had identified at the scene of the Little Fruit Stand Riot were rounded up for questioning. Also picked up was a neighborhood ex-convict, Robert Barnes. A general alarm went out for Wallace Baker, only recently released from Harlem Hospital. He surrendered voluntarily on May 4.

All spring the New York newspapers had been writing about a "blood brotherhood" of young black toughs who were said to have taken blood oaths to murder white people. This turned out to be a figment of the newspapers' imagination, for not a single member of the so-called blood brotherhood was ever found; but with the murder of Margit Sugar they cut loose in full cry. The worst offender was a black writer for the *New York Times,* Junius Griffin. One of his articles contained the following subheadings: "Trained in Karate and Judo"; "Offshoot Favors Violence"; "Then More Slayings"; "Police Deny Beatings"; "Hatred for the Police"; and "Police Take Precautions."

The precautions the police took were described by Police Commissioner Murphy as "wall-to-wall cops." In any case, the cacophony of the newspapers drowned out the screams of the suspects in the station houses— which were known in Harlem as the "meat grinder" and the "slaughterhouse"—where the police supposedly were reciting their constitutional rights.

The ex-convict Robert Barnes was released; later we would find out why. Altogether there were six suspects: Daniel Hamm, William Craig, Wallace Baker, Ronald Felder, Walter Thomas, and Robert Rice. The appeal by their mothers for aid fell on deaf ears. The NAACP insisted that no civil liberties

were involved, which was not the case. The chief investigator was Detective
Lieutenant Vincent Satriano. Mrs. Baker described her first meeting with
Lieutenant Satriano:

> I would never forget his face, nasty as he was that night in my house. He
> didn't ring the bell. He took his stick and just, you know, knocked on
> the door. So I said, "Come in." Look like there was about thirty of
> them, you couldn't tell. They were from the front to the back. I have
> four rooms straight through. I have a rack in the hall where you hang
> your coats. They just took the coats down, looking at the coats,
> throwing them on the floor. So I asked them what did they want? What
> was they looking for? They didn't say nothing then, just kept looking at
> the coats. So I said, "Have you got a search warrant?" This old nasty
> one I saw in the papers, he say, "No, I don't have a search warrant and
> I'm going to search anyway." Well, he did. So I asked them what they
> was looking for. They didn't say nothing. They just kept looking,
> flashing their lights. I said, "Well, I have babies back there, three
> babies, my three grandbabies." They was in the back sleeping. They
> didn't pay the babies no mind on the bed. They just picked up the
> mattress and the babies rolled on top of each other.

Less than a year later, Lieutenant Satriano was convicted of selling
counterfeit ten-dollar bills. But the evidence he produced against the defendants who became known as the Harlem Six was damaging indeed.

Not only did the NAACP turn the mothers of the Six away, so did the
Democratic clubs. Finally, in desperation they turned to the radical Progres-
sive Labor Party, which suggested they visit my office. Author Truman
Nelson wrote a flattering reconstruction of the day I first met the women:

> It is easy for me to understand how the mothers must have felt sitting
> before him for the first time, exhausted of hope, crushed in spirit,
> utterly functionless now as protectors of their children. Lynn is a small
> man, and black, and this smallness and blackness gives the effusions of
> indestructibility and fearlessness that he radiates a higher quotient of
> truth than if he were big and white and Zeus-like and out of touch. He
> has a way of topping his crescendos of attack with laughter, not bitter or
> acrid in the least, but almost joyous, exulting that his enemy, in the
> demonstration of his most hurtful power, has made himself so hurtful
> and mean that history will dismiss him as a pompous absurdity, a
> flyspeck on the rails now thrumming to the onrush of human advance.

I can well imagine that the mothers smiled there in his office for the first time since the blows had fallen on them. He is too good a lawyer to tell them he could save their boys regardless, but he did say that this case of the so-called Blood Brother murder is one pre-eminently showing the influence of dominant prejudice against a minority which is deprived of defenses; also that actual hard proof of the crime by the boys is missing, and the prosecution is depending on the existing state of prejudice to obtain conviction.

After talking with the women I realized at once that additional lawyers would be needed. My partner, an able and ambitious young woman lawyer, Gene Ann Condon, was the first to join me on the case. Gene Ann was Irish—she owned a little island off the coast of Ireland—and a real champion of the underdog. Gene Ann was blonde and attractive, a person of great honor, and her ability to think on her feet made her an excellent trial lawyer—that and an enormous capacity for hard work.

Next to join the defense team was William Kunstler, who has handled numerous controversial cases. Kunstler is an excellent attorney, a fighter. He has a phenomenal memory, is an extremely fast thinker, and projects the image of a man who *knows* his client is innocent.

I persuaded Samuel Neuberger to join the defense team. Neuberger was primarily a union lawyer—quiet, calm, scholarly—an attorney able to master thousands of pages of evidence so skillfully that even the most involved and difficult cases seem simple and easy to understand. Neuberger would be an excellent contrast to the colorful and flamboyant Kunstler.

Finally there was Mary Kaufman of Nuremberg trial fame. Mary had been the chief assistant to Brigadier General Telford Taylor, the main prosecutor of Nazi war criminals. Mary wrote many books about the famous Nuremberg trials. She was a very thorough woman, a meticulous researcher, and extremely emotional. She could rein in her emotions, however, and her closing arguments to a jury were often among the most moving I have heard.

It was an excellent defense team.

I went to the office of the clerk of the supreme court and filed notice of appearance and retainer. This notice was necessary if attorneys were to visit their clients. It was designed to prevent unscrupulous lawyers from visiting people who were in jail, collecting a fee, and then vanishing. In this case, however, I found my way blocked. A lawyer from Harlem, a political hack named George Sena who is now a criminal court judge, had filed as the representative of all six defendants. No one else was permitted to see them.

The rule in New York State for a capital case in 1964 specified that indigent defendants had to accept the lawyer the court appointed for them. The court had appointed George Sena, who would collect $2,500 from the state for each defendant. There was no doubt that the defendants were indigent, but they were convinced that if they had to accept a lawyer appointed because of political patronage, they were not likely to receive competent representation.

Phoenicia Craig, the mother of William, wrote a pleading letter to the assignment judge asking that I be allowed to represent her son. He turned her down. Motions by the other lawyers were similarly rejected. The judge said the defendants had to be protected from themselves; that the court knew better than they did what lawyers could provide the best defense. The judge added that "lunatics and minor children" had to be restrained from hurting themselves, and so too did the six defendants. I felt that the remark was racist, but typical. Too many white people view blacks as eternal children, unable even to manage the simplest affairs of daily living: black men are "boys," black women are "girls." Regardless, the judge's decision was unfair, especially since the Six could be sentenced to the electric chair.

We could have represented the defendants at our own expense, and I have often been asked why we did not. The reason was that cases of this nature can last a decade (indeed, this one did), and we did not have the financial resources necessary to sustain ourselves and at the same time provide the defendants with the all-out legal defense to which they were entitled. More important, we were not really abandoning the defendants. We were determined to make a constitutional issue of the denial of counsel of choice to indigent defendants; one that would ultimately have to be resolved by the United States Supreme Court. It was wrong that defendants whose lives were at stake had to be represented by an attorney whose only qualification was that he had important friends. Finally, we felt the law was on our side. In the 1930s the Supreme Court decided in the Scottsboro case that adequate legal representation meant counsel of the defendants' own choice. The New York courts had refused to abide by that decision. By forcing them to comply with the law, we felt we might save countless other defendants who, in the future, found themselves in situations similar to that of the Harlem Six.

Phoenicia Craig told me that her son was being beaten to force him to confess. She said the jail guards in the adolescent center in Brooklyn were stopping the elevators between floors so that they could do their job in private.

I obtained a writ of habeas corpus in Brooklyn Supreme Court from Judge

Julius Helfand. I was reasonably certain that William Craig would be found guilty, what with George Sena representing him, and I was equally certain that the defense team I had set up would win a new trial for him on appeal. But in that new trial I did not want to have to fight a signed confession. Juries place strong faith in a confession. They do not want to believe that the police in station houses in Harlem and the Deep South are often different from the helpful people—the police who direct traffic and find lost children—the police that juries (which are drawn from lists of registered voters) are most likely to encounter.

The writ of habeas corpus gave me the right to talk with William Craig. He confirmed his mother's account of the beatings and showed me bruises the size of golf balls up and down his back. I told him no matter how hard it was, no matter what the police did to him, he must not sign a confession. I hoped he was strong enough. He was nineteen, a writer of poetry and a painter, and he had become a Muslim during his imprisonment. He was six feet tall and weighed one hundred ninety poinds and always spoke with a soft, strong voice that carried the ring of truth when he said he had nothing to do with the murder of Margit Sugar.

"I want you to trust me, William," I said. "It may take a long time and you'll have to suffer, but we'll win this case." I don't know why I made this promise. Maybe it was because I knew that William Craig could not have plunged a knife into Margit Sugar.

William Craig's mother, and the other mothers, knew that the defense team was waiting to appeal what it considered would be an inevitable guilty verdict. And they knew that we felt strongly enough about the case to do it with our own funds. But the women wanted to help—they *insisted* on helping. They had no practical political experience, but they went out into the streets of Harlem. Truman Nelson described what they did: "For five straight weeks people signed up at their street meetings to help their boys. They collected money for the inevitable appeal, for they were sadly certain that the counsel assigned to their sons would enable the D.A. to get another easy conviction. Some days they collected as much as forty or fifty dollars. This showed great sympathy and interest, for the people of Harlem have to express their largesse in terms of nickels and dimes."

The trial of the Harlem Six began in March 1965. The defendants refused to talk to the lawyers who had been assigned to them; they had no faith in these attorneys. Midway through the trial William Craig stood up and denounced the judge, the district attorney, and the defense lawyers. The judge responded by committing the defendants to Bellevue Hospital for psychiatric examination. I was attending the trial whenever my own practice gave me a day off, and I felt that this was an outrage. The lives of the defendants were at stake and they had every reason to denounce what they considered to be an unfair trial.

The court was recessed while the defendants stayed in Bellevue for fifteen days. When the trial was resumed, one of their lawyers fell dead in the courtroom from acute alcoholism.

The defendants refused to take the stand in their own defense. The jury found all of them guilty of murder in the first degree. Fortunately, the Supereme Court had abolished the death penalty while the trial was in progress. The judge sentenced the Six to life imprisonment.

The case that was presented to the jury had been carefully constructed by the homicide assistants of District Attorney Frank Hogan. The circumstantial evidence heard by the jury was voluminous. The eyewitness testimony was skimpy, but it had not been shaken on cross-examination. Therefore, I remained convinced that the central issue on appeal had to be the denial of the choice of counsel.

Gene Ann Condon, William Kunstler, Samuel Neuberger, Mary Kaufman, and I submitted a brief in the appellate division of the New York Supreme Court. We lost this first appeal. New York did not want to admit that the rule set down by the U. S. Supreme Court in the *Scottsboro* decision was the law of the United States. Too much political patronage was involved and New York judges knew it.

There are two ways a person can become a judge in New York, and every New York attorney knows what they are: a judge can be appointed because he or she has rendered a service to the political machine that happens to be in power; or a person can buy the office. The cost of a judgeship in New York in 1976 was $42,000. These are arrangements that call for change, but the defense team understood them and was not discouraged by our setback on the first appeal. The defendants were disappointed, but they trusted us and were able to retain a remarkable composure.

I was convinced that at least four of the defendants were innocent. I had spent as many days as I could spare from my practice watching the feeble defense they had been provided. My belief that innocent people were in jail made me work harder, and my wife Yolanda complained about the late hours I was keeping. Working on the appeals often kept me in the office beyond midnight, but I knew this arrangement was infinitely preferable to the ones the defendants had.

I was afraid Robert Rice and Daniel Hamm might be guilty. Each had signed a confession, and I knew I was almost as impressed by that fact as the jury had been. There is something about a confession—forget how it might have been obtained—that carries great weight. Intimidation and fearsome physical force can be employed to obtain a confession, but when the punishment for murder can be electrocution there has to be a terrible reluctance to admitting the crime. With Robert Rice and Daniel Hamm I simply was not sure. I reminded myself of my visit with William Craig; I knew that different people have different levels of pain tolerance, and I decided—uneasily—that Rice and Hamm might also be innocent. In addition, it seemed too great a coincidence that all six of the accused had interposed themselves between the police and children during the Little Fruit Stand Riot. Police do not like to be challenged, and they become especially fearful and hostile when the challenge comes from people in an oppressed community. There was no doubt that the police went after these six because they had challenged their authority.

The American appeals system of justice can be maddeningly slow. The system is choked with an enormous backlog of cases, and there are inevitably delays and postponements. It was not until April 1968, four years after the murder of Mrs. Sugar, that our appeal reached the New York Court of Appeals. We had prepared our arguments with care and diligence, and my heart sank when my argument on the constitutional right to choice of counsel was received impassively by the Albany court. I argued:

> The right of counsel, as we conceive it, means the right to counsel of one's own choice. It is not the right to counsel that the court appoints, counsel that as far as the accused is concerned may be collaborating with the district attorney, counsel who is in the good graces of the prosecuting attorneys and the courts. This is not the counsel that the accused, whose life is at stake, would want to choose. The practice of the courts of assigning lawyers against the wishes of indigent clients is a practice based on property qualifications. A poor man who cannot afford to hire a lawyer for his defense against a first-degree murder charge, where the average cost would be at least five thousand dollars, is denied the counsel of his choice, but a wealthy man who can afford to pay the thousands of dollars has a much better chance of surviving. There is, in effect, a denial of the equal protection of the law, based on a class distinction.

The judges were not impressed by my argument, even though it was demonstrably the law of the land. But the court *was* concerned about the confessions. By this time there were three: Wallace Baker had confessed, but none of us took that seriously. His fractured skull had led to brain damage and he had been in a number of psychiatric institutions during the course of the appeal.

The defendants were not permitted to be present in Albany when we argued their appeal. All six mothers were there, however, sitting next to one another on a long bench, stolid and determined, their very presence a more eloquent plea for justice than any of the defense attorneys could have presented.

The arguments in Albany were long and involved, but in the end the Court of Appeals reversed the convictions of *all* the defendants because two of the confessions had been used against six people. In seeking a reversal of the original conviction we had used every argument we could muster, but we did not think this one was our most persuasive. Regardless, the court ordered the case sent back for new trials.

We were, of course, delighted for our clients—and for their mothers. These women never hesitated in their belief that their sons were innocent. The happiness of the defense counsel was tempered, however, because we were unable to carry our contention, that the denial of choice of counsel violated the Fourteenth Amendment, to the U. S. Supreme Court. We might have won an important victory for countless other defendants forced by the courts to be represented by second-rate lawyers.

The Court of Appeals ruled that Hamm and Rice should be tried separately, and that the four others should be tried together.

In four-and-a-half years the boys had grown into men. During their imprisonment they had seized opportunities to develop their minds and physical skills—with the exception of Wallace Baker.

Soon after our victory in the Court of Appeals, Bill Kunstler suggested that we reapply to the supreme court assignment judge in New York City and have ourselves appointed by the court as counsel of record. I was dubious about the proposal. I pointed out that we would have to apply to Judge Gerald Culkin, who had originally refused our request. I went along with Kunstler, however, because there was really nothing else we could do.

In January 1969 we appeared before Judge Culkin. All the defendants and their mothers were present. Kunstler presented a lengthy and persuasive argument. Finally, Judge Culkin turned his chair and faced a side wall. "These boys," he said, "wouldn't know a good lawyer from a good watermelon."

"That's a dirty, racist remark!" I shouted, jumping to my feet and glaring at Culkin. My heart was pounding and I wanted to climb over that lofty perch he sat behind.

"How would you like if I held you in contempt of court?" Culkin asked. He was angry too.

"You do that," I said. "You either do that or you apologize."

"This court finds . . ."

"Your Honor!" Bill Kunstler was striding toward the bench. I followed him, not certain if I would stop when I got there. "Your Honor," Kunstler said, "perhaps we had better take a five-minute break."

Kunstler was giving the judge a way out. He felt that if Culkin had a chance to think about what he was doing, he would back away. All the defendants were black. I was the only black lawyer in the case. Culkin had definitely made a racist remark, and it was unlikely that he would reap any benfits finding me in contempt.

As a young lawyer I overlooked many racist remarks because I believed the people did not know better. Now I cannot bring myself to make excuses for them. If people do not know better, it is their fault, not mine, and I am not going to give them the benefit of any doubt. Especially, I was not going to give Judge Culkin, who had life-and-death power over the defendants, the benefit of any doubt. I think also I have become more intolerant of racist language because I am not so vulnerable economically. It would be hard for anyone to destroy me or my family financially. But more, untold numbers of good people have for centuries worked for the achievement of a more just society, yet here, in 1969, a judge was still talking about "boys" and "watermelons."

Judge Culkin granted the five-minute recess. Bill Kunstler succeeded in calming me down, and when Culkin returned to the bench he said nothing about a contempt citation. A short time later he rejected our application to be appointed counsel for the defendants.

I wrote a letter to Presiding Judge Harold Stevens. I quoted what Culkin had said and asked that he be disciplined. Meanwhile, the *New York Times* published Culkin's picture along with his remark, and he became known as the "watermelon judge."

What occurred next was one of the most humiliating experiences of my life. When the officers of the Harlem Lawyers Association heard that Judge Culkin was under attack, they called a special meeting. They adopted a resolution backing Judge Culkin to the hilt and deploring my charge of racism. I shall never forget this degrading performance by the Negro bar in Manhattan. In addition, when the appellate division assembled to hear the charge against Judge Culkin, they completely absolved him. Robert Rice was tried in November 1970. The evidence against him was a confession and a fingerprint of his that was found at the murder scene. The lawyers assigned to him were Gussie Kleiman and Herman Postel. The only way for Robert Rice to overcome the confession was to take the stand and argue that it had been beaten out of him. This he did, and I thought he made an articulate and convincing witness. Rice was 6'1" and weighed 180 pounds. He explained that he believed the murder charge stemmed from his activities during the Little Fruit Stand Riot. Increasingly, I was beginning to believe that this could be true.

The witness who followed Robert Rice to the stand ruined the case for the defense. Gussie Kleiman called him to testify. He was a real-estate lawyer and a friend of the Rice family. At their request he had gone to the police station after the arrest to see if Robert was being physically abused. The real-estate lawyer was made to wait for hours. Then, at 2:00 A.M., he was allowed to visit Robert Rice in an upstairs room. The lawyer testified that when he walked in, Robert Rice screamed, "I did it! I did it!"

Gussie Kleiman is dead now, and that real-estate lawyer has descended into a deserved anonymity, but what they did was nothing short of criminal: Gussie Kleiman asked no further questions of the witness, and he volunteered nothing. It sounded to the jury as if Robert Rice was confessing to his own lawyer. The truth was something quite different. Robert Rice had thought that the white real-estate lawyer, a man he did not know, was the next relay of the plainclothes detectives who had been assigned to extract a confession. In his fear and exhaustion he said what he thought the new policeman wanted to hear. But the jury never learned the truth. They convicted Robert Rice, and once again he was sentenced to life imprisonment.

What happened to Daniel Hamm was hardly more inspiring. On the eve of his trial, his court-appointed lawyer persuaded him to plead guilty to three counts of manslaughter. It was the understanding of this lawyer that the sentencing judge (Judge Frederick Backer) had agreed to give Daniel Hamm *concurrent* terms. Instead, the judge handed out three *consecutive* terms, which amounted to a sentence of fifteen to thirty-five years in prison.

The trial of the remaining four defendants began in February 1971. Judge Backer presided. He had a reputation for great severity and he now sat only on murder cases. At least he was not devious: "I wish I could have them executed," he told the defense attorneys in his chambers.

Judge Backer was the most depersonalized human being I have met. He was cold and hard. He reminded me of Raskolnikov in *Crime and Punishment*.

Just before the trial began, I gained permission to represent William Craig, thanks to the courtesy of his court-assigned lawyer. This lawyer and I argued that William Craig had always wanted me as his attorney and that the current lawyer was more than willing to step aside. The judge agreed to this, but made me promise that I would not seek compensation from the state or accept money from private sources. I readily agreed to these conditions. I was dismayed by the harsh sentences given to Robert Rice and Daniel Hamm and I did not want the same thing to happen to William Craig, whom I had come to consider a friend. I also had deep respect for his mother.

William Craig had become an accomplished artist and poet during his years in prison, and he and I had enjoyed many warm conversations. He had grown to a height of 6'1", and his face had the gaunt and dignified look of an Abraham Lincoln.

During their second trial the defendants all had lawyers with whom they could communicate, even though the court had assigned them. The lawyers were young, agressive, products of the civil-rights revolution of the 1960s. The only holdover from the past was Gussie Kleiman, who had wangled the assignment for Wallace Baker. Baker was *non compos mentis* but not violent. Since he showed no hostility to Gussie Kleiman, his friends and the other defendants—Ronald Felder, Walter Thomas, William Craig—did not object.

Just before the trial began, the New York State legislature introduced an experiment for jury selection. In the past the lawyers for each side selected the jury. Now the judge alone was empowered to make the selection. Judge Backer exercised his authority with dispatch. The defense attorneys objected to this new procedure on constitutional grounds, but Backer brushed our objections aside and the jury was selected in one afternoon.

The prosecution's case closely followed the pattern of the earlier trials. Its chief witness was Robert Barnes, the ex-convict who claimed to be a friend of the defendants. Barnes was 5'7" and stocky, a fast-talking street hustler who seemed unable to look anyone in the eye, including the district attorney. Barnes testified that at 3:30 P.M., on April 29, 1964, he met with five of the others in a hallway on West 129th Street, where they made a plan to rob and kill the Sugars in their store. This seemed preposterous to me. I knew the defendants and I could not believe they had committed this murder, much less that they had plotted it in advance. But there was Robert Barnes, saying that not only had the murder been committed, but it was premeditated.

Barnes testified that he did not take part in the killing but he had agreed to meet the group afterward, in Robert Rice's apartment. Barnes further testified that this meeting took place and that Robert Rice described how the Sugars had been stabbed.

The only eyewitness at the murder scene was Ollie Roe, a seventeen-year-old black who worked as a delivery boy in the drugstore next to the Sugars' clothing store. Ollie Roe testified that just before 5:00 P.M. he heard a thump against the wall of the drugstore and that his boss told him to go out and investigate. When he looked in the store, he said he saw a number of black youngsters moving about around the body of Margit Sugar. Some of these youngsters he identified as the defendants. He said that he was frightened and had run and hid in the basement.

I did not believe the defendants were guilty, which meant that the witnesses were either lying or mistaken—or that I was mistaken. With younger witnesses like Ollie Roe, my strategy on cross-examination was to be friendly and try to win their confidence, and then catch them in a slip. I believe that being tough with young witnesses often alienates a jury. A young witness can break into tears and the defense attorney can be made to look like an ogre. I felt sad about some of these young witnesses. If they were lying, and I believed that they were, it meant they had not been able even to reach adulthood without being corrupted. With witnesses like Robert Barnes, the cross-examination was much easier. There was no need to go easy on him.

Except for that of Robert Barnes and Ollie Roe, the rest of the testimony and evidence was circumstantial. Altogether, the prosecution called thirty-nine witnesses. The cumulative effect was overwhelming.

The most damaging evidence against William Craig, other than the testimony of Ollie Roe, was the identification of a fingerprint, alleged to be his, on the outside of the door of the Sugers' shop. To me it was obvious that if the case was being fabricated by the district attorney, it would take little persuasion to convince an "expert" that a fingerprint belonged to a certain person. However, I hired an independent fingerprint expert and he told me that the print did indeed belong to William Craig. I asked William about the print but he could not explain it.

"Were you ever in that store?" I asked.

"I don't know. I honestly don't remember."

"It's important."

"Mr. Lynn, I really don't know. I'd like to say I was, but I just don't know."

"The store's in your neighborhood, isn't it?"

"Yes."

"Did you have anything to do with the murder of Mrs. Sugar?"

"Honest, Mr. Lynn, I didn't."

"Then you must have been in that store some other time."

"I must have been. I just don't remember it."

Wallace Baker was not even competent to stand trial. He paid no attention to what was going on. He drew figures in the air with his fingers and sang quietly to himself. Judge Backer denied every motion Gussie Kleiman made to have him examined by a court-appointed psychiatrist.

When the prosecution concluded its case, three of the four defendants said they wanted to testify in their own behalf. I thought this was a hopeful sign. Most people who are innocent want to testify. No matter how unjustly they have been treated in the past, they have an almost childlike belief that a jury will believe the truth. And people who are telling the truth have an advantage over those who are not—they cannot be caught in contradictions.

The three defendants all testified that they had not been at the murder scene on April 29, 1964, and that they all had alibis as to their whereabouts. I thought all of them were extremely effective. Walter Thomas had acquired a reputation for being a jailhouse lawyer—an inmate who helped other inmates prepare appeals—and he was crisply articulate. Ronald Felder, during the seven years he had been in prison, had concentrated on the study of existentialist philosophers, and his mind was remarkably acute. William Craig, the artist, displayed a quiet dignity and candor.

The mothers of the defendants never missed a day of the trial, and their eyes shone with pride as their sons proclaimed their innocence. I was proud too. Prison had not broken these young men; it had made them stronger.

Robert Lehner, the original prosecutor of the Harlem Six, conducted the cross-examination. He asked William Craig a long and complicated question which, paraphrased, went as follows: "Did you on the night of August 10, 1964, walk along St. Nicholas Avenue in Harlem with a bunch of other boys and did you not see another boy in your group slip up behind a white girl who was walking with a Negro and stab her in her heart and as she lay dying on the ground did you not walk up and open the Koran and intone some verses over her?"

"No!" William Craig's voice was an explosion in the courtroom, and I was as angry as he was. I vehemently objected to the question on the ground that nothing of the sort had ever even been suggested. I asked that the question be stricken from the record. Judge Backer overruled my objection on the ground that William Craig had already answered the question.

Only at this time did I become absolutely convinced that the entire Harlem Six prosecution was a political vendetta being conducted by the police and the district attorney's office. It was a conclusion that seemed incredible, but nothing else made sense. Robert Lehner had a very strong case; it was not necessary for him to invent an incident to secure a conviction. In 1965 he had, after all, secured the conviction of all six for first-degree murder. In the second trial of Robert Rice he had secured a murder conviction. And Daniel Hamm had been given a long sentence. With his question to Craig, Lehner had pulled a despicable trick. By mentioning the Koran, he was trying to stir up all the latent religious antagonisms associated with Moslems and Jewish people: there was the conflict between Arabs (Moslems) and Israel; Judge Backer was Jewish; five of the jurors were Jewish; most important of all, Margit Sugar had been Jewish.

There was still another insidious level to Lehner's question. He had spoken about a white woman being stabbed to death by a black for no apparent reason. The white woman, according to Lehner, had been walking with a black. Such a question was certain to arouse whatever racial prejudices were harbored by both the black and white jurors. Moreover, the Black Muslims had reputations as political desperadoes.

A prosecutor is supposed to represent the people, and his purpose is to see that justice is done, which is presumed to be what the people want. By asking the kind of question he did, however, Lehner showed that he was interested not in justice but in a conviction.

The defense attorneys called witnesses to corroborate their clients' alibis. Then came the final arguments. This case would be determined by which side the jury believed, so each of the defense attorneys hammered hard at contradictions in the prosecution's case.

Before making a summation I do not take notes. I try to sit alone or go for long walks and let the entire case become part of me. The summation is very important—if the last thing the jury hears before rendering a decision—
. .and I have worked very hard making myself proficient in this area of trying cases. Here is how I concluded this particular summation, a summation I felt was accurate—just how accurate I would not find out until much later:

> We have the reason on the part of the police. These were marked black men and you can be sure in the kind of seething cauldron that was Harlem in the summer—in the late spring of 1964, just before the great Harlem Riot—that the police would mark these boys as people who

must be eliminated if they were going to maintain and enforce what they conceive to be law and order in 1964. So, when this murder happened, there was no problem on the part of the police finding or determining who should be charged with the responsibility for the crime. They just went back to those activists in the Little Fruit Stand Riot and they picked them up, and, through this complex of testimony you have heard, they were charged with the murder. . . .

Robert Lehner talked to the jury for five hours. Judge Backer's instructions were fair. Then came the wait—and there is nothing more suspenseful than waiting for a jury that is deliberating a first-degree murder case. The defendants were calm, which is often a sign of innocence. The calm means they are confident that a jury will see that they have been telling the truth. Guilty people are almost inevitably nervous.

Two hours went by. The defense case was definitely not as strong as I would have liked it to be, so these two I considered to be the most important hours of deliberation: if the jury has not returned with a verdict within two hours, there is an excellent chance they will be deadlocked.

I tried not to think about the case. It was too hard on the nerves, especially in a case where I was so emotionally involved, to become party to the endless speculation that takes place while the jury deliberates.

The jury received the case in the early afternoon of April 18, 1971. They deliberated all that day, and the next day (they asked for portions of the testimony), and the day after that, and the day after that. I could not sleep at night. I had worked for almost three months without pay, I believed in the defendants, and I knew how great the disappointment would be if they were found guilty. The defendants, even though their futures were at stake, were more composed than the lawyers. They were innocent and they believed the jury would so rule.

On the fifth day, the foreman of the jury announced that they were hopelessly deadlocked. Judge Backer asked them to try again. The foreman said it would accomplish no good, and Judge Backer declared a mistrial.

The first story told to me about the deadlock was that on the very first day of deliberation, a short black juror, a clerk by profession, placed his foot on the threshold of the jury room and declared, "You can go on talking about this case as long as you want to. I don't believe they're guilty. I want you to know now that I'll never vote for conviction."

I choose to believe this account because in my experience I have noticed that a black man or woman may go along for years being obsequious and fitting the image that is expected. Then they dig in and strike a blow to justify their existence as human beings. The clerk's name was Gordon. If he was indeed the person who held out for acquittal—and it is known that the jury voted eleven to one for conviction—our system of justice owes him a great favor.

By another account it was really a white man, O'Brien, who hung the jury, and this certainly could be true. If so, American justice owes O'Brien a favor.

The hung jury gave the case a new dimension. People who had assumed the defendants to be guilty began to rethink their positions. Radio, television, and newspapers became more open to our point of view. We dared to move for bail for the defendants. It was denied and we appealed to the appellate division.

Judge Backer announced that he was appointing me as state-assigned counsel for William Craig, which meant that I would be paid for any work I did in the future. But he denied our motion to dismiss the case on the ground of double jeopardy. We expected this denial.

The judge selected for the next trial was Joseph A. Martinis. He granted Bill Kunstler's application for assignment to Walter Thomas. By September 1971, Lewis Steel, a top trial lawyer, who has represented Hurricane Carter, was assigned to Wallace Baker. At the same time, Ed Leopold, wealthy and scholarly, was appointed to represent Ronald Felder.

The statute allowing the judge to pick the jury had been repealed by this time. It was not an easy task to find jurors who had not formed an opinion about the case, however, because Manhattan is a politically sophisticated county and the people take pride in being well informed. Juror after juror was dismissed. Some of them were dismissed, not because they knew about the Harlem Six case, but because they knew about Bill Kunstler from his work on the Chicago Seven trial. We were looking for a certain type of juror: we wanted the juror to be young, because many older people are afraid that what happened to Mrs. Sugar will happen to them; and we wanted the juror to be intelligent because of the complicated nature of the defense.

One juror stands out in my mind. He was a black taxi driver and he asked for a private conference at the bench. The lawyers bunched around him as he spoke to Judge Martinis: "Judge, I don't think I can be altogether fair in this case."

"Why can't you?"

"Because there are some things that are not being brought out."

"What is not being brought out? Speak up! You don't have to hold anything back!"

The cab driver looked at me. "May I speak to him first?" he asked.

"No, you may not. I want to hear whatever is said."

The cab driver summoned his courage. "Ain't you the judge," he asked, "whose son killed five people in his automobile?"

The judge's mouth fell open and a flicker of panic showed in his eyes. There was really nothing he could say. His son, a heavy drinker, had indeed smashed up a car on the freeway, and five people had died. When the son escaped without a prison sentence, there was talk of corruption. Later the son was involved in another serious accident that was caused by drinking.

The cab driver decided to go all the way: "You get your son off without a trial, and now you're going to sit in judgment of these four black men?"

I thought for a moment that the cab driver was going to spit on the floor. Instead he spun on his heel and walked out of the courtroom. The silence of the lawyers was a judgment of the judge. Martinis was a product of the Tammany machine, and I felt he had been selected because District Attorney Hogan wanted a conviction. Hogan was a product of that same machine, and both men had reputations for going along with what the machine wanted. The machine did not want it proved that innocent defendants had spent more than seven years in prison, and Hogan did not intend it to be known that his office had fabricated evidence.

The jury selection took three weeks. Both the jury selection and the trial were held in Manhattan Supreme Court at 100 Centre Street. The courtroom was huge: it seated five hundred people, and each day of the trial it was packed.

Robert Lehner again handled the prosecution, and once more his principal witnesses were Robert Barnes and Ollie Roe. They were buttressed by fingerprint and medical experts, police detectives, and various denizens of the street world who helped fill in certain pieces of the mosaic. On this occasion, however, the witnesses went through a far more grueling cross-examination than had occurred in the previous trials. The experience of Robert Barnes was typical. He had admitted during the other trials that he had run afoul of the law in a few minor instances. This time, however, he was questioned about rape.

"Objection!" Robert Lehner was on his feet. "Your Honor, there is no court record to substantiate this charge!"

"That's true," I said. "And that's the heart of this case."

At this point the jury foreman asked if he could speak with the judge and the lawyers in private. It was an unusual request but the judge granted it. The foreman revealed that he knew the name of the woman who had been raped. She was the wife of a historian at Columbia University. Lehner demanded that the foreman be removed from the jury, and defense counsel objected. The judge took the matter under advisement. At this point the trial was five weeks old.

The strangest aspect of this part of the trial was the disappearance from criminal-court records of any reference to Barnes's arrest on the rape charge. Lehner was required by law—under the *Rosario* rule—to give us any information he possessed that might be favorable to the defense. Such material could go a long way toward explaining why Barnes was so cooperative with the prosecution. The fact was that he had never been tried on the rape charge—a charge of which he was guilty, according to our sources—but he could still be brought to trial. If Barnes was guilty, the district attorney had a halter on him. None of us suspected that the truth was even more sinister.

In theory, the *Rosario* rule is valuable because it helps assure fairer trials. The prosecution almost always has more resources at its command than the defense has, and the *Rosario* rule requires prosecutors to share their information. It has been my experience, however, that too few prosecutors abide by *Rosario*.

Judge Martinis allowed the foreman to remain on the jury , and we felt it was an important victory. In fact, Bill Kunstler and I had told the judge that we would resign from the defense team if the foreman were removed. This would have caused headlines and probably an investigation by newspapers that just might have revealed why Robert Barnes had no record for being arrested for rape. I felt the judge and prosecutor would prefer to let the foreman remain on the jury than open up that potentially grubby can of worms.

One of the stickiest aspects of this trial was how to explain William Craig's fingerprint on the door of the Sugars' store. I searched through the records of the testimony by experts and discovered that, in private, one of them had said the print could have been placed on the door two or three weeks before the murder.

The defendants did not testify during this trial. The other defense lawyers thought I had been reckless in the previous trial by letting them take the stand. Instead, we called witnesses to rebut testimony that was favorable to the prosecution. One such prosecution witness said he was forty years old, although he looked to be at least seventy-five. He said he was a friend of Robert Barnes, and that Barnes had told him he knew all about the Sugar murder case. The defense attorneys, unfortunately, missed the nuances of this testimony. This witness began shaking on the stand.

"Do you need a heroin fix?" Bill Kunstler asked.

The man did not answer. His trembling became more pronounced and I thought he might pass out and die right there.

"Well," Kunstler said, "is that what you need? Do you need heroin?"

"Yes," the man gasped. "Yes."

The man was hurried off the stand by Robert Lehner and, we presumed, given just such a fix, because when he returned to the courtroom he was at least able to control the terrible shaking. If Lehner did indeed give the man a heroin fix, he was committing a Class B felony, which carried a fifteen- to twenty-five-year prison term. It was that kind of trial.

The trial came to an end after more than three months. Lehner once again claimed that the defendants were part of a Muslim gang that murdered white people indiscriminately. Each of the defense attorneys summed up the case in exhaustive detail. Judge Martinis charged the jury, and once again it was time for that awful wait.

This time I felt we had a good chance. I thought we had a fine jury, one that had been chosen with the utmost care. At best, I told myself, the jury would acquit. At worst, they would be deadlocked.

The jury took three days, and then they told the judge they were hopelessly deadlocked. This time it was seven to five for acquittal. Martinis declared a mistrial.

The defense lawyers asked for bail and Judge Martinis set it at $75,000 for each defendant.

"There might just as well be no bail," I told the judge.

"Well, that's not the court's problem," said Judge Martinis.

There was no possibility of raising that amount of money. Four innocent men, already imprisoned almost eight years, would have to wait a little longer. We immediately filed an appeal seeking a reduction of bail.

Bail is used both as a form of preventive detention and as ransom— preventive detention because it is implied that the person may commit another crime; and ransom because the person is held against his or her will unless money is paid. Bail is effective only against the poor and middle class, because the rich can always raise the necessary funds. Our system of law carries a presumption of innocence; yet if that presumption is to be effective, people should not be held in jail until they are convicted. In this case the bail was particularly unfair because the defendants had been held for almost eight years, and two consecutive juries had been unable to convict. There are, unquestionably, a few instances where dangerous people should be held without bail, but these instances are exceptions.

Often, the bail system is corrupt. In Rockland County, New York, for example, where I live, there are 293,000 people and one bail bondsman. He has become a multimillionaire. A bail bondsman in Rockland County has to be licensed, and this man is the only person the county fathers have seen fit to license. Thus, one person out of 293,000 has the power to determine whether people who are allowed bail are given their freedom.

I was depressed the day I argued for bail. I had been on the case almost since its beginning; I had come to look on the defendants the way I did my own son, yet I was still unable to win their release. I walked out of the courtroom and across the street and down into the Independent subway station at Canal Street.

I was standing on the platform waiting for the train when a white man approached me. I recognized him when he identified himself as Herman Joseph. He had worked with a group that had raised defense funds for the original Harlem Six.

The train arrived and he sat next to me. "Conrad," he said, "there is something I have to tell you. It's been on my mind for a long time. Do you remember Ollie Roe, the drugstore delivery boy?"

Of course I remembered Ollie Roe. His eyewitness testimony was the main reason six people were still in jail. I did not want to talk about Ollie Roe.

"Well," said Herman Joseph, his voice almost a whisper, "Ollie Roe was a drug addict. I used to run a detoxification unit and I know. The D. A.'s office sent him to me. Ollie told me that on the night of the Sugar murder he was taken to a precinct house and asked to look through a glass and identify anyone he had seen in the store around the time of the murder. The only person he told me he recognized was Robert Barnes."

I told myself to relax. For the first time in this long case, hope was surging through my veins—but I had to be calm. What I had just heard was incredible, something straight out of one of the more obvious Perry Mason shows. I looked at Herman Joseph and waited for him to tell me it was a joke. But he wasn't smiling.

"Ollie Roe was afraid," Herman Joseph continued. "He was afraid they'd lock him up because of the drugs. That's why he lied."

My mind was racing back over the eight years of the case. Mysterious pieces of the puzzle clicked into place. What Herman Joseph said had to be true; it made too much sense not to be true. One of the killers had been the prosecution's chief witness! The eyewitness, Ollie Roe, had gone along with the concocted version for fear of going to jail.

"You mean," I said, "you've known this all these years and you've never told anyone?"

"There was a doctor-patient relationship."

"Are you a doctor?"

"No. But it's the same thing."

"The hell it is!"

Herman Joseph stood up. "I tried to help you," he said. "I felt bad about what I knew, and I tried to be of help. But I don't know you. If you repeat what I said, I'll deny it. I'll deny I even know you."

I tried to call the other lawyers the minute I reached a pay phone. Bill Kunstler was already on his way out of town. Ed Leopold was in court on another case. Lewis Steel was the only one available. I told him what I had learned. He said he wanted to interview Herman Joseph, and I said the man would refuse to talk. But Steel said he might not. He might talk if he felt it was off the record.

"Off the record?" I asked.

"Yeah," said Lewis Steel. "Off the record but on the tape recorder I intend to have hidden."

It took two days to track down Herman Joseph. We found him in his office at 80 Lafayette Street. Joseph was willing to talk—off the record. I could tell that his conscience was bothering him, and it should have been. He admitted that Ollie Roe had told him the only person he had been able to identify at the murder scene was Robert Barnes. I felt that Joseph was attempting to unburden his conscience in the hope that the defense attorneys, once in possession of the truth, would be able to win the release of the defendants. But Joseph was not willing to go the last mile and actually testify. I felt he was afraid he might be prosecuted for withholding evidence, and also that he feared retaliation from the police or district attorney.

Herman Joseph panicked when we told him we had the conversation on tape. He called Barbara Lamont, a capable black newscaster for WNEW–TV. He asked if she could arrange for him to meet with Judge Martinis, and Barbara asked why. He told her what he had told me and Lewis Steel, and she immediately arranged for the interview.

It was unethical for Judge Martinis to see or talk to anyone about evidence in a case without first informing the lawyers on both sides. I do not know whether he contacted the district attorney's office; I do know that he did not tell any of the defense lawyers. But Judge Martinis did see Herman on March 6, 1972.

The defense lawyers met with Robert Lehner on March 7, and we told him about the new evidence. Steel promised to deliver a copy of the tape recording.

On March 8 the defense lawyers met with Judge Martinis. We were not aware that he had already spoken with Herman Joseph, nor did he tell us about the meeting.

On March 13 we learned of another twist this strange case had taken. Judge Martinis had instructed his secretary to read Ollie Roe's testimony to Herman Joseph. "Is that what you meant to say to Lynn?" Herman Joseph was asked.

"Yes," said Joseph. "That's what I intended to say."

Two days later, on March 15, Bill Kunstler served notice of a motion asking for an evidentiary hearing to determine if the new information divulged by Herman Joseph required dismissal of the indictments. Kunstler also insisted on a meaningful reduction of bail.

Argument on Kunstler's motion was set for March 22. When that day arrived, friends and sympathizers of the Harlem Six were in an uproar. They sensed there was skullduggery in the judicial establishment. By 9:00 A.M. the street in front of 100 Centre Street, site of the Tombs and the criminal courts, was already filled, and extra police were called out to handle the crowd.

I managed to wedge myself into the packed courtroom. Many whites who had come early were occupying seats that blacks felt they should have had. People pushed one another, and angry words were exchanged. Wallace Baker's mother stood up and delivered a wonderful little speech. She told the black people that the supporters of her son should draw no color line. She pointed out that many whites had stood by her son when Harlem itself had not yet rallied to his aid. Her speech helped quiet the courtroom, and I went over and congratulated her.

Another problem arose when Judge Martinis refused to come out of his chambers. He said he felt threatened by the crowd and that he would not preside until the room was cleared. The court attendants were not about to tackle the angry spectators, so the case, it seemed, had come to a standstill. Finally, Judge Martinis said that he would hear the motions in the afternoon if the defense lawyers could convince the crowd to leave. Because I had been on the case the longest, and because most of the crowd trusted me, I was appointed by the other lawyers to ask the crowd to leave. And they did leave.

The afternoon hearing was set for two o'clock, and that was when the spectators returned. These people were familiar with the long history of the Harlem Six case, and it was as if by their very presence they believed justice would be done.

Judge Martinis once again refused to come out, and the lawyers went to his chambers to talk with him. Before anything could be said we heard the sound of wood cracking. The crowd had shoved the guards aside and was smashing the locks on the courtroom door. The guards did not draw their guns. There would have been a massacre if they had.

Judge Martinis was shaking with fright. He said he was not going to come out, and he adjourned the hearing until March 29.

I believed that on March 29 a reasonable bail would be set. I spent the rest of the week asking the supporters of the Harlem Six not to disrupt the next hearing. Bill Kunstler, Lewis Steel, and I went on radio and television to discuss the new evidence and to ask people to be calm.

The people were calm, and on March 29 we gave our arguments to dismiss the indictments or, alternatively, to grant reasonable bail. Robert Lehner opposed us bitterly, and once again I found myself musing about the nature of people who spend their lives trying to keep other people in prison. I did not even try to tell myself that he was just doing his job, because I would not have believed it.

When all the arguments had been made, Judge Martinis said he was reserving decision.

In the middle of April 1972, the bail was lowered to $5,000 for each of the defendants, except for Wallace Baker. Lehner insisted that a charge of assault was still pending against him from the Little Fruit Stand Riot. His bail was set at $10,000. Finally, just before the eighth anniversary of the jailing of the Harlem Six, four of the defendants walked out of the Tombs and were greeted with a tumultuous reception. The people who first hugged them were their mothers. Mrs. Rice and Mrs. Hamm were also there.

Judge Martinis had still not ruled on whether there should be a new trial. Instead, he called for another hearing on the evidence. I pointed out that it was highly unlikely the state could ever obtain a conviction, that the state had already admitted spending $3.5 million attempting to convict the defendants, and that another trial would only prolong this injustice.

The first witness called at the new evidentiary hearing was Herman Joseph. He admitted that he had talked to Barbara Lamont and Civil Court Judge Martin Stecher about his secret meeting with Judge Martinis. He admitted that Ollie Roe had talked to him privately about his testimony. He also admitted that he had talked to me. But he denied, just as he promised he would, he had said that Ollie Roe had told him that Robert Barnes was the only person he could identify at the Sugars' store.

Barbara Lamont, Judge Stecher, and Lewis Steel all took the stand and supported the information I had received from Herman Joseph. Judge Martinis, to our disbelief, ordered another trial. I believed that he was hoping the defense lawyers would make a deal with the prosecution; that there could be some face-saving before the new trial, such as our agreeing to plead our clients guilty to a lesser charge in exchange for a sentence of the time they had already served. I was in no mood to make such a deal. I wanted to expose the whole mess. But I was not the one who would have to go to trial, and therefore the defendants would be the ones who must decide about any deal.

The campaign to obtain unconditional release for the four defendants reached unprecedented heights. WPBS–TV in New York City ran a special program on the case. Lacey Fosburgh of the *New York Times* appeared on the show and urged that the case be dropped. William van den Heuvel, chairman of the board of correction for the city, demanded that the district attorney stop prosecution. Truman Nelson appeared on the program, and so did the defense lawyers.

Frank Hogan, contacted the next day, said he intended to go ahead with a new trial. It was at this point that Robert Barnes dropped a bomb.

From Clinton Prison, Barnes wrote a letter to the *Amsterdam News*. He said that he had lied in his testimony, but was now willing to meet with defense attorneys and tell the truth.

Bill Kunstler caught the next plane upstate to visit Barnes. He obtained a thirty-nine-page affidavit from Barnes, sworn to in front of the deputy warden, in which Barnes recounted in detail how assistant district attorneys, detectives, policemen, and investigators had coached him to tell his story. He also revealed that he had been promised immunity from prosecution.

Kunstler obtained this statement on July 3, 1972. On July 5 he obtained another sworn statement which gave even more details of the frame-up. On July 8 Barnes was taken from Clinton Prison and the authorities would not reveal where he was being held.

The arrogance of the prosecution! They had no case and they knew it. All they could hope to do was save some people who deserved to be prosecuted for sending innocent defendants to jail. The defense lawyers introduced the sworn testimony of Barnes into the court record and released the news to the press.

The prosecution announced that it was going ahead with the new trial and that Barnes, in a telephone conversation, had retracted the statements he had made to Kunstler.

The defense was fed up with Judge Martinis. He had the authority to dismiss the indictments and he refused to do it. We waited until he was away on vacation in August and then went to Judge Sidney Fine with our motions to dismiss based on Robert Barnes's affidavit. In early September, Fine denied our motions. We went to Federal Court and there, in December 1972, Judge Brieant proved to be just as intransigent as his counterparts on the state bench. Brieant denied our motions and ordered still another hearing on the issues.

I believe the greatest fear the prosecution had was that its role in the frame-up would be exposed and that careers would be ruined. I also thought they were afraid that the defendants would sue the state for false arrest and imprisonment.

On another front, Gene Ann Condon had been working tirelessly for the release of Daniel Hamm. The new evidence we had uncovered would weigh heavily in Hamm's favor. He had been convicted chiefly on the basis of his confession. The state parole board assured Gene Ann that Hamm would be freed on November 14, 1972. On November 13, Gene Ann was told that the provisional notice of parole she had received was revoked.

A few days later I learned what had happened. I ran into Assistant District Attorney Tannenbaum in a corridor of the courthouse. I knew he had been active in Hogan's office, trying to negotiate a plea of guilty from the defendants in exchange for a lesser prison sentence. The plea of guilty, of course, would stop the defendants from suing the state and would effectively quash any claims that they were victims of a frame-up.

"Why the change on Hamm's parole?" I asked.

"Conrad! You know the D. A. has nothing to do with parole."

"I know just the opposite. Why was the parole revoked?"

"Conrad . . . we're friends."

"We're not friends. Just give it to me straight."

"Conrad . . ."

Tannenbaum was trying to talk to me in lawyerese, and I was in no mood for it. The idea was for Tannenbaum to tell me what the district attorney's office wanted without actually spelling it out.

"You wrote a letter," I said, "and asked them to hold Hamm. That's it, right?"

"Would we interfere with a man's parole? Would we stick our noses into an area where the law says we don't belong?"

"Tannenbaum, I want to know what you're after."

"Assuming we were involved with Hamm's parole, and of course we weren't because that would be a breach of ethics, but assuming we were, then it would be a fair assumption on your part that we wanted a package that would include all the defendants."

"You wrote a letter to the parole board."

"Conrad. What can I say about these accusations?"

"You can call me Mr. Lynn. And I don't care what you do with the accusations. If you make this case go to another trial, if you make all these people suffer again, I promise you that heads will roll. I give you my most solemn promise on that."

"Conrad . . ."

"Mr. Lynn!"

"Okay." Tannenbaum's voice changed. "We can still discuss this matter. The D. A. wants to discuss it—not just about Hamm, but about the others too."

It was clear: any negotiations with the four defendants had to be part of a package with the two who were already convicted.

The defense attorneys talked the matter over with the four defendants. We explained that we felt they had a strong case and would most surely win. On the other hand, their lives were at stake, and anything could happen in a court of law. We said that all other charges would be dropped against them if they pleaded guilty to manslaughter, and their sentences would be the time already served. We also pointed out that a new trial presented the opportunity to expose what we felt was a monstrous frame-up, and that it was the prosecution that was on the defensive and desperately wanting some sort, any sort, of guilty plea.

The defendants wanted to think it over, and we met with them again three days later. They were quiet and very serious. They said they wanted the matter over and done with and out of their lives. They told us to go ahead with plea bargaining, but to be sure Hamm and Rice were part of any deal that was made.

That night my eyes filled with tears and I could not sleep. I knew the Harlem Four still considered themselves the Harlem Six and that the cynical

Tannenbaum had been right when he assumed the Four would not make a deal without the other two.

The district attorney's office could not have been more pleased with the arrangement. We asked about Hamm and Rice and were told there would be no objections to their release. To the defense attorneys that meant Hamm and Rice would soon be out of prison. It was a mistake we should not have made. The four pleaded guilty to manslaughter and were sentenced to the time they had already served. They were freed from all future prosecution for the murder of Margit Sugar. But Hamm and Rice were not released.

William Kunstler worked in Robert Rice's behalf, and Gene Ann Condon remained as attorney for Daniel Hamm. On July 17, 1973, Kunstler was able to report to Robert Rice the first good news that the young man had heard in years. A federal judge, Harold S. Tyler, had ruled that Rice was entitled to a new trial. He said there was evidence to indicate that torture had been used to extract the confession, that Rice's fingerprint had been faked, and that the testimony of Robert Barnes had been perjured.

Daniel Hamm was released from prison in the summer of 1974. When he stepped through the gates he was greeted by all six of the mothers and by the four who had already been freed.

Because of legal maneuvering, Robert Rice's new trial has still not been held. But he has a good lawyer in William Kunstler, and a strong case, and I am optimistic about its outcome. Of course, the Harlem Six case will not be over for any of us until Robert Rice is free and we all gather for the last time at the prison gate to welcome him back among us.

It was a sordid case and could have wrecked the lives of six promising young men. There was ample evidence that the real criminals were the ones who did the prosecuting.

But the case did not wreck the lives of the Six. They came away from it stronger than before. Ronald Felder went to college. William Craig became a professional painter and writer. Walter Thomas was reunited with his wife and young son and works for an architectural firm. Daniel Hamm also went to college. Even poor Wallace Baker made the most of his gifts: he is a community street worker in Harlem.

CHAPTER 2

Early Years

Poppa's early years in Augusta, Georgia, must have been pleasant—he was always talking about them. There, he had met Nellie Irving and they married in 1904. In the summer of 1906 Nellie Lynn bore her first child, Winfred William.

That same year the little family, which included Nellie's mother, Sophie Irving, followed their employers, the Belmonts, from Augusta to Newport, Rhode Island. I was born in the new home on November 4, 1908.

Our name for grandma was "Nanny," and she became convinced that I was destined to be a preacher before I was hardly able to walk. She never tired of telling me of the time when I was two years old and mother had taken me to a revival meeting near the seashore. The biting wind whipped through the somewhat threadbare blanket mother had wrapped about me and I caught a severe cold. Soon it had developed into pneumonia and it appeared that I had very little more time to live. Nanny said the fever reached 110 degrees, alternating with shaking chills. All the doctor's efforts seemed in vain. He brought in an associate, but one night he decided to prepare mother for the worst. She became prostrate with despair and fright.

Then Nanny took over. She heated bricks over the old coal stove, wound blankets about them and placed me between them. She summoned Nellie to kneel beside her and she began to pray for divine intercession. She never forgot the words that came to her then: "Lord, thy will be done. I ask you to save this little tyke but if you must call him home while he's so young, then you must have a reason beyond our understanding. We are poor sinners, Lord, but if you can spare him this one time, we will prepare him to be a faithful servant in your vineyard."

They kept the vigil all night. Just before four in the morning, they told me, the fever broke. Nanny saw the glazed eyes begin to brighten. She whispered, "Praise the Lord!" The battle had been won. I have been sick many times since then, but that occasion was undoubtedly my closest brush with death.

The little black ghetto which we moved on Banks Avenue in Rockville Centre, Long Island, was a fetid, swampy lowland. Poppa had been forced to move there after he found that he suffered chronic indigestion on his job as a cook in Newport. It was the worst kind of environment for my weak lungs, but the adults faced our condition with a stoic fatalism, bolstered with a Baptist predestinational faith.

The death rate in our damp valley was high, and Nanny had a morbid habit of taking me to every funeral. My earliest memories are bound up with walking down church aisles, hand-in-hand with Nanny, to the strains of the mournful funeral song of the slaves—"There's a Man Going 'Round Taking Names." I grew up as a deeply religious child and also as a Republican, in emulation of my father.

I remember the 1916 election campaign between Woodrow Wilson and Charles Evans Hughes. The day after the election the *New York Times* announced that Hughes had won. I got into a fist fight at school with a boy who insisted that Wilson had won. He bloodied my nose and, sure enough, the late count from California tipped the scales in Wilson's favor.

A few months after the election, Wilson persuaded Congress to declare war. Black men were drafted in segregated units to serve as labor battalions. There were only two black combat regiments—the Eighth Illinois and the Old Fifteenth of New York. Both were assigned to French divisions.

My father boasted many times of the fabulous exploits of the Old Fifteenth. It had been organized by Teddy Roosevelt, and on one occasion it had actually saved his life. It had gained its early fame in the battle of San Juan Hill, but in World War I the prevalent notion was that blacks were too cowardly to fight as infantry.

But the leaders of the French army, which had been dreadfully decimated on the western front, welcomed the Old Fifteenth as a fighting unit. In the bloody stalemate of trench warfare, the Old Fifteenth earned the reputation of never retreating an inch. But they paid a frightful price for their bravery. Fully two-thirds were killed or wounded. At last, in late 1919, it was announced that the Fifteenth was coming home.

A teacher of mine, Miss Gordon, persuaded my mother to allow her to take me to the Fifteenth's homecoming parade in Manhattan. This event forever shaped my opinion of the possibilities of black people.

I heard the distant tramp of marching feet. Then came the thrilling notes of trumpets and horns as Jim Europe's famous band, including Louis Armstrong, shattered the morning air. Since that time, veterans of many wars have assured me that on that day I had the good fortune to hear the greatest military band ever assembled in the Western world. Miss Gordon was waving and weeping, and I was waving too. Following the band came endless carriages of the wounded.

At last the ground shook to the rhythmic tramp of the able-bodied veterans bringing up the rear, in rank after rank of gleaming bayonets and rifles. It seemed to me then that no force on earth could have withstood the charge of those inspired black soldiers whose faces looked straight ahead, all the way into the future.

Malverne High School's first senior class assembled in September 1925. We were five in number; three girls and two boys. Our little classes resembled latter-day seminars, and two of the girls had made outstanding academic records. The three of us concentrated on aiding the laggard two. We were determined to have Malverne accredited by the board of regents in 1926.

Football appealed to me and that fall our team enjoyed its first undefeated season. The squad had only sixteen boys, so there was little relief for the linemen. I played left guard and made up for my lack of size with a fanatical will to win; and I believe the grim, persistent slogging in the line taught me the value of tenacity.

Winter came unusually early to Long Island in 1925 and all the Lynn children learned to ice-skate. My mother kept a watchful eye on us.

After the winter examinations it was clear that three of Malverne's seniors could qualify for college, but the two girls—Myra Lehman and Irene West—intended to marry and brushed aside the idea of further study. Myra Lehman did indeed marry Larry Noble, a close friend of my brother Winnie.

I had the tentative promise of a debating scholarship from Syracuse University, and the mother's club met early in the spring to plan a series of cake parties to raise additional funds to help me. I played no further sports my last few months at Malverne; instead, I concentrated on studying commercial subjects such as bookkeeping and business law. There was no teacher for these subjects but I had to learn them, and this brought my general average down.

My classmates had assumed I would be valedictorian, but the averaging of marks over the high-school years showed that I was number two instead of number one. Myra Lehman had the highest average. She thought that I had been denied the honor on account of race and said so. "Conrad should be valedictorian," she told our teacher.

It was decided to honor a salutatorian in addition to the valedictorian. Later, during the commencement exercises, the mother's club presented my mother with a check for $100 as a contribution toward my college expenses, and it was announced that Syracuse had awarded me a four-year scholarship in debating, which would cover roughly half my tuition fees. The Lynn family was thrilled.

I put in a full schedule of ten-hour days that summer, working with my father at landscape gardening and road cutting. When it was time to leave for Syracuse my tuition was secured, and I also had minimal funds for room rental off campus. In 1926 black students were barred from living on campus, with the exception of scholarship athletes.

I took the train from Lynbrook to Syracuse and then walked to a little rooming house on Harrison Avenue. It was about a mile from campus.

"My," said the landlady, "but you're so small to be carrying such big suitcases. Are you Conrad Lynn?"

"Yes, ma'am. Are you Mrs. Harrison?"

"I certainly am. Let me take one of those bags!"

She was large and brown skinned, a big-boned woman. I said nothing as she led me to my room. It would be a long time before I overcame my shyness.

That night she insisted I eat supper with her. I reminded myself not to make a habit of this. The twenty dollars I was paying her applied only to the room rent. All other living expenses I was expected to earn by working part time.

The first courses I took at Syracuse were philosophy, political science, biology, mathematics, Bible, and French. Bible and mathematics were electives. In addition, I was to receive academic credit for debating.

Dr. Ralph Himstead, the debating coach, was the first faculty member with whom I became well acquainted. He had a rather homely Swedish face and had transferred from Northwestern University.

"Conrad," he said, "you won't be much use to me unless you make the varsity debating team. Can you do it?"

"I don't know," I said.

"Well," he said, "I think you can."

Mrs. Harrison, the landlady, introduced me to a middle-aged man named Green. He explained that he operated a tailor shop not far from the rooming house and asked if I would like to make deliveries for him and become an apprentice. I said that I would, as soon as I saw how my school schedule worked out.

I soon became acutely aware that most of the students at Syracuse came from middle-class families, and a significant proportion from distinctly wealthy families. Cars were parked on every street leading to the campus, and a student who did not have at least a bicycle was pitied.

The distances between buildings were considerable, but I loved to walk. The air in Syracuse was much more bracing than the lowlands of Long Island and I lost no time climbing Mount Olympus to look out over the entire city.

I did not try to make friends—I was too shy—but the debating team forced me out of my shell. All the other members of the team were upper-classmen, but they were not condescending.

Dr. Himstead stressed the importance of acquiring a command of the subject matter and the question at issue; and because research was one of my strong points, other team members began to rely upon my memory for mounds of statistics and data.

Himstead was not satisfied to let me do just the digging. He found a place for me on the team in forensic competition. There, my earnestness and underlying emotionalism compensated for my lack of finesse, and there was no grumbling from the squad because a freshman was debating as a member of the varsity. The fact that I was not just the only black on the squad but the only black on the platform in all our debates seemed to give my teammates a certain satisfaction.

Professor Hall, my political science instructor, aroused my admiration. He was from Australia and had a gift for understatement that revealed a mordant, if subtle, sense of humor. He was also a master of his subject, and his sensitivity encouraged me to confide to him. His homeland, Australia, was regarded simply as a colony of Great Britain by most Americans, and many of his barbs were directed at U. S. big-power complacency and crudity. As a black youth, I had already begun to feel a second-class citizenship in the United States, and I shared his disdain of the national ego. Many of Professor Hall's hopes for the future were carried by the League of Nations, and his students were drilled in the intricacies of its charter.

Al Capone's mob was dominating Chicago during this period, and Professor Hall enjoyed bringing a large rock to place beside the lectern. When asked what the rock was for, he would reply that he needed elementary protection against the more aggressive forces in our country. Later, he joined the secretariat of the League of Nations in Geneva, Switzerland, and was present at the league's demise upon the outbreak of World War II.

I found a way to secure minimum subsistence by taking odd jobs in the homes of professors—scrubbing floors and baby-sitting. Occasionally, mother would send me a little extra money from her meager savings. It gave me an uneasy feeling when I found a five-dollar bill in one of her letters, because I knew how hard she had to work and how she must have scrimped to save that much. Poppa did not believe in a black boy going to college.

One winter afternoon I received such a bill in a letter; I stuffed it in my pocket and went to the library. I became absorbed in some subject and did not notice how dark it had become until I started back for my room. Sleet and ice had coated the hill that I had to descend. Hurrying along in the biting wind, I slipped and fell a number of times before reaching the rooming house.

I warmed my hands and feet and decided to buy a meal with part of my mother's gift. I reached in my pocket but the money wasn't there. Fighting back tears, I borrowed a flashlight from Mrs. Harrison and retraced my steps. When I reached the bottom of the hill, I found it had become too slippery for me to walk up. I got down on my hands and knees and painfully worked my way up the slope in anguish and growing despair. Some two hours later, I saw a paper fluttering under a piece of ice. It was the five-dollar bill. Overcome with relief, I made my way back to my room. The next morning I bought my first full meal in many days.

To supplement my income, I often toyed with the idea of taking Mr. Green at his word and becoming his tailoring apprentice. But a little incident made me hesitate. As a member of the debating team, I was required to wear a tuxedo in our formal engagements. One day I took the tuxedo to be cleaned and pressed in Mr. Green's shop. He looked at me with surprise.

"Did you buy this?" he asked.

"My folks did. I have to wear it in debates."

"Good. I was afraid you were one of those fraternity hounds." It was plain he disliked the upper-class pretensions attached to tuxedos.

My chronic poverty had become acute by spring. The reward of debating write-ups in the *Daily Orange* was no substitute for food. I fasted for three days, hoping against hope for some money from home. At the end of the third day I stumbled coming up the steps of the rooming house and had trouble getting up. Mrs. Harrison happened to be at the window. She came to the door.

"What's the matter, Conrad? Are you sick?"

"No, ma'am."

"You haven't eaten, have you?"

"No, ma'am."

"Come in here! And don't ever act like this again. When you're hungry, you let me know!"

She made me sip the soup slowly and asked questions about my family. I explained that my parents had seven children and only my father was able to work full time. He had my promise that I would earn my food and incidental expenses.

The next day Mrs. Harrison took me to Green's tailor shop, and he hired me as his delivery boy. Most of the clothes I delivered were destined for the big white houses on fraternity row. The sons of the rich, as far as I noticed, never saw any incongruity in the black debating-team member serving as their boy Friday.

Mrs. Harrison began paying me to take care of her pedigreed English bulldog. She left hamburger for me to feed him. He seemed a little overweight to me, so I cooked the hamburger for the two of us. It was fair because I shared my food—cereal and bread—with him.

My total weekly income grew to six dollars, but my needs also became greater. About once a month I took Josephine to a movie. She was a sweet, lovable, and intelligent girl. My only reservation was her height. She did not seem embarrassed when I had to hold an umbrella up, almost at arm's length, to reach above her head—but I was.

A mishap clouded our relationship. When Alpha Phi Alpha fraternity had its spring formal, they indicated whom all the invited freshmen should escort. For me they selected a small girl who claimed to be a dancer. We had nothing in common except height—she was an inch or two shorter than I.

I told Josephine that unless the fraternity changed the invitation to let me take her, I would not go. She agreed not to go either. A few days later the dancer, Christine Matthews, invited me to meet her at the Dunbar Community Center. She was attractive and charmed me, and I promised to take her to the dance.

I had a miserable time. She wanted me to escort her only so that she could see some boys from Colgate. I was too shy to ask other girls to dance. Besides, my skills as a dancer were miniscule and I was filled with guilt.

Josephine found out the next Sunday that I had betrayed her; she refused to talk with me, burst into tears, and ran out of the Sunday School room. But that afternoon she forgave me. I never broke our pact again.

Dunbar Community Center was the heart of the black intellectual set in Syracuse, and its hinterland. The key weekly event was the Sunday afternoon discussion of cultural, social, and political subjects. In this way the local blacks participated in the burgeoning Negro Renaissance. After everyone had a say, a designated "critic" would comment on the remarks and sum up the discussion. In April of my freshman year I was elected critic, and I remained in that office until I completed Syracuse University Law School.

Josephine was ecstatic, because at Tuskegee Institute, which she had previously attended, she had become familiar with the Negro past, particularly in America.

Looking back on these early attachments, it is hard for me to escape the feeling that many times life shunts aside its best spirits.

I never married Josephine, probably because of my short stature. I had read in a magazine that I could increase my height by hanging myself by a belt tucked under my chin and behind my neck. The fabric belt from my trunk fitted my needs. In secluded spots, wherever I lived for the rest of my undergraduate and graduate life, I hung myself almost every day. Nevertheless, I never exceeded 5'4½". Josephine was 5'10".

That first homecoming, in June 1927, was a happy occasion. The family buzzed with plans for the immediate future. Mother welcomed the suggestion of my sisters that we form a family orchestra and tour Rhode Island and other parts of New England where a number of Lynn relatives and friends lived.

Mother had insisted that music lessons begin the moment we learned to read. Winnie became an adroit pianist. At age seven I was trudging four miles to Hempstead for violin lessons. Arnold favored the saxophone. Sophia became adept with drums.

We spent the month of July traveling through New England playing in Negro church concerts. The financial return was modest, but the uplift for Mother was worth the venture. Winnie had run away from home earlier, and Mother seemed lighter in spirit than at any time since he had left us.

We played numbers like "Me and My Shadow," "Indian Love Song," and many Irish ballads. Our only Negro spiritual was a European version of "Deep River." No doubt we shared with the rather pathetic Negro "better class" of New England a slight shame of the black heritage in art.

Most of the black artists who had reaped significant financial rewards were uncle-tom comedians, tap dancers, and spectacularly foolish clowns. In a few years, Stepin Fetchit was to fix the stereotype indelibly in the American consciousness.

Upon our return I secured a job as a dishwasher on West Broadway in New York City, not far from the piers. It was exhausting, dirty work, but I earned more money than I had ever made before. My savings amounted to $200 when the fall term began.

My general inclination was toward the ministry, but when I returned to Syracuse in the fall, political science became my major and philosophy my first minor. I continued the study of the Bible along with French and biology. The year's debating subject was "Resolved that United States military intervention in Nicaragua is justifiable."

I moved into Alpha Phi Alpha fraternity house and became the official cook. It was rumored that in the previous year I had managed to eat on an average of 99 cents a week. Mrs. Harrison welcomed my decision to leave the rooming house. She considered me too much of a recluse.

The debating subject for our team compelled me to scrutinize in considerable depth the foreign policy of the United States. Teddy Roosevelt had been my childhood hero, but an examination of his role in shaping the Big Stick policy in Latin America removed the gloss from his reputation. I unearthed more and more facts, and Nicaragua's Sandino, whom the American press reviled as a ragtag bandit, began to look like a latter-day Robin Hood. Our team voted to take the negative of the proposition for the year.

Dr. Himstead never asked us to advocate a position we considered wrong. His object was to nurture *people,* not cynics. After discussion with the other members of the team—J. Welbourne Dearlove and J. Donald Kingsley—it was decided that I would carry the responsibility for proving that the American policy was in violation of international law.

My new interest in international relations led me to become friendly with a political science instructor named Candace Stone. Her tiny size and effervescent personality had earned her the nickname of Pan. She co-managed a living center off campus for women students, where weekly sessions of the Commonwealth Club were conducted. There, I began to feel a kinship with Chinese, Japanese, Filipinos, Africans, and Europeans; and I could tell that my omnivorous curiosity was leading me down new bypaths.

An interested spectator at one of our debates was a senior with a reputation for "oddball" thinking. This was Dave Dworsky, and he invited me to lunch at a nearby restaurant. Within a few minutes we were locked in a dispute over Kant's categorical imperatives. I admitted that I did not fully understand the *Critique of Pure Reason.* It proved an impossible task to convince him of the existence of a deity. If God, ultimately, was the pricking of conscience, how could his existence be posited outside the human mind? From Kant we passed on to Hegel and his March of the Idea through history. From Hegel, Dworsky led me inexorably to Marx.

For the first time, academic abstractions became sinewed with flesh and blood. I smuggled the *Communist Manifesto* into the fraternity house and into classes, but the indoctrination of a lifetime was not easily overcome.

Other currents were tossing me about, also. My French professor, Mr.

Aiken, spent a great deal of class time discussing a work he had just read: Oswald Spengler's *Decline of the West*. The cyclical theory of history fascinated me. I had declined to take history at Syracuse, because although it was my favorite area of independent reading I did not want the subject spoiled by obligatory assignments. But now it appeared that its intensive study in a comparative sense might unlock the future.

Dr. Piper in philosophy tried to block my transition to Marx, but he was undermined not only by Dworsky but by my teacher in social psychology, Mr. Allport, brother of the famous Harvard psychologist, Gordon Allport. Behaviorism did not seem to leave much room for the Godhead.

Dworsky told me he was going to debate Dr. Finla Crawford, soon to be head of the School of Citizenship, before an audience of trade-union workers. The subject was "The Significance of Karl Marx." I went along expecting the distinguished professor of government and history to put the upstart Russian immigrant in his place, but I underestimated the little Bolshevik. With an astounding display of erudition, Dworsky overwhelmed his older antagonist. I walked home with Dworsky in silence after the pyrotechnical display was over. The next day I applied for membership in the Young Communist League.

In 1928 candidates were not easily accepted into the YCL. It was necessary to pass through a period of probation. As part of the regimen, I had to get up one morning at five o'clock and distribute strike leaflets at the gates of the Brown-Lipe-Chapin gearworks. Our activity was strictly illegal.

Only a few minutes after I had begun, I was told to run; but I was too slow. A burly Irish cop grabbed my shoulder and hustled me into a paddy wagon. Next it was a cell in the city jail.

But luck was with me. Just a few nights before, I had taken part in a very exciting debate against Colgate in the Mizpah Auditorium. The tension was so great that I was overcome with emotion in the final speech of the night. The audience voted us the victors, and in that audience was John Peacock, Chief Inspector of Police. Now Peacock was staring through the bars at me.

"What are you doing in there?"

"I was arrested."

"What for?"

"Distributing strike leaflets."

Peacock unlocked the door of the cell. "Get lost," he said.

At the same time that I applied for membership in the Young Communist League, I announced a change of major from the ministry to law. The day after the Colgate debate, Dr. Bernard Clausen, the famed pacifist minister, who had acted as moderator, published a letter in the *Daily Orange* abjuring me to reconsider the change. I never answered him.

Just before the school year ended, in June 1928, I made my first radio broadcast—on behalf of William Z. Foster, Communist Party candidate for president of the United States.

CHAPTER 3

The Political Growth in College

I was the only member of the Young Communist League on campus, so it was not possible for the parent organization to establish a unit at Syracuse University. I was attached to the youth group in the working-class district of the city, but I was not permitted to take part in street activity because of my arrest and brief incarceration. It was probably felt that I was more useful at discussion groups, such as those at the Dunbar Community Center and the Commonwealth Club.

Members of the Commonwealth Club were incredulous in the spring of 1929 when I asserted that international financial imbalances centering in Germany did not augur well for President Hoover's predictions of uninterrupted prosperity. Most of the American and foreign students in the Commonwealth Club were mildly socialist with pacifist inclinations. Norman Thomas was their favorite guest.

The opposition I encountered in the Dunbar Center was concentrated on my espousal of a form of militant atheism. I was just beginning to read Clarence Darrow on this subject.

My first polite disagreement with Norman Thomas occurred at the Commonwealth Club in the spring of 1928. Thomas clearly saw the menacing advance of fascism, but he advocated meeting it with nonviolence. He seemed to look with equanimity on a coming fascist conquest of all Europe and predicted widespread sabotage and civil disobedience after such a catastrophe. To my question—Would not the action he predicted be violence on a less coordinated scale?—he would only reply that such a prospect was preferable to war.

It struck me that Thomas's appeal to college youth lay precisely in his lack of specificity. He aroused a "noble rage" without requiring that it be followed by decisive action. In the halcyon days of the "golden twenties," even the League of Nations appeared to have a future.

Thomas was particularly well received by the visiting female students from India. These young women, with their diaphanous, silken saris, the jewels in their nostrils, and the caste marks on their foreheads, were indubitably of the upper class. I had yet to learn of the misery of hundreds of millions they had left behind.

Pacifism was on the way to becoming the dominant liberal philosophy of the campus, foreshadowing the Oxford Peace Oath some years later. It was impossible for me, however, to ignore the recurrent waves of savage lynching in the South, and I could not help wondering why the propagation of humane values had so little effect in that region.

My first year in law school completed the requirements for my liberal-arts degree. Dr. Himstead became my professor of criminal law, and one day we had a private conversation:

"Conrad," he said, "I'm convinced that the most difficult problem this country will face in this century is the attainment of full citizenship and opportunity for the Negro."

"The stock market has broken," I said. "We may be in for a major economic decline."

"I know, and it's serious, but the government will overcome an economic crisis long before it will solve the race question."

As a Marxist, I could not fully accept Dr. Himstead's thesis. I was being taught that the basic antagonisms existing in modern industrial societies were between classes: the propertyless workers on one side, and the holders and controllers of property—the capitalists—on the other. I believed that the crisis precipitated by the crash of October 1929 would inevitably cause great unemployment, and that the dispossessed, white and black, would draw together to bring down their common enemy.

A number of students from other colleges visited the fraternity house on Cedar Street where I lived. Prominent among them were Adam Clayton Powell and Ray Vaughn from Colgate. They were part of a hard-drinking, whore-mongering crowd. It was not uncommon for Fred Douglass and I to carry Adam into the house so he could sleep off the effects of a night dedicated to the bottle.

I did not bother to wait for the commencement exercises in 1930. My liberal-arts sheepskin was mailed to me. That summer I worked as a "greaseball" in a Rockville Centre garage, a job my brother Winnie had secured for me. Winnie had returned to Long Island early that spring and had married a woman named Grace Seaman, from Cold Spring Harbor.

Winnie was worried about mother's health. She seemed to be aging rapidly—developing gray hair, becoming listless, and exhibiting an uncommon in attention to details. Father tried to make us believe she was going through a phase and insisted on having the regular big Sunday dinner with, as usual, Rev. Pierre BunCamper as the main guest.

I returned to law school somewhat reluctantly that fall. It had not interested me as much as I had expected, and I was openly bored by subjects like contracts, sales, wills, trusts, and civil procedure. Unless they were passed, however, I could not graduate, so I grimly applied myself to them.

I was the only black in the law school, and I took a good deal of kidding from Margaret Hall, the librarian. She thought it was crazy to be a communist and still expect to become a lawyer. "How are you ever going to pass the character committee?" she would ask. The character committees of the various judicial districts in the state, we well knew, had the ultimate say about who would be admitted to the bar.

Dr. Himstead also had qualms about my future. Once, in the presence of Mary Crouch, another student, he asked, "Conrad, how do you expect to survive?"

I laughed, but Mary, with a sad expression on her face, turned away. She knew he was asking the question of her also. Mary Crouch was in love with Dr. Himstead. He was a married man; she was the beautiful daughter of a judge of the court of Appeals of the state of New York; but she refused to become interested in any other man. Two years later she committed suicide.

Dr. Himstead was a Bull Moose Republican who wondered whether any drastic change for the better could be wrought in America without revolution. He was harshly anti-militarist and would not permit any ROTC member to wear a uniform in class. In constitutional law he delighted in discussing the intricacies of civil-rights cases with me, almost to the exclusion of the rest of the class. He knew that my anger about oppression could be brought out easily through needling.

Moore v. *Dempsey* was a case that grew out of the Elaine, Arkansas, massacre of 1923. A group of black tenant farmers in that benighted state had formed a union to secure living wages in the face of remorseless repression by the Confederate-descended landlords. The very idea of unionism meant communism in Arkansas, and the owners stirred up poor whites to smash the Bolshevik atheists.

One Sunday night the blacks were having a meeting in a little rural church, when the nightriders attacked and killed four of them. Some of the blacks fired back in self-defense and killed two Klansmen. Troops were called out to hold back the white mob. The black leaders were held for murder.

The mob terrorized the court, and the jury returned a verdict of guilty against all defendants after less than a half-hour's deliberation. The judicial process being a farce, the defendants were hurriedly sentenced to death.

Eventually, however, the defendants succeeded in bringing the case to the U.S. Supreme Court. Justice Oliver Wendell Holmes, in a decision infused with passion yet classic in its understatement of horror, reversed the convictions. Whereupon the mob stormed the jail and lynched the defendants.

I will never forget how Dr. Himstead set the framework for our discussion of the case. He seemed to be fighting the Civil War over again.

Some days later he reminded me of his prediction that the race question would outlive every other antagonism in America. I was growing to realize that history justified his reservations.

Dr. Himstead and I had many discussions in his office. His eyes always twinkled as he stared at me through the clouds of smoke from his ever-present pipe. He seconded my admiration for Oliver Wendell Holmes, agreeing that the great judge was not a liberal in the popular meaning of the term. He was rigorous in his thought, a strong believer in the inevitability of wars, and a supreme expositor of the common law. It was his writings alone that made civil law palatable to me.

My debating scholarship had expired at the end of my first year in law school, and my funds ran out near the end of my second. I did not want to worry mother because she had become quite ill, and I dared not ask my father for support because he had heard that I was a Red. I had been earning money by baby-sitting, and now Dr. Himstead busied himself among the law-school faculty to find me additional baby-sitting jobs.

In May 1931, I went to a political symposium with Pan Stone of the Commonwealth Club. Speakers from the Republican, Domocratic, and Socialist parties presented their views. But the Communist party spokesman, due in from Buffalo, did not show up. Pan prodded me to take his place.

I went to the platform and delivered a fiery denunciation of world capitalism in the midst of crisis, as it struggled to sustain itself by encouraging the rise of fascism.

That night the dean of the law school told me I was suspended from classes. I had visions of losing everything I had worked for. I immediately contacted Pan Stone.

Chagrined over the consequences of her reckless advice, she went into conference with Dr. Himstead, who had just been named vice-dean of the law school. Himstead and a few other prominent Republicans reminded the

tter for me to stay
ear of it. He said I
' own savings and

that final year at
aw school I was
they were consid-
James Allen, their
rk on the subject.
a crude parody of
called it ''Self-

ber of contiguous
ajority. Allen said
o solve America's
cal and economic

d this proposition
ere close; in fact,
ger than for their
xpression, and in
I had never heard
can South. I was
st movement this
vement Associa-
o Africa as their
passionate, even
thesis.

had furnished the
e line. Instead, I

He knew that my
d been based not
lack unemployed
ndon, in Atlanta,
n for jobs. These
forging a unity
ld proceed along

)een exercising my free-speech
en the ideological opponents of
ent civil libertarians. The latter
ays later.
my return to his class in civil
that he had never seen a radical
d not graduate if I did not pass
early in June did I hint to my

n that I mailed the letter home.
I packed hurriedly, but I had a

ne met me at the station, and I
it.
s mother's best friend, Vernetta
n shore of Maryland to work as
thirties and pursued her higher
Only the previous summer, she
d with her Lynbrook employer
at mother one morning and said,
t to anything, it certainly won't

rived—ministers, deacons, and
g the smaller children.
e. Nobody had told me she had
ayville, Long Island, a month

a gnawing sense of guilt, which
ns to her grave in the cemetery
had pursued my petty concerns
She was only forty-seven years
r sensitive spirit was too fragile

te enough money to finish law
to see me graduate. My sisters
d washing chores. There was an
ed home less and less often at
and kept an eye on the younger

children. When I suggusted that perhaps it would be
home rather than return to Syracuse, Winnie would no
could call on him to supplement monetarily whatever
my father's help would not cover.

My concentration was almost solely on my studie
Syracuse. The day after I had been suspended from
summoned to a Young Communist League meeting whe
ering the implications of a new direction to Party policy
authority on the Negro question, had just published a
When I read it, I discovered that Allen had develope
Stalin's thesis on the nationalities problem. Alle
Determination for the Black Belt.''

The book contained a map that outlined a large nu
counties in the South in which black people constituted a
that these people naturally made up a nation, and the wa
race question was to encourage this area to seek poli
independence.

I could hardly contain my amusement when we discus
at the YCL meeting. My contacts with the Deep South
my emotional affinity for Southern blacks was far str
Northern cousins. In all my reading of Southern Negro
conversations with acute black thinkers from that regio
of any demand for a separate black nation in the Ame
particularly familiar with the strongest black-nationa
nation has produced—Garvey's Universal Negro Imp
tion. Yet Garvey demanded only that blacks return
spiritual, political, and physical homeland. None of th
angry, voices of the Negro Renaissance had raised Allen

The Party leaders were obdurate. Stalin, through Allen
key. As a disciplined YCL'er, I was expected to follow
quietly dropped out of the YCL.

David Dworsky did not have the heart to chide me
arguments had not been answered. My strongest points
on theory but on facts. At that very time, both white and
had elected a nineteen-year-old black youth, Angelo H
Georgia, the heart of lynchdom, to lead them on a ma
outcasts, at the very botton of the social structure, we
across racial lines that made it apparent the revolution w
classic lines or it would not succeed at all.

I did not make my disagreement with the Communist party public. It did not seem to me that the Party was my enemy, and its activists still had my respect. As for them, they continued to act as if I were their prime exhibit on the Syracuse campus. Nevertheless, in debates with socialists and anarchists it was easier for me to defend my views after I had made clear my disdain for the new doctrine of black self-determination in the Deep South.

No one alluded to the effort made by YCL unit leaders to persuade me to quit law school immediately after I had been suspended the previous spring. These unit leaders had tried to convince me that world capitalism was on the verge of collapse, and they asked how a young black lawyer could make a living at a time of ever-growing unemployment.

They offered me a job as an organizer for the Party, which paid subsistence wages. I gave the offer considerable thought, but I decided, on balance, that American capitalism was not yet moribund, despite the surface symptoms. I turned down the offer.

My material prospects did not look good, however. Although my skill as a debater and the fact that I was the only black law student at Syracuse had elicited admiring comment, no law firm in the city or surrounding towns was prepared to offer me a job as law clerk. In fact, there was not one black lawyer practicing in the central New York area at the time.

A clerkship was essential for admission to the bar. This was not the first time, nor would it be the last, I had noticed that white people were willing to encourage a black to get an education, but became extremely chary about offering a job after he or she finished. At the time, I had no satisfactory explanation for this paradox.

When I received my bachelor-of-laws degree in June 1932, I still had no promise of a job.

CHAPTER 4

Teething at the Bar and the WPA

I looked diligently for work in New York City as a law clerk. It was easy to become discouraged. Winnie gave me ten cents each day for subway fare, and I would catch the BMT in Jamaica, where most of the family had moved, to the last stop at Fifty-ninth Street in Manhattan. Then I would walk the length of Central Park to Harlem.

The move to Jamaica was necessitated by my father's attachment to a woman after mother's death. The woman persuaded him to sell our home in Lynbrook to pay off the mortgage on her own home in Jamaica. Then she ordered the Lynn children out of her house.

Once again Winnie stepped into the breach, even though his own marriage had foundered on in-law trouble. He persuaded an aunt to take nine-year-old Samuel into her home. Arnold had just married and taken an apartment over a garage in an all-white neighborhood in Rockville Centre. Winnie found an apartment for the rest of us on New York Boulevard in South Jamaica and kept us together. When I suggested that it might be better for me to take a job as a porter at Penn Station, he refused to listen.

By this time the goal of a Lynn becoming a lawyer had assumed the aspects of a major gamble. After the graduation ceremonies at Syracuse, Dr. Himstead and Professor Levine pooled the one hundred dollars necessary to send me to the cram course for the bar exam at the university's football training camp on Lake Onondaga, a calm and scenic spot to study. To strengthen my moral fiber, Himstead called his half of the sum a loan. A few years later I paid it back.

The resourceful and generous Winnie found the twenty-five dollars needed for me to take the bar examination. He made it clear that he would be unable to put up another twenty-five dollars if I failed either half of the test. Luckily, the two-day examination included a number of questions on constitutional law, so I was able to pass on the first try.

Finding a job was more difficult, but in August the search for a clerkship bore fruit. James Johnson, of 200 West 135th Street in the heart of Harlem, agreed to take me on with no salary. I was fortunate, because he was the lawyer for the Dunbar National Bank, the first financial institution in Harlem, which was controlled by the Rockefeller family. In that capacity he handled a greater variety of legal cases than most Harlem attorneys.

It was not long before I began to take notice of Johnson's seventeen-year-old stenographer, Alberta Aspinall. She was what was known as a "high yaller" and had a sweet, shy smile and a beautiful body. At first, in my egotism as a lawyer-to-be, I tried to impress her with my importance. She was amused; for all her youth she sensed more about men than they knew about themselves. It was not long before my assignments in mortgage preparations were being neglected for a seat next to her typewriter. She was bright and curious. Soon she had me explaining the intricacies of Spengler's philosophy.

She would not go out on dates with me, but occasionally after work I walked with her to the IRT subway, where she would board for her home on Ninety-ninth Street near Lexington Avenue.

Alberta was a receptive audience for my fulminations about the depression. I would complain to her by the hour about the ominous rise of the Nazi party in Germany and explain the reasons for the Japanese assault on China, the boiling unrest of the black masses in the Caribbean, and the remarkable radicalization of poor blacks in the Deep South.

In the late spring of 1933 I was admitted to the bar. The character committee brought out that I had been a member of the Young Communist League, but I pointed out that I had become inactive mainly because of my disagreement with the program of self-determination for the Black Belt. Fifteen years later I could not have been admitted to the bar with such a background.

I immediately accepted an invitation to speak on the Syracuse campus. My theme was the developing social revolution, and I was not invited back until forty-five years later.

However, Pan Stone offered me a part-time assignment doing research for her doctoral dissertation on Charles Dana, the late editor of the *New York Sun*. In the course of that assignment I met a slim, impertinent, brown-haired woman from Oklahoma named Gene Phillips. We worked together on Pan's research and soon became luncheon partners.

Gene was neither a communist nor a socialist, but a skeptical leftist. She was intrigued by my lingering attachment to Communist party views, but she had had experience in a government-sponsored relief program in Oklahoma in which she detected, it seemed, the germ of a substitute for the proletarian dictatorship. Gene introduced me to a sister Oklahoman whom we nicknamed Love. Love lived, since her migration from the dust bowl, with her aunt, Ann Upshure, who was married to a crippled, black piano player, Theodore Upshure.

These new friends caused some confusion in my estimate of American white people. My judgment had been that Southern whites were almost uniformly antagonistic to blacks. The radical poor whites who followed Angelo Herndon in Atlanta, I thought, confined their loyalty to the political sphere. But Gene and Ann and Love seemed emotionally so close to the warmth I had hitherto observed only in the Southern Negro that I began to feel my beliefs might have a geographical rather than a racial origin. Few of my Northern friends agreed with this conclusion.

Just prior to my admission to practice, Mr. Johnson sent me to the New York County Supreme Court to submit a motion in a civil case. When the matter was called, I discovered the judge wished it to be argued orally rather than submitted on papers.

The temptation was too much for me. I argued the motion and it was granted!

Johnson pretended anger: "Don't you know you can't argue a motion until you're a lawyer?"

"Yes, sir. But the judge wanted me to argue it."

"That's because he thought you were a lawyer. Do this again and you're fired!"

I learned later that Johnson had boasted about the exploit to Alan Dingle, a lawyer down the hall, who was Harlem's foremost advocate.

Johnson began to pay me five dollars a week after I was admitted to the bar. He permitted me to take my own cases, prepare them on office time, and keep the fees. During the entire summer of 1933 I independently handled only two matters: dispossess defenses for tenants about to be evicted.

One day in the early fall, my sister Sophia walked into the office. She had become a stenographer for a real-estate broker, William Tomlinson, who shared a small office with a young West Indian lawyer, Darwin Telesford, on West 117th Street.

"I have a murder case for you," she said.

I looked at her in disbelief.

"I know the woman charged with the murder," Sophia said. "She's an American Indian."

I did not think I was prepared to handle a murder case, but I decided it would not hurt to take a look. The next day I visited my new "client," Anna Center, in the eastern wing of the old Jefferson Market courthouse. Anna Center was a somewhat phlegmatic woman just short of her thirtieth birthday. She and Sophia had lived in the same apartment building, and Anna had confided to her that another woman was cutting in on her man.

Anna found her rival one night in a bar. There was a heated quarrel and Anna whipped out a knife and stabbed her enemy. The woman stumbled out of the bar, collapsed in the street, and died.

A month passed before Anna was arrested. The bartender did not report the fracas because he knew he would lose his license. It was not until Anna became involved in another scuffle that the previous incident was uncovered. Anna had gotten the worst of this second struggle and had foolishly complained to the police. Her assailants, aware of the prior fight, accused her of murder.

When I first met Anna she had already been in jail a year. I took the case because she could not afford anyone else.

The first mystery to clear up was why she had been detained so long. By her own admission she had committed the murder. To bring the matter to a head, I sought a writ of habeas corpus.

The hearing on the writ was scheduled for Part I in general sessions. I was about to get a firsthand look at what passes for justice in New York. The case was called and the judge summoned me before him.

"Don't you know, young man," he said, "that the trial of this case is set for Part IV on the second floor this morning?"

"The district attorney didn't say a word to me about it," I said.

"He doesn't have to."

This was a pretty state of affairs. I wondered what to say next.

"Aren't you ready for trial?" the judge asked. "After all, you have a writ calling for the release of your client because you say the district attorney has been dilatory in prosecution."

Some veteran criminal lawyers in the room were smiling.

"I'm ready, Your Honor," I said, hurrying out of Part I in search of Part IV. I asked directions and found it. The judge called me to the bench.

"Are you ready for trial, Mr. Lynn?"

"May I have a short adjournment, Your Honor?" I had to talk to Anna, who was seated on the prisoner's bench.

"Haven't you been asking for a speedy trial?" the judge asked.

"I wasn't aware," I said, "that the district attorney doesn't have to notify defense counsel when a case is going to be called."

"I'll give you until Monday," the judge said.

It was then Friday. The delay simply meant three sleepless nights for me. The only defense Anna had was lack of premeditation.

On Monday, after I answered "ready," the judge had a number of cases called for sentencing. As he handed out heavy sentences for first-degree robbery, rape, and other felonies, I became more and more depressed.

About noon the judge called me to the bench. He said that out of consideration for my lack of experience he would agree to reduce the charge to second-degree murder if Anna would plead guilty. Then, at least, she would be spared the gamble with the electric chair. I relayed this information to Anna, but she said she preferred death to life imprisonment. I told this to the judge and he told me to sit down.

I waited another hour, using the time to speculate about why so many felony criminals were black. We composed less than one-twelfth the population of New York City, but four-fifths of the people brought before general sessions were black. Our case was called in the early afternoon.

"I understand this is your first murder case," the judge said, "but you shouldn't gamble with your client's life."

"I'm here to serve her wishes, Your Honor."

"It's all right to say that, Mr. Lynn, but you have an obligation to advise your client of what you conceive to be her best interests."

"I understand, Your Honor, but I can appreciate why she feels a sentence for second-degree murder is little different from a sentence of death."

The judge turned to the district attorney. "Mr. District Attorney, in view of the youth of the defendant, and because this may have been an act committed in the heat of passion, would you be willing to accept a plea of guilty to first-degree manslaughter?"

"If Your Honor thought such a plea would serve the ends of justice, I'd be willing to go along."

With more experience, I would have known something was strange here: a district attorney and a hard-nosed judge concerned about my client's "youth" and my inexperience?

"Now, young man," the judge said, "go tell your client about this chance we're giving her and report to me at two o'clock."

The offer began to bother me. I could not eat lunch. Why would the district attorney not proceed to trial for first-degree murder? I thought of calling Mr. Johnson for advice but rejected the idea. He was not a criminal lawyer.

The case was called again at 2:00 P.M. It was the last one on the calendar.

"Have you an application, Mr. Lynn?"

"Your Honor, my client does not want to accept the plea of first-degree manslaughter. She feels some justification for what she did."

The judge abruptly left the bench and disappeared in the direction of his chambers. The district attorney hinted that I had offended His Honor, and now all offers would be withdrawn and Anna would have to stand trial for first-degree murder.

I felt sick wondering if I had made a terrible mistake. I sat down with Anna and told her that it would be necessary to take a plea.

She patted my hand. "Whatever you think, Mr. Lynn," she said.

When the judge returned to the bench, I asked permission to withdraw the original plea of not guilty.

"Motion granted," said the judge.

"My client is ready to plead guilty to second-degree manslaughter."

The judge looked at the district attorney. That worthy frowned. The judge beckoned him to the bench and a whispered colloquy ensued.

Then the judge asked, "Do you waive the forty-eight hours before sentence?"

"I do, Your Honor."

"Stand up, Anna Center!"

Anna complied.

"Are you pleading guilty to second-degree manslaughter?"

"Yes, sir."

The judge went through the rubric of apprising her of her constitutional rights and concluded by sentencing her to six to ten years in the women's reformatory. I was crestfallen. I had hoped for a term of three to five years.

A court attendant followed me out of the courtroom and whispered in my ear, "If you had slipped me twenty-five dollars, I would have told you the D.A. didn't have the murder weapon."

The words lashed me like a whip, and I recoiled in disgust and anger. Was that the way to win cases? Shouldn't the D.A. have admitted he lacked the requisite proof? Or was the law just an unprincipled game? Many times it is, as the years would teach me.

I reported to Mr. Johnson when I returned uptown. He told me he would have fired me if I had not pleaded Anna Center guilty. He said I was reckless to gamble with the woman's life. But I could not help thinking about the difference a twenty-five dollar bribe would have made. A mixture of disgust with myself and with the court made me avoid taking any other criminal case for six years.

The winter of 1933/34 was particularly severe. Roosevelt was busy establishing the alphabetical agencies of the New Deal. Some of my young communist friends hinted that they had connections which would enable me to obtain a WPA job if I joined the Party. My convictions about communism as the only goal for progressive advance had not changed. Now, the Party was no longer pushing self-determination for the Black Belt. I applied for membership and was accepted. In a few weeks I was able to obtain a job as a coder on a WPA Project.

In the Public Works Administration and the Works Progress Administration, the Communist party perceived the opportunity to forge a mass base. Black and white unemployed in the larger cities rubbed shoulders together and debated what action to take to secure some sort of assistance. Roosevelt had been elected in the revulsion from the heavy-handed tactics of Herbert Hoover, at whose authority Douglas MacArthur cleared the unemployed bonus marchers out of Washington with bayonets. Now, Angelo Herndon's accomplishment of forging a fighting front of black and white workers in the Deep South had become a lesson for the theoreticians.

I joined the Jamaica branch of the Communist party in February 1934. The next day I applied for the job as a coder in the huge Western Union building at 60 Hudson Street in Manhattan. All the workers there were college graduates, and many of them held doctorate degrees. There were physicists, chemists, accountants, writers, teachers, lawyers, and mathematicians. As a new member of the Party, I was warmly welcomed by some of my co-workers. Even radicals of other persuasions were not unfriendly.

Herbert Harris, a mathematician and the most outspoken communist in the building, soon discovered that we were being cheated on our pay. We were supposed to receive twenty-one dollars a week, but actually we were getting eighteen. Someone in Washington was cutting himself in for a share. The news had an electrifying effect.

We stopped work and called shop meetings. Within thirty minutes the first white-collar strike in American history had been agreed upon!

The decision was made to march on the WPA headquarters on Lafayette Street the next day, a Saturday, to demand an accounting from the city administrator of WPA.

As we walked along the sidewalk the next morning, WPA workers poured out of every building along the way to join us. When we reached Lafayette Street, our ranks had swollen to twenty-five thousand shouting men and women. Some of them expropriated a telephone pole; and when the administrator failed to answer our knocks on his locked door, the pole was converted into a battering ram. I did not actually swing the pole but, instead, stood a little to the right of the door. As the huge steel portal began to sag inward from the tremendous pounding, I heard a peculiar shuffling sound inside.

Suddenly, the door swung open and out charged LaGuardia's Cossacks—the mounted police. Cries of mirth and derision changed to shrieks of dismay and terror as the horses trampled everything in their way. LaGuardia had stationed more than a hundred horsemen in the lobby to teach the presumptuous relief workers a lesson.

One man died that day, and he was not even a striker. As he came out of the subway kiosk at Chambers Street, an Irish cop, beet-red with fury, swung his billy on the head of the hapless passerby and cracked his skull as if it were an eggshell. The murdered man had been a cripple, and the cop, of course, was never prosecuted.

Three days later a silent throng of one hundred thousand people bore the casket through the winding, narrow streets of the lower East Side. Not a cop was in sight.

The city and the nation held its breath. But Roosevelt and LaGuardia were equal to the test. Official condolences were sent to the family and a violent reaction was averted.

But the ruling class was by no means stupid. We received our proper pay, plus a supplementary check covering all past deductions, and the hurriedly organized WPA workers' union was accorded instant recognition as representatives of the white-collar employees.

The administration had bent without breaking, in a manner that left the hotheads among us agog. LaGuardia and Roosevelt had ridden out the storm, and Marx was again proved right—that in America and possibly Great Britain, revolutionary change might occur without bloodshed.

As we marched behind the coffin borne by longshoremen through the hushed streets, we knew we were participants in an important occasion. The somber resolution on the faces all about me was convincing evidence of the will to fight. Other people in other countries, such as India, might endure unimaginable suffering for centuries in relative apathy, but a country such as the United States, born in revolt and nourished by unprecedented material opportunities amid almost continuous violence, could hardly expect its deprived to bear their ordeal quietly.

The government acted quickly to disperse the activists to various projects throughout the city. I was sent to Columbia University.

At Columbia we decided to publish a weekly newspaper, the *Projector*. I was book review editor. As a communist, my task was to persuade people to read left-wing literature. An early review was of John Strachey's, *The Coming Struggle for Power.* I derived inspiration from the author, especially since I had recently attended a debate at Mecca Temple in which he had participated and easily won. I was dubbed a theoretician after the review was published, but I shied away from that label. English utilitarians, and scholars such as Max Weber and Oswald Spengler, kept alive in my character a basic skepticism.

During the congressional elections of 1934, the Communist party ordered its lawyer members to keep a close watch at the polls to ensure that the Tammany machine counted the votes honestly. We were instructed to travel in pairs and to keep in touch with our respective headquarters. My base of operations was the Finnish Workers Hall on East 126th Street, and my partner, Eddie Kuntz, and I were to be available if trouble arose. Late in the afternoon there was a call: Tammany thugs were chasing Communist party poll watchers from the polling station at P.S. 89 on 135th Street and Lenox Avenue.

Kuntz was away so I hurried to the school alone. It seemed at first that the problem would be an easy one to solve. The Communist poll watchers were admitted back into the building.

I left the school, but no sooner did I reach the sidewalk than I was smashed to the pavement by a heavy blow to the back of the head. Several burly gangster types advanced on me, but I rolled into the gutter, got to my feet, and ran directly across traffic on Lenox Avenue. I did not stop running until I reached the Finnish Workers Hall.

James Ford, the black vice-presidential candidate, listened to my story. He said he would recommend that the Party pay for my broken glasses. Later, at home, Winnie thought my skull might be fractured, but a visit to a doctor proved otherwise.

The next Sunday, my election-day experience became part of the discussion at the weekly afternoon current-events meeting at the Episcopal mission in Jamaica. Queens had become the living space of the new Negro middle class. Father McKinney presided over a congregation consisting of post-office workers, railroad porters, civil-service clerks, a few schoolteachers, real-estate salesmen, insurance agents, preachers, small landlords, and several lawyers. Doctors were in the upper class.

Father McKinney was considered very liberal because he welcomed people of all shades of skin into his fold. We well knew there were churches of the "colored" persuasion in Washington, Baltimore, and Charleston that would not admit Negroes who were black or brown-skinned into membership.

Although Father McKinney encouraged talk without inhibition, a few of us were eager to develop activity programs on the left for blacks. In early 1935, the four Lynns who were still together—Winnie, Dorothy, Charlotte, and myself—moved to an apartment over a tailor shop on New York Boulevard near Brinkerhoff Avenue, an area of small stores and undertaking establishments. It seemed an ideal area for another forum similar to the Syracuse model. Thus, with a few other radicals, such as LeRoy McLean, Liston Nicholson, Byron Headley, and Priscilla Pemberton, I helped form the Jamaica Forum, which met in our apartment on Sunday afternoons and as often during the week as necessary.

A few days before our first meeting, I dropped in on the tailor downstairs. Aaron Osofsky was a Russian anarchist of the Kropotkin cast. Although he deplored violence, he was proud of the exploits of the Spanish Anarcho-Syndicalists, who even then were preparing for their bloody showdown with fascism. His conviction that power corrupts contrasted with my faith in communist discipline and authority.

Our first discussions in the Jamaica Forum centered on the depression and its world implications. Many of the young people had parents who had lost money in the collapse of various business ventures clustered about the Garvey movement. Jamaica had been the core of the Colored Merchants Association, and one of its grocery stores still survived there.

Most of our members were black, but we barred no one from our discussions, and soon we had a devoted white minority. Our general orientation was toward the Communist party, though we never made any formal affiliation as a group. This fit with the new preachment of the Party for a united front of all class-conscious elements of the population, to stem the march of fascism.

We developed techniques in the forum of penetrating large Negro groups, such as the NAACP, the Negro lodges, and the churches. One of our most effective "cadres" was a petite Jewish girl of such dark complexion as to be easily mistaken for a Creole. We listened as she related hilarious stories about gaining the confidence of the most conservative and respectable Negro women's groups, whose members assumed she was a Negro. Such organizations were inaccessible to me. They would have rebuffed me as a known communist.

The antiwar movement in the United States boomed in 1935 with the heightening of international tensions and the assault by Mussolini on Ethiopia. We organized an immense demonstration at Columbia highlighted by a speech by Heywood Broun, the popular sports columnist of the *New York World*. The editor of the *Columbia Spectator,* James Wechsler, had laid bare in his columns the huge munitions holdings of the trustees of Columbia, which amounted to two billion dollars. Before this sensation subsided, our *Projector* published photos of women WPA workers behind the butcher-shop counter of Professor Irving Lorge's father in the Bronx. Evidently, the government was subsidizing the business of the distinguished teacher's family.

Wechsler's last editorial, in May 1935, "Hail and Farewell" beautifully set forth the society we sought:

> The path to an ordered, cooperative, profitless society is a long and perilous one; once attained, that goal will not be a wonderland of sweetness and light. It will be, let us say, the closest we can now conceive of the best of all possible worlds—without perfection or unbroken bliss or undiminished joy. It will provide the base upon which a civilization can be built; it is a prerequisite to that civilization but not the end-all of it. With the achievement of such a system our possibilities and progress will only be potential; but we cannot begin to emerge from our present dilemma without the erection of such a foundation.

I wonder what the editor of the *New York Post* thinks of those lines now?

One afternoon I went to see a motion picture with a Russian friend, Pyotr Epifanovich, at the Alhambra Theatre on Seventh Avenue near 126th Street. Just before the picture ended we heard a violent commotion. Everyone rushed outside and we followed.

As we reached the entrance, someone spotted Epifanovich and yelled, "There's a white son of a bitch! Let's get him!"

I moved in front of the man and asked what was wrong.

"The cops killed a little kid in the five-and-ten!"

An excited, angry black mob filled the street. I recognized a few of the demonstrators. They had attended our street meetings in the area. I pointed to my friend: "He's with us. He's one of my friends and he's from Russia."

The man who had wanted Epifanovich's blood calmed down. The Harlem people did not cotton to communism as a doctrine, largely because of its espousal of atheism, but they felt that communists were, at least, on their side.

With some difficulty I extracted Epifanovich from the crowd and hustled him back to Columbia. He was badly shaken. For the first time he realized that the mere color of his skin had endangered his life.

The Harlem riot raged on into the night.

Major damage was done by innumerable fires, set largely in the 125th Street area. Many black people were killed. But the riot gave a great boost to a peoples' movement, stemming out of Abyssinian Baptist Church and led by Adam Clayton Powell.

The cynical, irreligious playboy from Colgate had become the pastor of the largest Baptist congregation in America. I had lost contact with Adam during the early 1930s, but I remembered Fred Douglass telling the story of how Adam's preacher father had delivered the baccalaureate sermon at Colgate upon his son's graduation. He had begun by saying he had heard that his son had been passing for white at Colgate, but he wanted the students to know that Adam was black. Adam buried his head in his hands in humiliation.

From that day on, Adam flaunted his alleged African origin. In point of fact, the aquiline features, the light brown, straight hair, and the "high yaller" complexion, made Adam indistinguishable in appearance from a New England Brahmin. He had given us a lame story at school that there was an Indian ancestor in his family tree, but it was crystal clear that any Negro blood in him had been highly recessive.

In keeping with his role as a man of God, Adam helped calm the angry black masses after the riot had run its course. Had he been a revolutionary, the Democratic party's efforts to forestall any movement to overthrow the government would have undergone a severe test. Also, fortunately for the government, Adam had difficulty working in harness with other Negro leaders. A. Philip Randolph and Frank Crosswaith represented the union voice among the blacks in Harlem. Randolph was an effective speaker, but his mannerism of affecting a Harvard or English accent—I could never determine which—limited his appeal to the man in the street. But he was the darling of the white liberals and pacifists. As such, he spent most of his long public life pouring oil on troubled waters.

All the black leaders, however, united on immediate demands for significant employment of Negroes in the stores on 125th Street. Although these stores drew 99 percent of their income from the Harlem community, their owners disdained hiring blacks in any capacity save the most menial. Indeed, there were restaurants, such as Childs on 125th Street in the heart of Harlem, that as late as 1932 had refused to serve blacks at the counter. Many blacks accepted this standing affront without a murmur.

This racial lag might account for my distaste for the Negro middle class in New York City at that time. Not only did I carry over a hint of hauteur from law school, but the uncle-tom stance offended me. And I mistook the reciprocal distaste for my atheism as a sign that this group had never shaken off its servility to whites. Yet the lesson did exist of whimpering serfs at the onset of the Russian Revolution becoming, overnight, fearless revolutionaries. Perhaps a remnant of self-hate contributed to my myopia.

Supremely confident, Adam Clayton Powell was not encumbered by such drawbacks. In bull sessions at college it had been apparent that he had a deep contempt for the house domestics who contributed the major income of his father's church. But at public services in his imposing auditorium in the 1930s, he quickly demonstrated that he was a master of dissimulation. He did have an electrifying gift of speech.

The *People's Voice* became the organ of his movement, and Communists labored faithfully along with a few churchgoers to turn out its columns. Many of today's black bureaucrats got their start working for Powell's paper. Because they worked harder than anyone else, the Communists soon became the major influence on the paper.

At about this time the Party transferred me from the Columbia unit to the Harlem unit, where the experience of debating tactics with manual laborers was an eye-opening one for me. It soon became clear that many of these comrades had talents of a superior order. They had simply lacked the opportunity, or had not grasped it, to prepare themselves scholastically. Environment alone is not responsible for all degradation. All too often I witnessed the decline of persons with great native endowments, who were deficient in only one quality—the will. Drink or drugs completed their dissolution.

By the time the United States entered World War II, Adam Powell had forged a faithful following into a political machine that sent him to Congress again and again. There, his brash outspokenness for the little people made him an indispensable link in the civil-rights revolution.

CHAPTER 5

Political Differences and the Spanish Civil War

Communist party members, devoted students of R. Palme Dutt's *Fascism and Social Revolution*, were preoccupied with the onward march of Mussolini and Hitler. In the Harlem unit, we watched with horrified fascination as Ciano led the Italian fascist airmen in blowing up women and children in Ethiopia. Ciano did not hesitate to write poetry about the glory of the spectacle of huge bursts of blood and limbs erupting from the earth. We did not know at the time that Stalin had a contract with the Italian dictator to supply oil for his planes.

Hirohito's minions were decimating China. Hitler was preparing to march into the Rhineland. But no place held a more passionate concern for us than the dark Spanish terrain. There a government pledged to socialist change had been elected, but the fascists, with the connivance of international capitalism, were determined to overthrow it. Even before Franco had begun his uprising, Italian airmen had received orders to bomb Republican strongholds.

In France, we had seen how in 1934 the united front had temporarily forestalled the bid for power of the croix de feu. At the beginning of 1936 the united front tactic had been expanded into the Popular Front policy. At first, the significance of this policy was unclear to me.

The Harlem branch of the Party designated me as one of the delegates to the city committee in January 1936. At the first meeting I attended, I was struck by the lack of discussion about the ominous international events that were bringing a new world war ineluctably closer. When I asked if Russia was really selling oil to Mussolini, Weiss, the Harlem leader, mumbled something about the Soviet Union needing currency to secure strategic materials to prepare for its inevitable showdown with Hitler. The colonial sufferings, said Weiss, were regrettable, but the fate of the world depended on what happened in the advanced industrial nations. He said that this was where my major attention should be directed.

I soon had the opportunity to test this advice. That month I secured an assignment to the Workers' Education Project, which was devoted to teaching union workers, in order to enable them to function intelligently in their own self-interest, with one another as well as with their employers. During my free time I handled a few legal cases. Experience with the Party had convinced me that I had better obtain as much practice as possible.

The organizing drives of the Committee of Industrial Organizations in 1934 and 1935 had demonstrated the potential for militancy of the American working class, but Roosevelt and his New Deal cabinet rode with the punches and won over such key leaders as Walter Reuther and Philip Murray. It seemed clear to me that an American revolution was not imminent. Only the rush to World War II could provide another opportunity comparable to 1914–1918.

On the Workers' Education Project I met some of the best political minds ever collected under one roof. They were men and women dedicated to the cause of labor, and they represented every party and tendency on the left. For the first time, Trotskyists, Lovestoneites, Stammites, Socialists, Anarchists, and Henry Georgeites mingled with orthodox Communists.

My local reputation as a polemicist preceded me. Eddie Welch, Ella Baker, Pauli Murray, and Hezekiah Riley—all black intellectuals—shoved reading matter under my nose, critical of the Communist party. But the tactic boomeranged. A Communist is as much of an emotional being as he or she is a rational animal, and from 1928 on—with varying ups and downs—my basic loyalty had been to the Communist party. And I read only in the Party's press about its clashes with other elements of the left.

When the leadership noticed my spirited defense of the official line, it decided to use me in factional disputes. My most persistent opponent was an Italian-American schoolteacher, Agnes Martocci. She was a Socialist and the most articulate and truthful debater I had ever met. It was not unusual at a public meeting for the Party to assign three speakers to contain her.

I had one natural advantage. As a black, I represented the most oppressed masses anywhere in the world, whether we were speaking of the United States, the Caribbean, or Africa. The Socialists were hampered by the Norman Thomas line, tirelessly repeated, that no special bid needed to be made to blacks to win them to socialism. Black people, Norman Thomas pointed out, were part of the working class, and when the working class achieved power, blacks would share it.

World events were making a shambles of that thesis. It was true that in France the workers had beaten back the fascists, and Leon Blum, the able Socialist leader, had been elected by a popular front in which the Communists functioned. When Blum ordered the massacre of the Algerian revolutionaries in air raids at Setif, I insisted in a stormy meeting that the Socialists and their allies had to bear full responsibility for that terrible crime.

By now it was becoming clear to the Trotskyists and Lovestoneites that my commitment to the violent revolution was too deep for me ever to become a member of the Socialist Party. The former two groups redoubled their efforts to win me over.

I particularly admired Eddie Welch, a big, brown-skinned, hot-tempered man with a vitriolic tongue, which he used with the resonance of Paul Robeson. (It was not until forty years later that I learned in Harry Haywood's *Black Bolshevik* that Eddie had been a Communist youth delegate to the Sixth Congress of the International in Moscow in the twenties.) One evening at a political meeting in Harlem of the American League Against War and Fascism, he noticed a picture of Stalin on the wall. Eddie strode down the center aisle, pushed aside the chairman of the evening, and ripped down Stalin's picture.

He turned to the astonished audience and said, "Black revolutionaries should not stand for homage to the bloody collaborator of Mussolini in Ethiopia and the French in Algeria."

I was surprised to find myself standing and cheering. Party members gaped, and the Socialists looked at me in bewilderment. It was obvious to everyone that my position in the Communist party was becoming untenable. My loyalty to the colored people of the world was far greater than my loyalty to a political party. I had used the Communist party as an instrument; the goal was the liberation of the nonwhite peoples of the earth.

Just about this time the Spanish civil war began, and deep differences on the left were put aside for a while. The Communist party busied itself selecting comrades to enter the International Brigade. I sensed that the Party regarded me as too unreliable for such an assignment. But my early childhood friend, Tom Page, was picked to go, and many of my acquaintances in other parties volunteered.

Spain proved to be the last test of the classic tactics of revolution. Marx and Engels had been fascinated by the barricades of the French Revolution; but they had been forced to learn by the tragic end of the Paris Commune that romantic illusions about the efficacy of masses in the streets needed revision.

This no doubt, was one reason Engels became an authority on war in an industrial age.

Most of the young intellectuals in America, Canada, England, France, Italy, Germany, and other countries who filled the ranks of the International Brigade were expressing a heroic romanticism; but the terrible consequences of division in the ranks of people dedicated to a better future for oppressed humanity were demonstrated in Spain with grim finality. Jealousy and fear existed among the forces of the right—Mussolini, Hitler, the Catholic hierarchy—but their differences were submerged in order to restore the status quo ante. And the leaders of the so-called democracies—England, and the United States to a lesser degree—demonstrated their basic class solidarity through their "nonintervention" policy, which effectively barred aid for or to the elected Spanish government. Stalin delivered help to that government mainly to secure dominance by his agents.

But that was not the entire story. Beneath the personal and political rivalries within the left in Spain were irreconcilable views on how humankind attains true humanity. The Anarchists believed that people in combat must assert their full individuality and then pursue a common course only after freely giving consent: through this method they block the deadening hand of bureaucracy. The Communists stressed the need for tight organization and unquestioning obedience as the only way to defeat an enemy in the field. Complicating this basic division was the insistence of the Socialists and the P.O.U.M., largely Trotskyist, that Stalinist domination in the ranks of the government forces would mean only a new totalitarianism for the Spanish people.

Following the larger conflict from afar, and the conflicts within the left through underground sources, I knew that answers were needed to the awful dilemmas being presented.

In December 1936, Trinidadian oil workers struck against the British overlord on the Caribbean island. Alarmed out of all proportion, the English government dispatched warships to put down what it called a revolt: the population had shut down the harbor of Port-of-Spain in sympathy with the black strikers.

In January 1937, I attended a city committee meeting. The previous day, British sailors, operating the big guns of their battleships, killed twenty-three strikers and wounded hundreds of others.

I did not bother to ask for a place on the agenda. I stood up and proposed that the New York City committee of the Communist party back financially the Trinidad Oil Workers Union. I pointed out that the New York City division of the Communist Party in 1934 had the sole responsibility for supporting the Cuban revolutionaries in their struggle against Machado; surely it could do no less for the black workers in the West Indies.

The chairman of the meeting ruled my suggestion out of order. He said that it had not been proposed for the agenda, and, in a parallel of bourgeois forms, there was no discussion of the merits of my proposal. I walked out, and several West Indian comrades left with me.

The next day I was given notice that I would face a Party trial in the Finnish Workers Hall. It did not come as a surprise, because no one was permitted to resign from the Communist party. In the Party's lexicon a break could only mean expulsion.

The next day I was walking down New York Avenue in Jamaica and a young Party confidant, Leo Friedman, saw me coming. He hastily crossed to the other side of the street.

A clearer picture emerged in the next few days of who my friends would be. Some Communists defied orders and continued to speak to me. Among the blacks, these were largely West Indians. It was obvious an exodus from the Party of black intellectuals had taken place. The trend had begun before the first National Negro Congress in 1936 in Chicago. I talked with Angelo Herndon, who shared a seat in a railroad coach with me on the way to the congress. He confirmed information I had received from members of other left parties about the bloody purges then underway in Russia.

When we arrived at the congress, no information of this nature had been discussed. The Party had assigned us to devise ways to penetrate Negro organizations and recruit members. The Party, of course, had planks for better job opportunities for blacks, for building tenant-farmer unions in the South, and for making home relief more adequate. These were all well and good, but they did not quiet my burgeoning doubts. In the future, might not the application of the Popular Front doctrine involve the sacrifice of the black person's interests for a goal or temporary advantage of the Soviet Union?

The emotional ties I had formed in the Communist party caused me to resolve not to join any other party. The tragic consequences of left-wing division were all too apparent in Spain. Also, Roosevelt had just demonstrated in the 1936 election how cleverly the Democratic party could co-opt the slogans and even some of the programs of the left, in order to broaden its appeal to the underprivileged. Some of the president's supporters who had a socialist past, such as Fiorello LaGuardia, even campaigned with socialist rhetoric. Alf Landon never had a chance. Roosevelt carried every state except New Hampshire and Vermont.

FDR showed his true colors shortly after his inauguration. The island of Puerto Rico was governed as one of the few admitted colonies of the United States, but it had a strong nationalist tradition. Along with Cuba, it had risen in fitful revolt against Spain at various times in the nineteenth cenutry. During the Spainish-American War, General Nelson Miles landed his forces on the island to bring it, as he said, peace and liberty.

The Puerto Ricans soon learned they had merely exchanged masters. In fact, the limited autonomy they had won from Spain was brusquely nullified by the North Americans. Although the United States government granted nominal independence to Cuba in 1902, the Jones Act confirmed Puerto Rico as a colony.

The island was populated mainly by Catholics. One Sunday morning, early in March 1937, a nationalist leader named Pedro Albizu Campos conducted a march in the city of Ponce to celebrate a Te Deum mass in the cause of freedom. The American authorities had forbidden the march. As the unarmed Puerto Ricans, in holiday garb, filled the street on the way to the cathedral, U.S. marines closed in behind them. The order was given to fire. More than twenty men, women, and children were killed, and hundreds were wounded. I had no inkling at the time, but Pedro Albizu Campos would become my friend and play a major part in my life.

Roosevelt never apologized for the atrocity that became known throughout the world as the Ponce Massacre—evidently he believed the Puerto Ricans had been taught a salutary lesson. Nor did the condemnation of the wholesale murder in the left-wing press find any echo in the major North American newspapers. Once again it was apparent that the press moguls exercised a well-coordinated self-censorship of any news that would reveal that capitalism operated, de facto, as a dictatorship over minority people. The European press, however, did not fail to publicize the story of the Ponce Massacre.

The Communist party leadership had a difficult time with the colonial situation in Puerto Rico, just as it did with the Trinidadian oil strike. It was not as easy to decree a hands-off policy for its members about Puerto Rico as it had been to do so for Trinidad. Puerto Rico was a colony of *its* government, and some leading Puerto Rican militants, like Corretjer, were Communists.

The Party constantly kept at the fore the thesis that the main enemy of humankind was the fascist Axis—Germany, Japan, Italy. Inexorably, the Axis was compelled to expand by violent means, and the democracies had to be shored up to save civilization. If this position undercut the class analysis of society and implicitly rejected the conclusions about the nature of imperialism reached not only by communist thinkers such as Lenin and R. Palme Dutt, but by noncommunists like Hobson, Rudolf Hilferding, and Charles A. Beard, the Party leadership showed no signs of being aware of it.

My differences with the Communist party had considerable repercussions within my family. My sister Dorothy, who made an impressive record at Hunter College and had been a member of the Young Communist League there, entered the Howard University Medical School on scholarship after being rejected by the Cornell University School of Medicine. Cornell's letter of rejection had laid it on the line: "You will not be admitted, first, because you are a woman and second, because you are a Negro." Medical school took Dorothy away from the New York scene and she took no further part in left-wing political activity.

Winnie supported no political party, but he distrusted the economic premises of communism. He had worked hard as an auto mechanic throughout the depression and held the position that a person who really wanted to make it could get ahead.

My brother Arnold shared my attachment to the colonized peoples.

Charlotte and Samuel expressed interest in my dispute with the Party but took no overt position.

Regardless, I felt it to be a fact that wherever the Popular Front had achieved power, it suppressed unrest and dissent at home and prepared for war with the Axis. Thus, Socialists like Norman Thomas, who abhorred war above all else, found themselves bedfellows with rightists like Charles Lindbergh in the America First Committee.

Using hindsight, it is difficult to demonstrate how the world would have survived in any acceptable way without the defeat of Hitler and his cronies. The purists in politics make choice seem simple, but life is not readily reduced to formulas.

Meanwhile, a whole generation of young revolutionaries was being consumed in the Spanish civil war. At the outset we were thrilled by the exploits of the International Brigade and the new Republican Army. At the same time I could not help but feel melancholy over the persistent circumstance that black colonials were constantly used to consolidate the conquests of the oppressors. Ever since I was a boy and heard Arthur MacArthur tell how the Old Fifteenth had served Teddy Roosevelt so well in Cuba, and how Senegalese had served their French masters so well and at such cost in World War I, I wondered when these people would fight for their own freedom. Now the Moors were attacking the ideology of freedom itself: at the very time they were serving Franco they were acting as Moslem conquerors for reactionary Catholicism.

I did not gain a perspective on the centuries-old butchery of colored peoples by Western nations until many years later, when I talked with a North Vietnamese army captain in Hanoi.

Technology has always been the most faithful handmaiden of war. The American Indians were no less its victims than were the African slaves and the numberless millions of Asia. Now, the Spanish civil war seemed to be signaling the demise of the noblest configurations of Western humankind. Was there any hope for people save in a revolution to abolish classes?

On WPA we had plenty of time to speculate and argue, but I knew this program was only an emergency stopgap. It was essential for me to build up a law practice so that I could shed relief work altogether.

CHAPTER 6

On My Own

As a prerequisite to becoming an independent lawyer, I felt it necessary to move from James Johnson's office for the Dunbar National Bank. He had exercised exemplary patience with my radical proclivities, but he must have experienced considerable embarrassment explaining me to his patrons. No doubt, he felt that my youthful radicalism would gradually be submerged in the inevitable compromises that the practice of law involves. But he was active in the Tammany machine in New York City, and we both felt less strained after I moved.

Actually, moving consisted only of taking my office desk across the street to the real-estate office of a young black woman. She knew that I could be useful to her in her mortgage and sale transactions of houses, stores, and apartment buildings. In return for my advice she did not require me to pay any rent. A year after I left him, Mr. Johnson was appointed collector of the Port of New York. We never associated again on a professional or social basis, but he maintained a friendly attitude toward me. In the fifties he moved to Westchester to join the upper bourgeoisie there.

My estrangement from the Communist party affected my legal associations. I was one of the founding members of the National Lawyers Guild in New York City, which, as a Popular Front vehicle, served an important role in recruiting young lawyers to support progressive and left-wing causes. After all, there was no other organized group of lawyers devoted to aiding and defending the poor and dispossessed. But the guild attracted few Negro lawyers. Some of them had discovered that by quietly playing the Tammany political game, by ignoring the indignities endured by their less-favored brothers and sisters, they could feather their own nests. A few could even ascend to minor judgeships or middle-level administrative posts in the Establishment.

Ninety-seven percent of the members of the New York City Bar were white, and they held a near-monopoly on cases involving blacks. It was often discreetly pointed out to the potential black client that the judges were white and the black lawyer was, thus, at a disadvantage in court against white lawyers.

In the South, white lawyers did not seek black clients, so a class of black lawyers with black cutomers sprang up there. However, custom barred Negroes from pleading cases in the Deep South, so whenever a court appearance was necessary a white lawyer was hired.

Neither North nor South offered much opportunity for a black lawyer. During this period, black lawyers in Harlem secured no more than 15 percent of the legal business of that community. A major reason why anti-Semitism was rife among black professionals was that the white lawyers practicing in Harlem were largely Jewish.

Because I was both on WPA and a radical, my cases were not confined to blacks. One-third of the retainers I received in the late 1930s came from white people. Such retainers enchanced my reputation in the eyes of black clients, and white lawyers never ceased regarding me with curiosity whenever they saw me in court with a client of their race.

I tried my first contested divorce case in the summer of 1937. Prior to this, I had learned to dispose of uncontested divorce matters where both parties had agreed to separate and the "guilty" party would provide the other with the evidence of adultery required before a decree could be granted. New Yorkers were sophisticated enough to arrange these matters before seeing a lawyer. The lawyer was just the mechanic.

But a contested divorced was something else. The scene was the Surpreme Court of Nassau County in Mineola, on Long Island. The courthouse was an impressive three-story structure, its red bricks wreathed in vines as it sat behind a deep lawn.

My client was Arlene Spires. She was seeking a divorce from a philandering husband, and support for her three small children. My opponent was an elderly Negro lawyer from Queens County named Lipscomb. The judge was Thomas Hooley, who had employed my father as his gardener many years before. I could remember dusting off law books in his office when I was fourteen.

Early in the trial, Lipscomb pointed at my client and called her a "nigger." I demanded that the judge order him to apologize. The judge instead grinned contemptuously and waved me to sit down. It was obvious his funny bone had been tickled. It was all I could do to regain my composure. Was this Mississippi or New York?

Our evidence was overwhelming and my client was awarded her divorce, but I never forgot the humiliation of that day.

In the summer of 1937 I took a job as a substitute teacher at Julia Richmond High School in New York City. My class consisted of five girls: two blacks, two Italian-Americans, and a Puerto Rican. They had all failed the bookkeeping examination, not because they were stupid but because they were mischievous and restless. My job was to prepare them for the regents test, and it turned out to be the hardest work I had ever done.

First, I had to convince them that their individual progress was important to me; and second, each one had to be persuaded that she was intelligent. At the end of six weeks I was on the verge of a nervous breakdown, but it was gratifying that four of the five passed their regents. I joined the teachers union before I left the job.

By the end of 1937 it had become apparent that I would be able to make a modest living as an attorney without depending on my WPA salary, but I did not stop teaching altogether. I held classes for union members on their legal and organizational problems, and also for the poor who were on home relief or WPA. A great many of the lessons were devoted to a revolutionary analysis of current events. I imagined, considering my government-paid job dialectically, that in this manner I was hastening the demise of capitalism.

In late spring, 1939, I became involved in my second substantial criminal case. It involved a black inhabitant of the noisome community of Scotic. Scotic was the area of garbage dumps for the villages of Rockville Centre, Lynbrook, and Malverne. It was hollow land, behind a New York City water reservoir, and it was hidden from the roads that ran north and south by trees. Relief was so meager and restricted for the black unemployed of the surrounding towns that many families, evicted from their rented lodgings, had moved to the dump. They broke up old crates and flattened tin sidings to erect rickety homes. Then they picked over garbage to find scraps to eat.

It was a terrible existence, one that I was emotionally unprepared to encounter. The raggedy children ran when they saw me, not out of fear but from shame. None of them attended school, and truant officers made no attempt to visit their hovels. Scotic was not in any incorporated village, so no government felt responsible for the community. It was in the County of Nassau, however; and county police made forays into the area from time to time, looking for escaped criminals.

My client was charged with felonious assault with intent to kill. He was accused of blowing a man's leg off near the hip with a sixteen-gauge shotgun. I visited him in the county jail, and he showed me the same pathetic faith I had detected in Anna Center in 1933. He readily admitted committing the crime, explaining that the man had been fooling around with his wife.

The trial was held in an ornate, walnut-paneled courtroom. The jury rolls were restricted in practice to the middle and upper classes of white people. Henry Grant, my client, was obviously not going to be judged by a jury of his peers.

The district attorney had the shotgun admitted into evidence and laid it on a table in front of the jury. Its ammunition was displayed, and a picture of the bloody shreds into which the leg of the hapless victim had been torn was also introduced.

I did not put Henry Grant on the witness stand. He had a long record of previous arrests and convictions, and the jury would have been further alienated when the district attorney brought this out on cross-examination.

The defense consisted essentially of a summation. I had made a careful study of the history of Scotic, and I presented it in detail to the jury. It seemed to me that the jury was on trial, because it represented the sanctimonious communities that had condemned black people to be animals and had kept them hidden from view. I told them, finally, that whatever manner of man Henry Grant might have been, I too had been raised in the same county, and by the slightest turn of fate our roles could have been reversed. I finished the summation in tears, for what I had said was true.

The judge told the jury that what I said was true, but that they should not mistake my speech for the facts in the case.

Henry Grant was found guilty, and the judge sentenced him to three to six years in prison. By 1939 standards it was a light sentence.

Politics was never far from my mind, even when I was trying cases, because so many cases were really political in one way or another. And, of course, there were constant political discussions. Even after I had been expelled from the Communist party, many of my friends asked why I did not try to wangle my way to Spain. My answer derived from a conception that the main enemy of the black people was in the United States. It was our own government.

Few of the ideas of racial superiority enunciated in *Mein Kampf* were original with Hitler. He could neither improve upon the theories of racial supremacy developed in the *Dred Scott* opinion nor refine upon the tortures devised in the seventeenth, eighteenth, and nineteenth centuries for recalcitrant black men and women.

The grim tragedy of the Spanish people continued to unfold, as the major powers maneuvered for the inevitable showdown with the Axis when 1938 neared its end. I did not think it possible for Stalin to conclude an alliance with England and France. The ruling classes were far more afraid of the social revolution than they were of Hitler. Numerous influential groups in both countries, as in America, were eager to make a pact with Hitler in order to curb the ominous upsurge from the lower depths.

As part of its effort to persuade Roosevelt into favoring an alliance of the "democracies" against Hitler, the Communist party, with varying degrees of covertness, backed the Democratic party candidates in 1938. The fact that control of Congress by the Democrats meant control by Southern seg- regationist committee-chairmen in the House caused hardly a passing com- ment in the *Daily Worker*.

The Popular Front movement made gains in the mass organizations. From the American League against War and Fascism to the Congress of Industrial Organizations, the activity of dedicated cadres resulted in major influence for the Communist party. The new technique of the sit-ins was leading to rapid unionization of workers on assembly lines in the huge industrial combines.

The Socialists, with a strong base in unions such as the International Ladies Garment Workers and the Amalgamated Clothing Workers, com- peted bitterly with the Communists. Their great ace was the well-nigh universal loathing of Americans, black and white, for the Bolsheviks. And the Socialists never tired of pointing out that the first Communist country in the world had been transformed into a totalitarian dictatorship.

The Popular Front made headway with the clergy of all races. The Communists played down the doctrine that religion was the opiate of the people and were rewarded with the support of Adam Powell and Harry F. Ward.

Other splinter parties on the left provided lessons in ineffectuality. The Socialist Labor party, the Socialist Workers party, and the Anarchists had such canned, doctrinaire approaches that they appealed only to the mes- merized faithful. I believe most Americans are too practical to elevate dogma over reality and are inclined to applaud what works. Their dominant political instincts are infused with the memory of carving out careers on the frontier, conveniently forgetting how they murdered Indians in the process. The obscure rhetoric of the minor parties was bracketed with the bleating of crackpots, such as the Prohibitionists and the Vegetarians.

The year of decision was 1939. The corrupt, class-loyal statesmen of France and Britain had given the green light to Mussolini and Hitler at Munich. The ruling circles in France feared the workers far more than they did Hitler. Indeed, major sections of this class were willing to collaborate with him to preserve their domestic ascendancy. The Popular Front in

France, representing a mélange of social groups, had neither the perspective nor the courage to sweep away capitalism when it had the power. Now, in 1939, it was in full retreat.

Stalin had made overtures to the Front for an alliance, to include England, against Hitler. Chamberlain and Laval rebuffed his efforts. These two men cynically manipulated the desire of their populations for peace, and their press never tired of portraying the barbarity of the Russian bear. Hitler had goose-stepped into the Sudetenland, and it was only a matter of a few months before he would swallow all of Czechoslovakia. A year earlier he had marched into Austria, and only the pathetic resistance of the Socialists indicated the presence of a workers' movement there.

Stalin shifted gears and began a secret discussion with the Nazis. He was menaced by Japanese aggression in Siberia and sensed that Chamberlain would like nothing better than to see the Germans roll over Russia, while the Western powers waited to pick up the pieces. Therefore, Stalin decided to buy time.

On August 23, 1939, radios throughout the world crackled with a startling announcement: Stalin and Hitler had signed a mutual assistance pact. The West's cards had been trumped.

The stroke was clever and callous, and it left the rank-and-file supporters of Communism at sea. After all, the number one enemy of humankind was Adolf Hitler.

Even the Trotskyists had been taken aback by this coup. As perfidious as they had painted Stalin to be, they had never imagined he would actually forge an alliance with the Nazis. Some believed Stalin might be playing for time, but they feared Hitler was more ruthless and powerful—especially, that he had not given up his fanatical conviction that Bolsheviks were the ultimate enemies of "Christian civilization." Hitler, with his raw materials assured and his rear secure, sent his Wehrmacht and Luftwaffe against Poland on September 1. The soldiers of the Pilsudski dictatorship fought surprisingly well, but it was over in thirty days.

The French and British had declared war on Germany but had done little else. This was the period of the "phony war." In the United States, the *Daily Worker* shrilly assailed British and French imperialism and suddenly recognized that it was worthwhile to support the colonial revolts in Indochina and Algeria. Sympathy even for the West Indian dissidents began to creep into the Communist press, and former acquaintances in the Party began to smile upon me again. Perhaps some use could be made of the intransigent stand of colored peoples after all.

At this juncture Leon Trotsky, in the October issue of *New International*, organ of the Socialist Workers party, called for a revolt of all the workers of the world against their national rulers.

The issue was banned from the mails! The editors consulted me about the possibility of lifting the government injunction. They rightly believed that the issue suppressed had most felicitously expressed the final thought of Marxists. Trotsky had written:

> "The second world war had begun. Without any question it proved that society could no longer live on the basis of capitalism. Thus the proletariat was subjected to a new and, perhaps, decisive test." If the war provoked a proletarian revolution, the world and the U. S. S. R. would return to the classical Marxist perspective. On the other hand, if the proletariat does not "take into its own hands the direction of society," the world might evolve in the direction of a monopolistic and authoritarian capitalism. "As onerous as the second perspective is, if the world proletariat proves itself in fact incapable of fulfilling the mission conferred upon it by the course of historical development, nothing else remains than to recognize frankly that the socialist program, founded on the internal contradictions of capitalist society, has ended as a utopia." (quoted in Maurice Merleau-Ponty, *Humanism and Terror*, p. 151.

The editorial board of *New International* consisted of sharply contrasting personalities. James Burnham was a shy, reticent Irish-American. C. L. R. James was the scintillating West Indian orator and the author of *The Black Jacobins*. Dwight MacDonald was a wealthy social critic and art partron, who presented a somewhat sardonic counter to the board's left politicians, Joe Carter and Max Schachtman.

I agreed to see what could be done about lifting the government ban of *New International* from the mails. I suggested that instead of resorting to court action we pursue administrative remedies in the Post Office Department in Washington.

I called my former constitutional law professor and debating coach, Ralph Himstead, who was stationed in Washington as the general secretary to the American Association of University Professors. Himstead set up an appointment for me at the Post Office Department and, after a three-hour session, I was able to have the ban lifted. My new clients were delighted.

In the winter of 1939 Stalin moved to secure his northwestern flank. He sent the Red Army smashing into Finland. He may have expected a quick victory because the Finns were vastly outnumbered, but they put up a tremendous fight. The Fourth International split on the issue of the invasion. The official line of the Trotskyists had been that Russia was a degenerated workers' state, deserving, in the last analysis, of support against any capitalist nation.

The editorial board of *New International,* examining the Russian state anew in the light of the Finnish invasion, broke away from the Socialist Workers party and founded a new group, the Workers party. The editorial board took the magazine with them as the organ of their new party. In its pages there raged a new debate: whether Russia was a bureaucratic collectivism or whether it had evolved into state capitalism. If Russia had become a bureaucratic collectivism, it still contained new forms of production. If it had become state capitalism, then the great Communist experiment had come to an inglorious end. C. L. R. James expounded the latter view, Max Schachtman the former.

The debate came to a sudden end with Hitler's spring 1940 offensive against France. The Panzers, supported by thousands of dive bombers, broke the hinge of the Maginot line at Sedan and used the military tactic called blitzkrieg. In six weeks France surrendered, and Hitler was at the English Channel.

The United States still adhered to the Neutrality Act, and Stalin was increasingly nervous. The Japanese warlords gobbled up the French possessions in Indochina. The Eastern European nations hastened to climb aboard the Reich's bandwagon.

England stood alone. Churchill became prime minister and began his imperishable admonitions to his countrymen to stand firm.

My attitude towards England had always been ambivalent. Its poets, novelists, and playwrights had captivated me, and the astringent skepticism of its great philosophers and scientists from Newton through Hobbes and Locke to Mills and Bertrand Russell had acted as needed counters to the romanticism of Hegel, Marx, and Nietschze. But I had always been revolted by its imperialist depredations and held it largely responsible for the depopulation and subjugation of Africa.

Nevertheless, England's stand in the summer and fall of 1940 was unforgettable.

Not long after France had fallen, the Workers party held a meeting in a hall on Irving Place in New York City. It was to be a valedictory meeting since the magazine would soon cease publication. Everyone was sunk in gloom. Logically, fascism was about to triumph everywhere. The Bundists, the Coughlinites, and the Ku Klux Klan had never been so buoyant.

C. L. R. James was the only speaker and he was magnificent. His address lasted seventy-five minutes, and he seemed equally at home in English, Yiddish, and French. For sheer emotional power, Adam Powell had no peer; but James, in the purity of diction and the felicity of his ideas, swept all before him. Never had I witnessed such a performance. James *proved* that despite all appearances Hitler could not win.

The meeting unanimously delegated to James the authority to write the entire next issue of *New International*. It was titled "Capitalist Society and the War," and it must be a bibliophile's prize now.

In December 1940, the Rapp-Coudert Committee summoned me to appear before it. The New York legislature had set up this group to harass leftists parallel with the Dies Committee on the national level. I was told in a conference that I was expected to reveal the names of Party members with whom I had been associated in the WPA teachers union. I declined to give the information.

Next, I had to appear at the Association of the Bar building in response to the committee's subpoena. This time they closeted me with a coaxing young woman, who hinted at unspoken delights if I would cooperate. This interview was faintly amusing. Finally, a lawyer warned that I would be taken before a judge of the state supreme court who would hold me in contempt if I did not testify. I invited the lawyer to fulfill his duty in any way he felt best. It did not seem to me that I would come off second best in a public showdown. Informers and betrayers had not yet achieved the status of valued public servants.

I went to the headquarters of the Workers party and told McKinney, the party's national labor secretary, who was black, of my refusal to testify against Communist party members.

"You damn fool," McKinney said. "Why didn't you testify against those rats?"

"Are you serious?"

"Hell, man, they're the enemy. You hit them any way you can hurt them."

I was astounded at the depths of his hatred. Was this the length to which factional fighting was carried?

The rank-and-file Communist may have been a dupe in some ways but he was not vicious. Quite the contrary. Throughout the 1930s I had witnessed in some instances the incessant activity of Communist party members on behalf of the dispossessed and disinherited of all races. The Party was the first to come to the defense of the Scottsboro Boys, even though later they were suspected of diverting some of the funds raised to the Party coffers. Many a lynching would not have come to light had it not been for dedicated cadres of Communists in the Deep South. I did not hesitate to oppose Party members in debate when it came to the meaning and proper application of Marxist doctrine, but fingering them for the police or FBI was another matter. Opinion on this issue was mixed in the Workers party. I gradually stopped attending their meetings.

By this time I had moved to 125th Street to share an office with a West Indian lawyer named Joseph Allen. Allen was a conservative, but he had the West Indian's respect for the radical intellectual, and we never had clashes because of my political habits.

My income had risen to the point where I had no pressing economic worries. My needs were modest since I neither drank to any degree nor smoked. It was clear that the advent of war in Europe had chased away the depression. The nation's immense productive apparatus busily turned out weapons and food for the European belligerents, the great bulk of it for England and its supporters in the Commonwealth.

It was about this time that I proposed to Gene Phillips, a winsome young white woman mentioned above. My qualms against marrying white women were dissipated by her charms, and I proposed. She hesitated. Shortly thereafter she visited her parents in Oklahoma—her father was a wealthy doctor. She came back to tell me her father had solemnly promised that if we were married, he would come hunting with his rifle for that "nigger lawyer," She was convinced that he meant it and we decided to remain boyfriend and girlfriend.

A few days later I learned of the death of one of my closest Syracuse friends, Fred Douglass. The circumstances of his death were hazy, but I could not help but think that he had never recovered from the brutal rebuff he received from Adam Powell in 1938.

Fred Douglass had become an intransigent radical after I left Syracuse in 1932. He became a member of the organizing committee of industrial unions in that area, and also a foundry worker. After the bitter defeat of the Little Steel Strike in 1937, Douglass found himself blackballed.

He visited me in New York and asked if I thought Adam Powell might have an opening for him in his Job Campaign.

"Well, Doug," I said. "You were Powell's best friend in Syracuse. Why not go to Abyssinian and talk to him?"

He did. He handed his card to Powell's secretary in the anteroom, waited for two hours, and then was ushered into the office.

"Do I know you?" Powell asked.

Doug was so hurt by the cold denial in that voice that he picked up his hat and walked quietly out. It was not the first or last time Adam Clayton Powell would make it plain that unless he saw some immediate advantage to himself in a friend, he would refuse to acknowledge him.

CHAPTER 7

Pilgrimage to Washington for Jobs

When I was able to sustain lasting interest with any friend, man or woman, it depended in large part on our mutual depth of commitment to political thought and action. After the outbreak of war in Europe in 1939 most of my associates realized that it would only be a matter of time until the United States entered the conflict.

To me, therefore, the campaign of the America First Committee, and the parallel campaign of the American Communist party against the United States becoming a belligerent, had an air of unreality about it.

The Wehrmacht attacked Russia on June 22, 1941, with fifteen thousand planes and twenty thousand tanks on a two-thousand-mile front. The Soviets reeled back in confusion.

Editors of the *Jamaica Gleaner* asked me to write a story estimating the probable outcome. I pointed out that Stalin had decimated his general staff in the bloody purge. Tukhashevsky, possibly the most brilliant young military mind since the first Napoleon, had been executed, and only a few veterans of the civil war remained to direct the defense. Hitler's forces, directed by von Rundstedt, Guderian, Goering, and others, appeared incomparably more powerful. I predicted the Russians would last six weeks. At that, my guess was three weeks more generous than Hanson Baldwin's.

The American Communist party did an abrupt about-face. On June 21, 1941, they were denouncing the Western imperialists. On June 23, 1941, they published a special addition of the *Daily Worker* calling all Americans to the sacred task of defeating history's worst monster, Adolf Hitler.

As funny as this seemed, I still found myself on the side of the Communists. There had never been any doubt in my mind as to who was the chief enemy of humankind at the time; and a rudimentary understanding of the balance of forces showed that the intervention of the United States would decide the war. The Russians might have fought the Germans to a stalemate, but they could not have been victorious after so terrible a bloodletting.

Without American aid they could, at best, have hoped for mutual collapse and unimaginably bloody chaos.

The Communists were now in favor of scrapping the Neutrality Act, and the Socialists, who were not as agile or as cynical as their erstwhile Popular Front bedmates, were left alone as its sole supporters. Almost for the sake of consistency alone, it seemed, some Socialists continued to call for no American involvment in the war.

In October, the Russians finally held before Moscow, and for the first time the great Nazi lunge had been contained. Many on the American left began to reappraise the Russian tactics. Was it possible that Hitler was courting the fate of Napoleon? The Russians were selling space and manpower at a fearful rate to give the Americans time to throw their full weight into the struggle. Roosevelt's cabinet was split, with Ickes, Hopkins, and Wallace generally more pro-Russian than the others.

Pearl Harbor resolved the developing differences. Roosevelt had been busy maneuvering Japan into a corner, and now there was no choice but for America to fight, which is what the President wanted. China had proved a morass for Hirohito, but the collapse of France had opened up the riches of Southeast Asia to him. He saw his only chance of escaping the tentacles of the American octopus in one mighty surprise blow. He succeeded in uniting 99 percent of the American people behind Roosevelt.

Roosevelt set about mobilizing all the country's resources for war, but he did not try to alter basic social patterns. By longstanding practice, Negroes were excluded from all skilled occupations, leaving them to work only as servants or to survive on home relief. Thousands volunteered for the army, navy, and air force. The navy and air force turned down almost all the black volunteers. When blacks were accepted, they were relegated to roles as cooks, messmen, grease monkeys, and laborers. Things were not much better in the army. Blacks were expected to be quartermaster troops and to form labor battalions.

Prospects for blacks on the civilian front were also bleak. Most war industries offered blacks only the most menial jobs. Blacks watched their white neighbors driving new cars and buying new homes. The NAACP's executive secretary, Walter White, was frequently at the White House visiting Eleanor and Franklin Roosevelt, but this did not change matters an iota.

At this time I was becoming better acquainted with the pacifists. Their undeviating opposition to the war fascinated me. Were there really those whose principles never wavered?

The gathering place of absolute pacifists in Harlem was the ashram near Mount Morris Park. Ruth Reynolds, Bayard Rustin, Pearl and Fran Hall, and the Reverend Mr. Holmes held forth. The house was organized in accordance with certain customs of India, where Mahatma Ghandi was trying to introduce fundamental social change and gain independence by campaigns of nonviolence.

The pacifists introduced me to the draft-resistance law. Many of them had refused to register for conscription, and when apprehended they faced five years in prison. The courts would not even allow these young idealists to testify in public trial about their reasons for opposing war, so their impact was limited.

I admired their selflessness and courage, but my youthful fascination with war and my conviction that underlying populations would never win their freedom by nonviolent means prevented me from joining them.

Through the ashram I met members of the Catholic Workers, which afforded me my first association with Catholics. They certainly did not fit the stereotypes of that faith which influenced me over the years. The Catholic church had been the strongest bulwark of Franco, and to many of us it seemed the major enemy of the social revolution. But the Catholic Workers were communists—an interesting mélange of Platonists and libertarians. Dorothy Day, their founder, had at one time been very close to the American Communist party. It seemed to me that we shared a nostalgic attachment to the Party, while recognizing the evils fostered by its leaders.

In 1941, A. Philip Randolph proclaimed a march on Washington to protest the failure of industry to integrate blacks into the war prosperity by affording them jobs. The craft unions opposed the admission of blacks, saying they were unskilled and illiterate or semiliterate. Actually, many blacks had been trained in crafts in the South—in bricklaying, carpentry, plumbing, and other trades. A tradition in the South dating back to the pre-Civil War era ordained that these manual crafts could be performed by slaves, mainly because most whites looked down on such work. This tradition broke down with the industrialization of the South after World War I.

White tenant farmers were driven off the land, and their only recourse was to take the jobs formerly held by black men. Even the Negro barber who cut the hair of the white gentlemen was being replaced. The mass migration of black people to the North dates from this time.

In the North, however, the migrants met a solid barrier to employment in the rules and constitutions of the craft unions, which barred them from membership; and in most places employers would not hire them unless they could prove they were union members. George Meany's Local No. 2 of the Plumbers in the Bronx, for example, had become notorious for its policy of blatantly excluding black craftsmen. It was Meany, incidentally, who later boasted that he had never called a strike or walked a picket line.

Randolph's technique was a ploy typical of a Socialist: the last thing a Socialist wanted to do was discredit a Democratic president. Of course, the march had been organized with the aid of Benjamin McLaurin and Bayard Rustin, both Socialists.

Thousands of young blacks were organized to march. Then, Randolph telegraphed Franklin Roosevelt asking him to issue an executive order barring discrimination in employment on account of race. When the march was on the verge of taking place, Eleanor prevailed upon Franklin to issue the order. Randolph, of course, called off the march.

The deceit in this maneuver was that the march had been organized as unconditional. Many of us backed the preparations because we felt it would provide the opportunity for a revolutionary confrontation with the government. This, of course, was the last thing the Socialists had in mind.

My law offices were in the same building where Randolph had the headquarters of his Brotherhood of Sleeping Car Porters, and I was on the executive committee of the youth group backing the march. When I learned through his secretary, DeVera Johnson, that Randolph was about to call off the march, I called an emergency meeting of the executive committee. At this meeting we condemned the pusillanimity of the older leadership, but essentially we were helpless because Randolph controlled the buses and the money. It was another lesson proving that revolutionary action cannot be expected from liberals.

The job situation for blacks did not improve, despite Roosevelt's executive order, and the growing race friction in the army made it apparent that nothing was being done to extirpate racism and bigotry on the home front.

At this impasse the dedicated egalitarians of the Harlem ashram decided to witness for justice. We organized a walk from the Harlem YMCA to Washington. We were pledged to complete nonviolence, we expected to be fed and housed by well-intentioned citizens along the route, and we planned to follow the famous Lincoln Highway the entire way.

One morning in early September 1942, we gathered at the YMCA. Among us were Margaret and Charles Lawrence, a young black doctor and her teacher husband; Hope Foy, a black dancer; two young white Mennonites; Ruth Reynolds; Rev. Holmes; and myself.

Our first casualties were the Lawrences. Charles severely cut his foot as we entered Central Park, and his wife dropped out to take care of him. At the Twenty-third Street ferry we compromised on the decision to walk every step of the way and accepted a ride across the Hudson to Jersey City.

New Jersey was called the "Georgia of the North" by blacks, so we were not surprised to be greeted by physical threats from hostile whites. Some roustabouts on the dock threatened to throw us in the river, but the police intervened. The white racists who threatened us, much like the government itself, seemed to have learned nothing about America's oft-proclaimed equality.

That night I debated with the pacifists the principle involved in allowing the police to employ force in their behalf. A minority of the group felt it was inconsistent to permit the police to protect us physically, and that they should have presented their bodies in a demonstration of Satyagraha, or soul-force.

For the most part the weather remained dry. Near the end of the third day we approached the environs of Princeton, and the police chief met us at the town's limits and read an ordinance forbidding the distribution of leaflets. He said the law had been passed to prevent littering.

"Littering?" I said.

"Right!" he said. "We want to keep our streets clean."

"We want to call the nation's attention to job discrimination," I said, knowing the moment I said it that I was wasting breath.

"The law's the law," he said.

Somehow I persuaded the chief to lead me to the town attorney. That worthy debated with me the application of a Supreme Court decision, *Griffin v. Georgia*, to the Princeton ordinance. In *Griffin* v. *Georgia* the Supreme Court had ruled that a similar ordinance unconstitutionally interfered with freedom of the press. Grudgingly, we were permitted to hand out our leaflets.

At night generally we were able to stay in an empty church. And in Trenton, Father Divine's followers treated us to a sumptuous chicken dinner.

The fifth day found us wearily trudging along the banks of the Delaware River, a few miles from Philadelphia's city line. We were so tired we barely noticed the glow of the rising sun. A suggestion that we stop to worship on a gentle slope leading down to the river was quickly accepted. Most of us were footsore and dispirited, and Washington seemed a long way.

A young black theological student, Wayne Nickerson, opened the service. As a professed atheist, I was assigned to the outer fringe of the group to ward off interruptions. Just as the service began a red-haired, red-faced man came running down the hill.

"I'm McLoughlin of the *Bulletin*," he shouted.

I put my finger on my lips to signal him for silence. He took off his hat, stopped his rush, and sat down beside me. Nickerson had quietly begun reading from Isaiah, 40:31: "But they that wait upon the Lord shall renew their strength; they shall mount up with wings as eagles; they shall run and not be weary; they shall walk and not faint."

Everyone seemed invigorated. When a volunteer to be the day's leader was called for, the young dancer, Hope Foy, raised her hand. The leader had the toughest task because he or she looked only at the endless road ahead. Those who followed could look at a companion just ahead.

McLoughlin had come to make fun of us, but the sight of Hope wrapping bandages about her feet and setting her face toward Philadelphia drained the humor out of him.

I had to leave the group just before they entered Philadelphia, to handle a case in New York City. I rejoined them north of Wilmington, Delaware, a few days later.

In Philadelphia, the authorities tried to persuade Ruth Reynolds to stop walking because her feet were trailing blood on the sidewalks. She refused, and it was necessary to arrest her in order to place her in an ambulance and take her to a hospital for emergency treatment.

Ruth was back with the group, however, when I rejoined them. She went the rest of the way, never complaining.

About nine miles from Wilmington a band of nine or ten white youths began to threaten us. We tried to ignore them but they moved closer and became more menacing. They were young racist toughs and their courage was buoyed by the realization that no one would fight back. Here it comes, I thought!

Just at that moment a black WPA worker who had been stolidly swinging his pick walked over to me. "Don' git scared," he said. "Ain' nobody gonna hurt ya. Don' git scared."

In the fury of his trembling voice I knew a lowly black had become a man. He was so determined that he was ready to die, and everybody sensed it, not the least the Delaware boys. Without saying another word they turned and walked away down the street with exaggerated casualness.

It was one of the thrilling moments of my life. The march, the belief in the dispossessed, the essential rightness of it all—it was worthwhile. We walked into Wilmington unmolested. I will never forget that brave WPA worker.

The decision was made to no longer walk at night. This meant we had to take shorter rests during the day.

Father Divine's followers provided us with food in Wilmington, and the Quakers secured a Protestant church where we could sleep. We wished that A. Philip Randolph had brought tens of thousands of marchers; but this was something, it was directing attention to a vital issue, and now, tired and sore, the end of our trek was in sight.

New and revived industries dotted the landscape between Wilmington and Baltimore. Most of the white workers we encountered on our walk ignored us, but without overt hostility; and the black workers were less demonstrative than they had been before. We were, after all, walking South: all public accommodations were now strictly segregated.

Before we reached Baltimore we learned that elaborate preparations had been made for our arrival. Juanita Jackson, the dynamo of Baltimore's NAACP chapter, had secured a large Negro Baptist church in which to greet us.

We had to take a trolley at the edge of town to be at the meeting on time. The crowd was large and the meeting friendly, but the people seemed a bit puzzled. They must have thought we were extreme.

Ruth Reynolds insisted that we take a trolley back to the town limits and walk through Baltimore. Most of us demurred: we would never conform to our announced schedule of reaching Washington on the fifteenth day if we went backward. But Ruth's suggestion made me wonder again about the wisdom of totally committed people who elevate form over substance. Had we devoted as much time to convincing the middle-class Negroes in that Baptist church of the merits of desegregation as we spent on the sterile argument of whether we were betraying our mission by not walking every step of the way, our net impact could very well have been greater. At any rate, common sense prevailed and we did not take the trolley.

The walk through the Maryland countryside evoked mounting hostility. Mississippians could hardly have been more hateful than those white Marylanders who resented any effort to win equality for black people. When we reached Laurel on the night of the fourteenth day it was apparent to the administration that without a federal guard we would never reach Washington alive, and that a mob attack upon us would reverberate throughout the world.

Roosevelt, with the consent of Maryland's governor, sent his metropolitan police to throw a protective cordon around us that night at our little encampment by a Negro church. The next day we walked the last twenty-two miles to Washington.

Neither the President, Eleanor, nor any member of the cabinet met us. An obscure secretary at the White House accepted our petitions. I had a strange feeling of uncompleted mission as we turned away. It was not the first time that pacifist projects would make me uneasy. I had no doubt they were sincere, and I knew many of them were ready to make the ultimate sacrifice for their beliefs, but it seemed to me that the elevation of nonviolence and orderliness as means, often vitiated the desired end.

We had walked all the way from New York City to Washington, D.C., without giving the slightest response to threats of violence. We had conquered our impulses, it was true, and disciplined our spirit; but what gain had been made for the cause of equality of opportunity in employment? It was not discernible to me.

The war went on and grew larger, and shortages of manpower developed in industry, thus giving white women and black men unprecedented opportunities to work. But these openings could not be attributed to our demonstration.

The walk had acted as a catharsis for the white people who participated. They had done penance for the sins of their fellow whites. But for the black walkers it had meant suppression of indignation and a lesson in humility. I doubted that this result was desirable.

Happily, some of the black youths were radicalized by the experience and deserted the pacifists to become revolutionary Marxists. They no longer believed that America afforded any real possibility of assimilating the Negro as a human being. Only in an overthrow of the existing social structure by violent means was there any hope for the underlying population..

CHAPTER 8

The Case Against Segregation in the Army

As much as I detested Hitler, my conception of World War II as a savage struggle between competing imperialist alliances prevented me from volunteering for service. Russia's role, however, made this analysis seem incomplete.

My brother Winnie—Winfred—was ordered to report for induction into the armed forces, but our family had very strong feelings about the government's humiliating conscription practices. We were opposed to lock-step regimentation and were particularly offended by the contemptible roles assigned to black men. In fact, it was a persistent belief among white people that Negroes were natural cowards and, therefore, could be trusted only in menial roles.

A lottery system had been devised for the white majority, but such was hardly the case for blacks. Each state director of Selective Service was assigned a quota of blacks that he was to call. When the army wanted a certain number of blacks, the state director passed the order to local boards, and blacks were called by name, not by chance. Of course, black recruits were kept in strictly segregated units, and their commissioned officers were almost invariably white.

Blacks throughout the nation were becoming indignant about the daily assaults on black soldiers by white civilians off post. In Monroe, Louisiana, black soldiers were murdered because, imagining they were citizens like white people, they dared to wear their uniforms in town.

Winfred wrote a letter to Franklin Roosevelt, with a copy to his draft board, stating that he would volunteer for the Canadian army because it was not segregated. He opposed Hitler as the embodiment of racial bigotry, but he refused to submit to induction into a segregated army that seemed to him to ratify his "inferiority."

Winfred did not show up for his induction date and was arrested and lodged in the federal government's detention house on West Street in Manhattan. I had not expected the government to accept a showdown on the issue so quickly, but I underestimated the self-righteousness of Roosevelt's democratic crusaders.

I went to research. I delved into law books and discovered an amendment to the draft law that had escaped public attention: "In the selection and training of men for service there shall be no discrimination on account of race or color."

In August 1940, the NAACP had persuaded the vote-seeking administration to accept that amendment as a modification of the draft law.

The law was clear. Blacks had to be selected for service on the same basis and with the same machinery as whites. I went to the Eastern District Federal Court in Brooklyn and sought a writ of habeas corpus, a remedy that requires a government official to produce the prisoner in court and justify the detention.

I contacted the NAACP the day before argument was to take place in court. That organization refused to have anything to do with the case.

I trudged over to the Civil Liberties Union. Thurgood Marshall, now a U. S. Supreme Court justice, then special counsel for the NAACP, pleaded with the Civil Liberties officials *not* to help in the case. The Civil Liberties Union reluctantly admitted that they had an informal understanding with the NAACP not to take a case involving black people if the NAACP disapproved.

This was simply one of numerous disagreements I would have with the NAACP. Even today, to many white people, the NAACP is a fire-breathing, radical organization. In reality, it is often quite conservative.

I was depressed, and worried about my brother. But that night I received a telephone call from the great Arthur Garfield Hays, general counsel of the American Civil Liberties Union and a former partner of Clarence Darrow. Hays told me that Pan Stone, my former mentor at Syracuse, had urged him to interest himself in Winfred's case. Pan, incidentally, was the niece of U. S. Supreme Court Chief Justice Harlan Fisk Stone.

Hays told me he was convinced that Winnie was no mere draft dodger but an opponent of racial discrimination. Therefore, he said, he would be happy to appear with me in the federal court.

I was overjoyed. Arthur Garfield Hays was one of the finest and most compassionate attorneys in the world. I listened carefully as he instructed me on what papers I should have for him the next morning.

I arrived early at the court and Mr. Hays was already there. He said very little to me. He read my file very carefully and at 10:30 A.M. he was ready.

Judge Mortimer Byers ordered our case moved up to number one position. The bridgeman intoned, "United States versus Lynn," and Hays stood up with the aid of his cane. He was a man of enormous dignity and impeccable credentials, and it was impossible not to be impressed and filled, just a little, with awe.

The judge would not look at him. He said, "I have before me the petition for a writ, the writ of habeas corpus, the return to the writ. Writ dismissed. Next case!"

The courtroom gasped.

Hays limped slowly and calmly toward the bench.

"Mr. Hays," the judge said sharply. "I have decided the matter. No argument will be permitted."

A whole country full of Mortimer Byerses would not equal one Arthur Garfield Hays. Hays continued straight up to the bench.

"Your Honor, I intend to show why you should accept argument on so critical an issue as this."

The judge's face turned red. Then white. This was no upstart Conrad Lynn who was standing in front of him, but a premier civil-rights lawyer—yet he was pulled by other considerations, too.

The courtroom glittered with brass. The adjutant-general had sent a bevy of officers from Washington. The judge advocate general was represented by a platoon of lawyers. The administration was taking this threat seriously.

But what was the threat? All we asked was that black people fighting for the country be treated equally.

Hays spoke quietly, and the judge, despite the preponderance of the military in the courtroom, dared not interrupt. Hays said he thought we were sending soldiers into battle against the Nazi superman philosophy because we were committed to the proposition that all men were created equal. At last, history's great scourge, said Hays, was being met by the massed might of all the freethinking people of the world. What a disgrace, what a mockery, Hays concluded, it would be to refuse to listen to a young black man who asked only that the government live up to its own professed beliefs.

Judge Byers was no thinker, but he knew better than to hold Arthur Garfield Hays in contempt of court. He knew enough, also, that the government did not want public ventilation of its practices toward black inductees. Finally, he knew enough to tell the government's lawyer to sit down: Hays had just given the best extemporaneous court argument I had ever heard, and there was really nothing to say in rebuttal, despite what the eager-beaver military lawyer thought.

Judge Byers simply reiterated that the writ was dismissed. People who are in charge can do that, no matter how much in the wrong they might be. Byers said that Winfred had not actually submitted to induction, so he had not suffered the discrimination anticipated.

"If the prisoner goes into the army," said Hays, "will you issue another writ of habeas corpus?"

"We'll cross that bridge when we come to it," the judge said, not very cleverly.

Hays came over to me and said he believed the judge would issue a writ if Winnie would submit to induction. Would Winnie agree? I said I thought he would if Hays would explain the situation.

Winnie did go in. He was taken to Camp Upton on Long Island for basic training. I prepared a new petition for a writ of habeas corpus and submitted it to Judge Byers. He refused to sign.

He would not talk to me, of course, but his secretary explained that the judge did not believe a writ could be issued to an army officer in wartime through a civilian judge.

I was outraged, but as a revolutionary Marxist I was not particularly surprised. I did not put much faith in the honor of a capitalist judge. Arthur Garfield Hays, however, was indignant. He felt the judge had double-crossed him. Of course, we spoke to newspaper reporters and the case received widespread publicity.

(Judge Byers has been dead for some time and it is difficult for me to feel any enmity toward him. It is considered a mark of ability for judges in this country to evade basic matters of principle when deciding cases: don't be controversial and don't rock the boat. This is particularly true in wartime. I recall scores of cases I had pending during the Vietnam war on the legality and constitutionality of that conflict, yet it was impossible to get the Supreme Court or any of the subordinate courts to consider the issues. By adhering to the precedent that the court will not decide political questions—although, of course, it does this all the time—judges have an easy way out. In view of the way most of these people obtain their offices, it is surprising that moral cowardice is no more prevalent than it is. Also, Judge Byers had considerable support for his reluctance to issue the writ. The government was behind him, and most lawyers are conservative and timid.)

The day after Judge Byers refused to sign the writ, I was tipped off that

Judge Marcus Campbell, a seventy-six-year-old federal judge living in semiretirement, felt Judge Byers had compromised the honor of the federal judiciary and would take upon himself the signing of the writ. I immediately submitted the papers to him.

Judge Campbell did sign the writ. I rode out to Camp Upton and served it personally on an unwilling Colonel Downing, Winnie's commanding officer. Downing was the stereotype of the military man who believes civilians fail to see the bigger picture and merely get in the way. Regardless, he accepted the writ with ill grace and Winnie was assured of a day in court.

It was a chilly December morning, 1942, and I was happy that Arthur Garfield Hays was with me. I was concerned dearly for Winnie—what could I have ever been without him?—but there was a larger issue involved also: the right of black people to fair and equal treatment.

Judge Campbell permitted argument by Hays and myself for the petitioner, and by lawyers attached to the attorney general's office and officers of the judge advocate general. The state director of Selective Service testified, frankly, that blacks were not called by lot but whites were, but he also asserted that blacks could be segregated in the armed forces because of congressional statutes. I said this 1866 law was superseded by the August 1940 amendment to the Selective Service Act, which forbade discrimination because of race.

Judge Campbell dismissed our writ. He said that if our argument was granted, too many blacks might seek to be released from the armed forces. He did not think the discrimination practiced in selection so odious as to justify opposition.

Winnie was returned to Camp Upton and I immediately began organizing political opposition to this officially sanctioned discrimination. Then, on January 15, 1943, I submitted to the draft: this was part of an agreement with Winnie that I would test the "training" phrase of the "no discrimination amendment." As soon as I was assigned to a unit for basic training, I intended to seek a writ of habeas corpus for myself.

My reception center was Camp Upton, and my immediate commanding officer had been Winnie's superior (Winnie had already been transferred to Fort McClellan in Alabama).

"Are you Winfred Lynn's brother?" the commanding officer asked.

"Yes, I am," I said.

"Well, as long as I have anything to do with it, you'll remain a private in this man's army."

At the time the man seemed a little funny. He was an officious pip-squeak just out of West Point, and he felt an obligation to teach black men their places. But it was not long before I learned that in the army the private is a prisoner, and his tormentors, from buck sergeants on up, can make life hell for him.

Every man in my company at Camp Upton had been classified as a Negro. Of course, they ranged in complexion from men who were indistinguishable from Caucasians to coal black men of apparently pure African strain. A few had attended college. One of these was Freddie Hewlett, a six-foot, light-skinned, brown-haired husky from Jamaica, Queens, whose father, it was said, had been a bodyguard of Dutch Schultz, the prohibition-era gang leader and rumrunner.

I was ordered on my second day in camp to go to the sewer-disposal basin. This was a huge pond of urine and dung, covered with a greenish slime. The noxious stench was almost overpowering. My job was to pound the dung so that it would become soft and liquefied enough to pass through pipes. I used a wide-bottomed mallet.

Every day except Sunday I had to *march* to this assignment. The stench of the dung clung to my fatigues and the dreadful odor made me dizzy with revulsion and self-loathing. Obviously, this was intended as punishment for daring to challenge the army's segregationist policies. It was necessary, however, for me to avoid any infractions before being sent to basic training.

But on my ninth day of tryst with excrement, I reached the limit of my endurance. The next morning after breakfast I went to my tent, put on my dress uniform, and sat down. When the sergeant came to find out what had happened to me, I told him my turn on the shitline had ended and he might as well get ready for a court-martial. He scratched his head and walked away to consult headquarters.

"What's the matter, Lynn?" It was Freddie Hewlett.

"I told that sergeant I wasn't going to pound shit any more, that's all."

"So that's it! I thought you were going to take that stuff lying down."

Before noon Freddie had assembled a group of privates. He clapped the sergeant genially on the back, almost knocking him down. Freddie had already gained a reputation as a fearful rumbler, and the sergeant was clearly frightened. Freddie was behind me, and the black GIs were behind him, and the sergeant was perplexed.

Freddie Hewlett, incidentally, had an effervescent personality that won everyone to him. He was handsome and down-to-earth. The most appealing thing about him was that he never used his charm for vicious purposes. Later, he became a doctor.

At noon the sergeant ordered us out for drill. The order for me to pound dung was never rescinded; it was simply ignored by both sides. My commanding officer was a shrewd article. He had me marked as a focus for discontent, and he did not intend to let it happen. Within a few days I received orders to go to basic training.

Madison Barracks had been a cavalry post of the old regular army. It was set in a lovely valley surrounded by gently rolling hills on three sides, with Lake Ontario on the fourth. My first shock was to discover that most of my barracksmates were white: evidently, my mail to Winnie had been opened—he was a hot potato to the army—and I had told him that my test of the army discrimination pattern would occur when I was sent for basic training. But obviously the army was prepared for me. Madison Barracks was the first unsegregated training unit in the American armed forces!

My commanding officer was Major Bailey, an insurance executive from Watertown, New York. He was very friendly and said he did not understand how a lawyer could be a private. He asked if I had applied to officer candidate school, and I said I had not. He had me take an intelligence test and my score was quite high (at Columbia as a teacher I had become adept at taking various forms of IQ examinations).

Basic training became quite interesting after I discovered I enjoyed firing guns, and the rifle range became a favorite place of recreation. I did not mind the long marches. Walking had always been a favorite avocation of mine.

Major Bailey promoted me to corporal, and in that capacity I went to him with a request from the other black soldiers in the outfit. They wanted to be allowed to form a separate unit for drill purposes. This did not conflict with my general orientation in favor of integration, because at that time it seemed that blacks excelled in certain activities. The drill routine came to life with their precision and verve. Major Bailey turned down the request, but many times, informally, the blacks drilled together in the rear of the barracks, and they were something to see!

Racial differences break up social monotony. It would have been inconceivable to me at the time to imagine that a white singer could take part in a gospel quartet. However, whites have so closely conformed to black intonations and rhythms that it is sometimes impossible to distinguish whether the performer is black or white.

Major Bailey told me he had recommended me for officer candidate school. Headquarters of the Second Army Command sent a Major Wolf to interview me, and it was soon apparent that he was attached to G-2, the intelligence division of the army.

"Why were you rejected for West Point?" was Wolf's first question.

I had completely forgotten that my father had wangled a recommendation while I was still in high school.

"I couldn't pass the trigonometry requirement," I said.

"Are you the lawyer for Winfred Lynn?"

"Yes, I am. There's still work for me to do on the appeals."

I explained the situation to Bailey after Wolf had gone. He was fascinated, and far from being estranged by the story, he seemed miffed with the Selective Service machinery.

In January 1944, an opportunity opened in a battle military police battalion that was scheduled to join the Ninety-third Division in Italy, and my job was to go along as a court-martial clerk.

All the soldiers in this outfit were black and soon I was on good terms with the rank and file. Every man was over six feet in height.

The day before embarkation we were assembling our gear on the armory floor. Colonel Huntzinger, the commander, walked over to me and said I was under arrest. The GIs were astonished.

"What's the matter, Lynn? What did you do? What can we do?"

It had not seemed appropriate to me to discuss Winnie's case with the men because I thought the issues would seem somewhat abstract, and, also, they did not seem at all unhappy to be in an all-black outfit. Segregation, per se, did not bother the black men. What did upset them were the menial and humiliating jobs that were concomitants of segregation. I gave the men an explanation of the case and they were for me. They went to Colonel Huntzinger, but he insisted I would have to stay behind. Obviously, the army thought I might be a bad influence in combat or might seek habeas corpus at an embarrassing moment.

In April 1944, my brother Sam invited me to come to his graduation exercises at Tuskegee, where he was an air cadet. All the brothers and sisters were proud that the youngest Lynn was about to become a pilot in the Ninety-ninth Pursuit Squadron, the first black flyers' outfit activated by the air force. I received permission to go and traveled, in uniform, by train. Passengers going to Alabama had to change at Washington.

The coach was crowded but I managed to find a seat. Just as the train was pulling out of Richmond, a white MP holding a pistol came up and ordered me to follow him. I was surprised until I looked around. Every other person in the coach was white. I had violated the segregation laws of the state of Virginia.

We reached the doors between the cars and the MP ordered me to jump.

The train was traveling about 20 miles per hour and I thought about arguing. But then I looked at the gun, and at his angry face, and realized I was going to have to jump no matter how fast the train was going. Better to jump now.

I slid about twelve feet on the cinders of the embankment but counted myself lucky that I suffered only bruises. The injury to my pride hurt much more.

I found a telephone right away and called the offices of the Lynn Committee Against Segregation in the Armed Forces in New York City. That night, Norman Thomas fired off a telegram of protest to the War Department, and the next day most newspapers in the major cities of the North and West carried the story.

I caught another train, dutifully remained in the Jim Crow coach, and rode leisurely on to Tuskegee. What struck me was the density of the black population in the little towns we passed through in South Carolina, Georgia, and Alabama. Evidently, a passenger train going through any of these hamlets was an event, and the blacks congregated along the tracks to wave. There were so many black faces that I could easily understand why white people were so easily agitated. If these black people ever began to stir and assert their humanity, the social structure would be in danger.

We had quite a reunion in Tuskegee. Sam, aglow about his oldest brother Winnie, had told all his classmates about the Winfred Lynn case, and they came up and pounded my back and told me to keep after it.

Sam rode back with me to New York City after the ceremonies at Tuskegee. We did not have to submit to Jim Crow on the returning trains; the air force had worked out an accommodation with the railroad so that new black officers would not be humiliated so soon after receiving their commissions. I was amused by the fury on the white faces we saw at the Atlanta station as they studied the second lieutenant's uniform in which Sam was modishly clothed. The military life was considered the exclusive prerogative of the Southern gentleman. Who would have imagined that the time would ever come when a "nigger" would be posing as an officer in the city that Sherman had burned to the ground?

Late in the spring of 1944 I persuaded Major Bailey to give me a week's pass so I could participate in the preparation and argument of Winfred's case in the United States Court of Appeals for the Second Circuit, in New York City.

A three-judge panel heard the case, and an adverse majority opinion was not long in coming down. The court held that segregation in the armed forces was justified both by federal statute and by custom, and that the antidiscrimination amendment did not clearly show the intent of Congress to change this practice. If I had needed further proof of the racist nature of this society, the decision furnished it.

Charles Clark, former dean of the Yale Law School, wrote a dissenting opinion.

Dwight MacDonald had begun to publish a new magazine called *Politics*. In the first issue he published my brief on the Lynn case. His profound comment on the crucial position of the black masses, which he wrote as a preface, was as significant as my more detailed and impassioned effort. As a consequence, Winfred's case became more generally known than is customary in lay circles.

My thrust was to show that racial discrimination invariably redounds to the benefit of the oppressor and to the detriment of the oppressed. Judge Clark had gone me one better by holding that even if a Negro benefited by a difference in treatment because of his race, the action was still demeaning. Unfortunately, Judge Clark died before his view fully prevailed in the law. It has not yet prevailed in practice.

Arthur Garfield Hays filed a notice of appeal and sought certiorari in the United States Supreme Court. The balance of 1944 was taken up by him with the enormous amount of paperwork involved in his application.

A few days after the circuit appeals court decision, I was transferred to Northport Veterans Hospital to become part of a caretaking company for soldiers who had become insane as a result of military service. I regretted leaving Lake Ontario, and I particularly regretted saying goodbye to Major Bailey. He was a just man, and I am sorry I have never seen him since.

Our mixed company at Northport was composed of men who had been designated for limited, noncombat service. A number of educated black men managed to wangle some slight physical disability into a cause for such classification. For example, Joe Black, who later became a major-league pitcher, was in our outfit. So, too, was Sidney Poitier, who became my barracksmate. These men did not take kindly to Northern Jim Crow practices.

One night a buddy, Jim Worrell, dropped into a little Italian-American restaurant for a beer. The place was near the waterfront. The bartender bluntly told the soldier that he didn't serve "niggers." The menacing attitude of his rough patrons made Worrell decide not to make an issue of the matter then.

By the next morning our whole outfit had heard the story. As Captain Hatten remained blandly unseeing, the boys took one of the army trucks and loaded it with strapping black GIs armed with ax handles and crowbars. In the early afternoon, just when the restaurant was beginning to fill with its regular clientele, the truck backed up to the door, the ramp clanked on the sidewalk and the soldiers, with Sidney Poitier in the lead, rushed into the bar. They weren't angry enough to attack the white customers. They simply shooed them out. Then, they applied the crowbars and ax handles to the tables, chairs, the counter, the glasses, and the stock of liquor. In ten minutes the place was in splinters. The terrified bartender had escaped out the rear door.

The soldiers returned to the base, where their story was received with whoops of laughter and applause. The captain pretended not to hear, but I could detect a barely hidden grin behind his placid exterior. (He was a Mississippi redneck from Hattiesburg.) He answered his jangling phone laconically. In a little while an indignant delegation of town dignitaries waited in his anteroom. About a half-hour later the delegation came out looking bewildered and crestfallen. Hatten lost no love on Northern whites. He had given me a perfunctory order to prepare a list of the errant soldiers for court-martial. It was simply impossible for me to identify anyone. He pressed the matter no further. No member of the raiding party was ever punished, and the uproar in the press soon subsided.

CHAPTER 9

*The War Ends and We Stage
the First Freedom Ride*

I received a letter from Mr. Hays in January 1945, telling me that the U.S.
Supreme Court had denied certiorari in Winnie's case on procedural
grounds. We had initiated the action by serving a writ of habeas corpus upon
Winnie's commanding officer at Camp Upton, whose custody he was in at
the time. By the time the case reached the Supreme Court, Winnie, of
course, had a different commanding officer in the South Pacific. Since
Winnie was no longer in the custody of the man we had served the writ upon,
the Supreme Court held that the case was not properly before it. This craven
evasion of the issue did nothing to enhance the reputation of the Court.

I discussed the problem with Mr. Hays in New York City. We decided to
seek a writ of habeas corpus in the Supreme Court itself, directed to the
adjutant general of the United States army, who was in charge of personnel
matters for every soldier, wherever he might be stationed.

The Lynn Committee was indignant about the obvious sophistry of the
court's decision, but it had expanded to become involved in other cases for
black servicemen who had experienced egregious discrimination in the army
or navy. Notable among the committee's successes was the case of a young
Seabee, Isaac McNatt. He had been subjected to humiliating treatment at one
of the U.S. bases in the West Indies, primarily because he was an educated
black man. McNatt organized opposition to discrimination and was court-
martialed and given a dishonorable discharge. The Lynn Committee vigorously prosecuted the case in the public press and secured an honorable
discharge, not only for McNatt, but for thirteen other black Seabees who had
associated themselves with him.

At the camp at Northport, I spent considerable time introducing black
soldiers from the South into the more subtle pressures from the North. In the
spring of 1945 I took a black soldier from Sparta, Georgia, to see Paul
Robeson in the role of the Moor in *Othello*. The black soldier had never seen

103

a play, and when we arrived late he was afraid to go in and sit next to white people. The side door to the theater was open, so we were able to watch the action from the outside.

Soon Paul Robeson seized the throat of Desdemona, played by Uta Hagen, and began choking her. The black GI was terror-stricken: "He can't do that to that white woman! Let me get out of here!"

I tried to reassure him that it was playacting. He insisted on dragging me away.

"That nigger had no right to put his hands on that white woman," he said, "whether he was acting or not."

On April 12, 1945, I happened to be in Times Square when the announcement of Roosevelt's death came over the loudspeakers. Within minutes, the square was jammed with two hundred thousand people. The faces of middle-aged black women were streaked with tears, and I once again realized how patriotic most blacks were. A revolutionary perspective was embraced by only a tiny minority, and these had tenuous connections, if any, with the bulk of the disadvantaged race. If the United States was the land of the historic oppression of the black person, it was also the country of his greatest opportunity.

The Supreme Court made its final decision on the Winfred Lynn case in June 1945. It was unable to avoid the issue on procedural grounds again, so it answered our application for an original writ of habeas corpus with a single word: "Denied!" Thus, the court demonstrated that it would not hold that onerous 1866 statute unconstitutional, although it was in derogation of the Fifth and Fourteenth Amendments. Also, the Court was unwilling to adopt the thesis that equal protection of the laws, or equal treatment, meant the same treatment without regard to race or color. In effect, the Court nullified the nondiscriminatory clause in the draft act.

There was no outcry from the NAACP. That organization considered our case an exercise against patriotism. In this stance they were supported by the Communist party, which denounced Winfred and me in the *Sunday Worker* as enemies of the crusade for freedom.

At the time of the decision, Winnie was attached to a chemical warfare company in the South Pacific. He told me later that he had never been called on to use gas or other noxious weapons, but his company stood ready to reply in kind if the Japanese did.

When Winnie was released from service, he took special courses under the GI Bill at Cornell in insecticides and herbicides for use in the landscape gardening business. He became a specialist in the elimination of weeds and unwanted insects by the latest scientific devices and so turned his wartime training to constructive purposes.

A favorite topic of discussion at Northport was how long our detachment might have to stay on after the war. The bulk of the men we took care of were neuropsychiatric casualties of the war, and their prognosis was not good. At this time a number of complaints were registered by white parents and wives of the disturbed veterans over the allegedly rough treatment the patients received from army attendants. Some of these complaints were justified. The men with the least educational background were assigned duty as attendants. Brutality was just as rampant when white soldiers were added to the assignment. The white soldiers came from the South, and their educational training barely equaled that of the blacks. None of the soldier-attendants had adequate training for the job, and most were afraid of the "crazies."

The *Pittsburgh Courier* sent a reporter, Jimmy Fuller, to the institution. I knew Fuller well. We had met after the freedom walk to Washington. He was a veteran investigator and a friend of the oppressed, but he had acquired a cynicism about the possibility of improving conditions. Still, he was not so cynical that he would refuse to give decent proposals a try, and he always stood ready to expose egregious instances of injustice to public view.

I took Fuller to one of the most violent wards and held the door open for him. The moment he stepped through I locked it behind him. When he was finally released from the ward, he wrote one of the most perceptive stories I have read. It was moving and powerful in its depiction of the fear of an uneducated, untrained attendant faced with the incoherence and unpredictable behavior of people whose nerves and minds have been shattered by unmentionable experiences.

The Lynn Committee against Segregation in the Armed Forces took up the cause of the ill soldiers and their serviceman-attendants in order to counter the scare reports appearing in the *New York Daily News*. Dozens of inspector generals visited Northport, and the public was assured that the situation would be improved. It wasn't, of course.

Atom bombs were dropped on Hiroshima and Nagasaki and new impetus was given to our maneuvering for discharge. We had become so inured to the staggering toll of lives in both theaters of the war that the full meaning of these events did not immediately impress themselves upon us. I learned from correspondence with friends in Italy that General Mark Clark was pressing Harry Truman to continue the Allied momentum into Russia to knock off the menace of communism once and for all.

The more intelligent members of our unit knew what this would mean:

hopes for the liberation of all the oppressed people of the world would be dashed for generations to come. Whatever the horrors Stalin had visited upon his countrymen, Russia represented the needed balance to the arrogant American white supremacists. We hoped the Russians would discover the secret to the atom bomb, *pronto*. I had little doubt they would succeed, because the scientific emphasis of Marxism had maintained a high level of research and theoretical advances in the physical and chemical sciences in spite of the war.

I felt it was important to compel the government to bring the troops home; and, indeed, American radicals in the armed forces all over the world mounted a vociferous campaign for demobilization. Soldiers stationed in America pitched in enthusiastically. I learned that vast numbers of troops were pouring into Fort Dix en route from Europe to the Pacific or on their way home. I secured a transfer to Dix.

The black soldiers at Fort Dix, most of them veterans of the European campaigns, were disgruntled by the favoritism shown German prisoners of war. While the black soldiers spent their duty hours digging trenches for camp latrines or collecting camp garbage, the German POWs busied themselves with white-collar assignments at headquarters. I recognized this as a deliberate training of the black soldiers for their return to civilian life. Many black and white soldiers fought side by side as the war neared its end, and segregation was forgotten. What was not forgotten by the high command, however, were the lessons learned after World War I. There were bloody riots in East St. Louis, Washington, and Chicago, and after this war the white majority wanted to return blacks to second-class citizenship without a dangerous delay.

The new President, Harry S. Truman, was a borderline Southerner, from Independence, Missouri. Truman was asked during the 1944 campaign what he would do if a black girl walked into his store in Independence.

"I would boot her out," said Harry Truman.*

Summer changed to fall and we were restless with the slow pace of demobilization. I wondered whether I should give up the law trade. It seemed too tricky and devious for me. The thought of trying to outwit district attorneys, private lawyers, and administrative officials held no appeal. Calling a judge "Your Honor" every day, when there was a good chance he was no more than a petty political hack or a currupt bribe taker, hardly

---

*From an article in the *Socialist Call*

seemed compatible with my confused mood of frustration and discontent. I was revolted by the little meannesses that have to be endured every day in American society.

I was discharged from the army in October 1945, and joined the "52–20" club, which was composed of unemployed veterans. I needed time to think before deciding whether to return to competitive activity. I took a small room on Morningside Avenue near 120th Street in Manhattan and soon found myself coaching a boys' football team in a nearby park. It was relaxing and invigorating. It was several months later that I was offered, and reluctantly accepted, a job with the law firm of Riddick and Doles.

The firm was located on the corner of 125th Street and Seventh Avenue in the heart of Harlem. My pay was thirty dollars a week, and I worked twelve hours a day. The partners had taken me on because they were far behind in handling their cases, chiefly because they were highly gregarious men who spent most of their time drinking with old army buddies. They obtained an impressive amount of cases that way, but did not have the energy to process them.

It was fine with me to do most of the work. It was the best way to regain the skills and statutory knowledge necessary for a resumption of the trade.

One day Doles brought me a complicated contract involving Adam Clayton Powell. The pastor was buying an all-white apartment house on Riverside Drive. The sellers were represented by Simpson, Thacher and Bartlett, one of the great law combines of the country. Neither Doles nor Riddick wanted to summon the concentration needed to lock horns with these bullish legal eagles: Riddick was a criminal lawyer and Doles was constitutionally lazy. I was given the case, and eventually Powell got his apartment building.

I began to realize that the great attraction the law had for me was the mental strain it exacted. Also, I was slightly arrogant, and nothing was more sobering than to run into a superior mind that made me acknowledge I was not omniscient. Since humility was not one of my inherited characteristics, bruising conflict in the office and courtroom enabled me to be a tolerable companion in social life.

I left Riddick and Doles after six months and moved into an office with Joseph Allen, at 271 West 125th Street. I agreed to share the salary of his stenographer.

The fate of Riddick and Doles is instructive. Riddick, a heavy drinker, became a judge in the criminal courts, but alcohol soon killed him. Doles became a collector of customs for the Port of New York. He became involved in a scandal with a white woman and had to relinquish his job, ostensibly for other reasons. He died also a comparatively young man.

The law for a black man is a hazardous trade. Criminal lawyers have a tendency to become alcoholics. Civil law is a more exacting intellectual pursuit: the blacks who succeeded in it were absorbed into the major white firms or government service. The notable black civil-law firms in New York City could be counted on one hand. During the 1950s the black population of New York City passed the one million mark, but 85 percent of the legal work for blacks was performed by white firms.

Already, new civilian associates were beginning to replace my army ties. Through the Lynn Committee I met a group of radical, anticommunist intellectuals, which included Nate Glaser, Eddie Robinson, Dave Bazelon, and Paul Goodman. Their virulent anticommunism led them to a certain acceptance of American institutions, however wryly they expressed it. To me, Russia, with all its ugliness, was a necessary counterweight to American imperialism. Also, I was not interested in framing a philosophy that would make life tolerable for me in this country. I felt a growing divergence from older friends, such as Murray Kempton, Dwight MacDonald, and Gene Phillips, who lacked my implacable hostility to the basic assumptions in our society. Most of these white thinkers were on their way to economic success and a degree of public recognition. We remained friendly but grew gradually apart.

Late in December 1946, George Houser, one of the founders of the Congress of Racial Equality (CORE), telephoned me about a project to test the legality of segregating passengers in interstate travel. The U.S. Supreme Court had ruled, in the case of a young black woman named Irene Morgan, that Virginia could not require her to move to a back seat on the bus when she crossed from the Maryland side. The decision, callously, was not based on her right as a human being to travel undisturbed, but on the rules of interstate commerce: like an article of freight, once she had paid her fare she could not be moved around until she reached her destination.

The decision had been hailed as a landmark in assuring equal rights for black people. CORE had noticed, however, that Southern states were ignoring the ruling and that blacks were still accepting segregation on buses and railroads.

In conjunction with the Fellowship of Reconciliation, a pacifist group, it was proposed that a "deputation" of white and black pacifists travel south on buses and trains to test the ruling of the Supreme Court. Contacts were alerted in the major cities of North Carolina, Virginia, Kentucky, and Tennessee.

The organizers included George Houser; Bayard Rustin, field representative of the Fellowship of Reconciliation and of the American Friends Service Committee; Joseph Felmet, Southern field secretary of the Workers Defense League; Rev. Aubrey C. Todd, pastor of the First Congregational church of Asheville, North Carolina; Worth Randle of the Cincinnati Committee of Racial Equality; James Peck, editor of the Workers Defense League news service; Rev. Ernest Bromley, minister of the Methodist church of Stonewall, North Carolina; Wallace Nelson, a youth worker in the Lexington Conference of the Methodist church; Homer Jack, secretary of the Chicago Council against Racial and Religious Discrimination; and William Worthy, who soon would become a famous writer. I was asked to accompany the group as their lawyer.

Not all the organizers could make the trip. Homer Jack, Aubrey Todd, and William Worthy did not make the test. Igal Roodenko and Nathan Wright joined us so we would have two teams totaling eleven people. Local groups in the Southern cities promised us hospitality and legal aid, if necessary. Women were barred from the project because white Southerners would have considered it an intolerable provocation, and some of us would certainly have been killed. As it was, the racists were hardly expected to keep their hands off.

We began the trip in two separate buses. My bus was traveling through the interior from Washington through Richmond and on to North Carolina and Kentucky. The other bus followed the coast with Raleigh, North Carolina, its first destination.

Nothing happened until we reached Richmond. There, the police warned us that our flouting of the law of the Old Dominion would not be tolerated. There were plenty of police on hand, seemingly impatient for action, but there were plenty of newspaper reporters too. I explained to the police that the Supreme Court had overturned the travel segregation law of Virginia and that I was confident they would show respect for the high court's edict. Actually, I was not confident at all.

Somehow we got out of Richmond without incident. I sat in the front of the bus with Wally Nelson. Our three white companions sat in the rear.

We arrived in historic Petersburg in early evening and stayed overnight on the campus of Virginia Union University, an all-black institution supported largely by church funds. I was surprised to find in talking with students that many of them were unwilling to admit they had suffered discrimination in public transportation. Evidently they were embarrassed that they had made no effort to oppose Jim Crow, collectively or individually. Most of these blacks were from the Negro upper class in the South and had been shielded by their parents from the slights and insults of the white world. They pretended that racial oppression did not exist for them.

Early the next morning we received our seating assignments for the next leg of the journey. Wally Nelson, a short, barrel-chested black pacifist from Philadelphia, was to sit in the "white section" of the bus. I was to sit in the rear with George Houser. On our way to the bus station, however, we noticed that Wally Nelson was unusually tense. We asked him what was wrong, and he admitted that he might not be able to remain nonviolent if someone assaulted him. Houser asked if I could refrain from reacting forcefully if attacked. I said I could, and Wally's role was assigned to me.

We boarded the bus together. I sat in front of a soldier, three seats behind the driver. The rest of the group sat in their allotted places, and the bus quickly filled up. Just before the driver started to pull out he noticed me in the mirror. He shut off the motor and walked back to face me.

"Mister," he said, "colored people down here sit on the last row of the bus."

"They do?"

"Yes, they do. Would you please move?"

"I picked this seat because it's convenient for me."

"I'm just enforcing company rules. You'll have to move."

"I don't think you understand," I said. "The United States Supreme Court ruled some months ago that Negroes cannot be separated in interstate bus travel anymore. That's the law of the land."

"I don't know anything about a Supreme Court rule. All I know is the company rule, and I can't move from here until you move."

The bus driver was not hostile. He had not raised his voice. He was simply confronted with a difficult situation and did not know what to do.

I looked around quickly. A white woman immediately in front of me turned, smiled, and turned back. The white soldier behind me leaned forward to confide that he was from New Hampshire and on my side. But not everyone was so friendly. A white man in the middle of the bus shouted, "Get the police!"

The bus driver went looking for a policeman. It was ten minutes before he found one and returned. The cop told me I was violating Virginia law and asked if I would get off the bus voluntarily. I said I would if he put me under arrest, and he told the bus driver he would have to find a magistrate to sign a warrant.

People on the bus were being inconvenienced, but only a few complained. They seemed to sense that a much larger issue was at stake. Unfortunately, a considerable crowd of local citizens had gathered outside the bus, and they were threatening to beat me up, and worse. Black people in the crowd looked apprehensive.

The bus station porter, a diminutive, roly-poly black man of uncertain age, placed his foot on the lower step of the bus and looked at the crowd.

"Let's take this nigger off!" he said. "We don't want him down here!"

I felt sick and sorry for this black. He was so demoralized and dehumanized that he would curry favor with whites by trying to be even more hostile than they were.

But to everyone's surprise, no one stepped forward. At this juncture George Houser, long an advocate of progressive causes and a brave person, stepped to the entrance of the bus and identified himself as a Methodist minister. He told the crowd that a number of us, black and white, were making a test to see if the state of Virginia was willing to give due respect and obedience to a rule of law announced by the United States Supreme Court. That court had held that a crate of oranges being shipped from Florida to New York could not be disturbed in transit, so a human being could not be forced to change his seat on a bus simply because he was crossing state lines.

The people outside the bus were unsympathetic. They considered us intruders who were disturbing a way of life.

The policeman returned with another officer who unfolded a warrant.

"Will you leave voluntarily?" the second officer asked.

"No," I said.

"Then you're under arrest." He read the warrant slowly and deliberately. "All right," he said. "Let's go!"

I asked him to put his hand on my arm; otherwise it might appear that I had consented to the arrest.

The bus left without me. I was told to sit on a bench outside a cell until someone showed up with bail money. The jail seemed to be empty, and I did not know why I was kept outside the cell. I was, after all, under arrest. In the late afternoon I was arraigned and released when a black lawyer produced the twenty-five-dollar bail.

I was told by the police that my life would be in danger if I returned to the bus station. An ugly crowd was milling about. The police drove me to a little railroad stop four miles outside Petersburg, flagged down a train, and put me aboard. The train was headed for Raleigh.

Meanwhile, the bus went to Durham. I went to a church in Raleigh where Bayard Rustin and his team had gathered. It was a highly emotional moment, and all of us knew our cause would not be defeated.

The two test groups joined in Chapel Hill, North Carolina. Charles Jones was the pastor of the Community church and he greeted us as his guests. It was not possible for him to put all of us up, however, and some of his friends volunteered to help. One of these was a tall white woman named Nelle Morton.

"You're most welcome to stay at my house, Mr. Lynn," she said.

Her house turned out to be located in the North Carolina woods, but I knew I had made a mistake even before we got there. A black man alone with a white woman in North Carolina in 1947, or even now, was asking for trouble. It came the next morning.

All the tires on her car were punctured. Later, a rock came crashing through the front window of Rev. Jones's house with a note attached: "If you don't get those niggers out of your house by tonight, we'll burn it down."

Local taxi drivers had stirred up a lynch spirit. When some young members of the Communist party heard about what was planned, they stationed themselves on Jones's roof with rifles for protection. I was having dinner at Rev. Jones's house when the rock came through the window, and outside we could see a mob of whites, growing by the minute and crazed with hatred. The police were nowhere to be seen. The reason no concerted rush was made was the presence of the virtually suicidal young Communists on the roof.

We had to make a run for it to get out of Chapel Hill. Cars were loaned to us by professors at the University of North Carolina, and we sped away toward Durham. Halfway there we changed cars and doubled back to Greensboro. In Greensboro we divided our forces again and continued our journey through the South.

Unfortunately, we did not escape North Carolina unscathed. Bayard Rustin was taken off a bus, slammed into jail, and hung by his thumbs.

We went to Kentucky and Tennessee and were not challenged. Although segregation was accepted as legal in those states, people who defied the law were seldom arrested. No bus driver challenged us and no citizen demanded that we conform to segregated seating patterns.

Before our freedom ride was completed I was called back to New York City to make a report on our journey one Sunday afternoon to Broadway

Tabernacle at Fifty-second Street. Bayard Rustin was still in the North Carolina jail, and my peroration focused on him. The parallel with the crucifixion of his being hung by the thumbs was not lost on the Christian assembly, and as I sat down the organist softly struck the thrilling strains of one of the great hymns of the Protestant reformation:

> There is a fountain filled with blood
> Drawn from Immanuel's veins . . .

In the audience that day were many ardent young people who were to form the core of a movement in New York City to end segregation in their own metropolitan area.

Among them was a tall, striking redhead named Mary Louise Garretson. She had come to the meeting from her home in Scarsdale, in Westchester County. She lost no time in attaching herself to our little circle and we quickly become intimate friends.

Her parents became alarmed and bundled her off to Scotland to spend a summer with distant relatives. Her letters to me betrayed a certain hysteria, and I had a slight feeling of guilt that I had used my political mission to ensnare this young woman. One day I telephoned her in Edinburgh and told her that if she would calm down we could marry upon her return.

She hurried back to the States and we married, but such a hurried union was foredoomed. Having been surrounded by servants from birth, she knew nothing of how to keep a house or, indeed, how to live on my modest income. She became pregnant almost immediately and, before her delivery in New York Hospital, showed intense anxiety over how the child would look.

Baby Suzanne Marie was a tiny, pink redhead. Her mother was overjoyed, and even the disapproving parents of Mary welcomed the newcomer to their home. But I was well aware that in a few months the African ancestry would make itself manifest in the child's face. I told the mother so, but she could not believe it.

One day when the baby was five months old, Mary was wheeling it in a carriage in a courtyard near her home. Two women passed and one said to the other in decisive tones, "That looks like a nigger baby."

To all intents and purposes that incident ended the marriage. A few days later Mary fled to join her Aunt Louise in California, and in a few months she obtained an uncontested divorce in Las Vegas.

I returned to Virginia to stand trial in Petersburg. The judge, a Virginian named Bowen, found me guilty, not of violating the Virginia segregation law but of disorderly conduct. "This man," said Bowen, "from New York City, knew he was violating the law of Virginia and would be disorderly and I find him guilty."

The black citizens in Petersburg had poured out for the trial. Seven black lawyers defended me, including W. Spottswood Robinson, now Senior Judge of the United States Court of Appeals for the Fourth Circuit. In so doing they showed great courage. It was one thing for a Northerner to challenge Jim Crow. It was quite another for Southerners who had to live there.

I appealed the conviction and it was overturned in the state Hustings Court. The bus driver had testified that he was happy to have me as a passenger, that he was only following orders and that at no time was I disorderly.

It was then that I turned my attention to the movement which had begun with our meeting in Broadway Tabernacle. In 1947 blacks were not allowed to use the lockers at most of the public beaches in the metropolitan region of New York City. We selected Rockaway Beach for our first demonstration and picket line. The pickets were largely white students or recent graduates from prestigious colleges in the East. A few blacks were interspersed. My brother Sam came in his air force lieutenant colonel's uniform. The beach was desegregated promptly.

We met far more resistance at Palisades Amusement Park, across the Hudson River in Fort Lee, New Jersey, where Jim Peck was savagely kicked and beaten by a cop. However, we won that battle in the end.

But far more serious problems were looming ahead of us. Churchill had heralded the onset of the cold war at Fulton, Missouri. He was beginning to marshal the forces of capitalism for a showdown with Soviet Russia, and he found a willing pupil in Harry Truman. The forces in the United States that wished to change the status quo in the direction of a more humane society for all its inhabitants were charged with desiring to foist a communist state based on the Russian model upon the American people. It would not be long before I would be compelled to take a case challenging the new repressive direction of the government.

CHAPTER 10

The Fight against McCarthyism

In April 1949, the student council of the City College of New York declared a strike after a vote by the student body showed overwhelming support for the action. The cause of the strike was Professor William Knickerbocker, who had been accused of blatant anti-Semitism. The students were also incensed with William C. Davis, an economics instructor who had refused to allow white and black underclassmen to share dormitories in Army Hall, which housed student veterans. The students demanded the dismissal of both men.

The *New York Times* of April 12, 1949, quoted Knickerbocker: "I am absolutely convinced that I am being used to further the cause of Communism in the college." The *Times* also quoted Leroy Galperin of the student coucil: "This strike cannot be called a Communist strike because of the people leading it or the people involved. . . . If there are more than twenty party members, I will eat everyone above that number."

The next day the *Times* ran an editorial: "Its longevity, the forms the agitation takes, the picket cries of scab, rat, Fascist, the identity of some of the agitators, all point to a Leftist if not Communist inspiration. We do not believe that any sizable number of Communists are taking part in the strike; we do agree with Professor Knickerbocker when he says that 'if it were not for the Communists, there would be no strike.'"

Members of the student council—William Fortunato, Leroy Galperin, Robert Oppenheimer, Albert Ettinger—visited my office that same day and said they wanted to sue the *Times* for libel. They knew I had become a volunteer lawyer of the ACLU that year. All of them were anti-Communist and believed the *Times* had struck a blow at their cause by smearing it with a red herring. I agreed to accept the case after considerable hesitation. I hesitated because I doubted that libel was clearly present. Given the temper of the period—the cold war was in full swing—most people would be persuaded to speculate that the student strike was called to further a Communist campaign rather than to protest ethnic bias. Also, the articles were cleverly written and bore a certain air of impartiality.

115

I began a civil suit against the *Times* for $500,000. The newspaper retained the firm of Lord, Day and Lord, a legal powerhouse. One of its relatively minor members was Herbert Brownell, later to be appointed U. S. Attorney General, and he was assigned to handle the defense.

Brownell's answer to the suit was a seventy-one page attack on Communism. I moved to strike out most of the answer as irrelevant, designed to becloud the real issues, and prejudicial to a jury. In reality, his answer was quite amusing. It was a consistent compendium of outrageous lies against the Bolsheviks that would have made even William Randolph Hearst envious.

Even the court found that Brownell's answer was unconscionable and ordered out the paragraphs to which I had taken exception, and more, besides. Lord, Day and Lord in the person of Brownell appealed, and the appeals court found against us and assessed costs of six hundred dollars against my clients.

The court might as well have assessed a cost of one million dollars instead of six hundred, because they could not afford to pay. I could not afford to pay for them, either, since at that time, as now, my client list was hardly dotted with corporations and rich individuals who kept me on large retainers. I called my sister Dorothy and asked to borrow six hundred dollars. She sent it, but the lesson was clear: the courts are fundamentally the instruments of the rich. A client generally gets the justice he or she can financially afford, and seldom can the poor invoke all the remedies of the law. Dorothy's six hundred dollars was all that allowed us to stay in the case.

The case was tried before Judge Dennis Cohalan and a jury in supreme court, New York County, on October 27, 28, and 29, 1953. Justice is not only a sometimes thing, it is also exceedingly slow. It was more than four years since my clients had come to me. McCarthyism was riding high nationally.

Judge Cohalan was bitterly anti-Semitic, anti-black, and anti-Communist. In short, he was like many other American judges. Cohalan refused to allow me to question perspective jurors. Fortunately, I was able to place one ardent, intelligent young Jewish woman on the jury. She was all I needed.

The lawyers for the *Times* piled up the evidence about the "red activities" of the students: any expression, any innovation, any hint of independent thought was portrayed as being subversive and a threat to the republic. Much of my time was taken up objecting to accounts of Stalinist horrors as irrelevant.

Judge Cohalan did his part. He lectured the jurors on their patriotic duty to uphold American values. Lord, Day and Lord and Judge Cohalan figured the jury would dispose of the matter in minutes, but they failed to consider the intelligence and courage of that single Jewish juror.

An entire day went by. And most of the next day. This was not supposed to happen and you could see it written on the judge's face. Finally, at 4:00 P.M. on the second day, the jury announced that it was hopelessly deadlocked (the Jewish woman had been the sole holdout for the plaintiffs). Throughout my career, people like her have occasionally given me some hope in our legal system.

We lost the case in the second round. This time the defense lawyers were able to show that the plaintiffs had prospered since graduation in their respective careers, and therefore the judge said they were unable to prove they had suffered damages.

The student council case was just one of the controversies I became embroiled in during the period of Joe McCarthy. The ACLU had become a victim of the cold war and expelled Elizabeth Gurley Flynn from its national board because she was a prominent Communist, something she never hid and that had been well known for years. Arthur Garfield Hays (a founder of the ACLU) and I protested the ACLU's action in letters and articles to newspapers and magazines. I resigned from the ACLU and joined a new group called the Emergency Civil Liberties Committee. Because so many people were being hounded out of government jobs, teacher positions, and even private assignments, the committee employed most of its energies defending people accused of being Communists or fellow travelers.

At times my reaction to this program was ambivalent. I had never concealed my Communist past or my revolutionary commitments. Therefore, it was hard for me to work up sympathy for someone I knew to have been a radical in the past, who was now trying to present himself as a "twentieth-century American" who had never contemplated overthrowing the existing capitalist structure.

There were some clients I had to warn not to risk prosecution for perjury. Nevertheless, most white leftists I knew in the 1930s and 1940s managed to weather the storm, entrench themselves in the system, and become the materially prosperous standpatters of the 1960s and 1970s.

At times I thought perhaps I was being too hard on these people. I was self-employed and not as vulnerable as someone who was at the mercy of an employer. But my license to practice law was constantly endangered, and it was not uncommon for a disgruntled client to complain about my political views to the bar association in an effort to have me disbarred.

The antidiscrimination groups that became active after our freedom ride (which, incidentally, was a forerunner of those to come, and the first in American history) were largely unaffected by the anti-Communist hysteria. Most had no leftist backgrounds, and the most radical had been Socialists or Trotskyists and thus possessed impeccable anti-Stalinist credentials. Truman's executive order of 1948 desegregating the armed forces—brought about by pressure—took considerable steam out of the antisegregation movement and gave so-called liberals the excuse to join the hue and cry against Communists.

The FBI records showing that I had been expelled from the Communist party in 1937 made it difficult to portray me as a red dupe. Of course, the history of suppression of basic liberties in the Soviet Union was grist for the mill of reaction. Every aggressive action taken by the U. S. government since World War II was justified as rescuing people from Communist enslavement. It seemed to me to be an essential technique in the unremitting effort to cajole the American populace into choosing the road to fascism.

In 1954 I was involved in an important and somewhat bizarre case in Kentucky—another case that might be considered unbelievable by rational people. On May 17, 1954, the U. S. Supreme Court ruled that segregation inherently denied equality in law and practice to black people. But ten days before that important decision, Carl and Anne Braden in Louisville, Kentucky, had been thrown in jail because they sold their home in an all-white neighborhood to a black couple, the Wades.

Life became a nightmare for the Wades almost the moment they moved in. Rocks shattered their windows, the Ku Klux Klan drove by firing rifles into the house, and finally the home was demolished by a dynamite blast.

Carl Braden was charged with inciting the bombing and held under an old Kentucky statute for fomenting insurrection.

Carl Braden was convicted and sentenced to fifteen years in prison.

In other words, in this preposterous case the Klansmen who had done the bombing did not go to jail, but the white man who had "incited" them by selling the house to a black couple received a lengthy prison sentence!

I was retained to represent the Bradens. He was allowed to see me only after he had paid a high bail, pending the appeal. We discussed a civil suit that had been brought against him following the criminal conviction. The bank holding the mortgage on the house bought by the Wades was bringing a foreclosure action to regain the property, and the Bradens remained liable even though they had sold the house.

I stayed with the Bradens in Louisville. Their lives had been threatened many times. While I slept, Carl Braden stayed in the attic with his rifle. Floodlights played outside, making it impossible for the cowardly Klan to take him by surprise at night.

The Bradens agreed with me that the crucial battlegrounds for black people were in the areas of education, housing, and employment.

While I was working on the brief in the *Braden-Wade* case, the editors of the *American Socialist* asked me to write an article about the New South, and I consented, titling it "The Southern Negro Stirs." I quote it to illustrate precisely how I felt at the time:

> The most inspiring area in the United States today is the Old South. The rest of the country exclaims in horror at the Till mutilation murder and the sickening whitewash of its perpetrators. The cowardly Belzoni shootings, the bullwhip and shotgun reigns of a Sheriff McCall in Florida, or a Byrd, or Strider of Mississippi, expose the hideous visage of race dictatorship for all the world to see. . . .
>
> Numberless anonymous little Negroes who trudged to the polls to vote, who dared to challenge Jim Crow on buses, who petitioned for non-segregated schools, are compelling a polarization of forces. In most instances these actions have been without the sanction of their major spokesman, the National Association for the Advancement of Colored People. Winfred Lynn was denied support when he refused to submit to induction in a segregated army. Irene Morgan did not have official approval for sitting in the "white" section of a bus in 1946. The national office of the NAACP hesitates to endorse the fight of Andrew Wade and his white friends, the Bradens, for a home in an unsegregated neighborhood of Louisville. . . .
>
> In the South, the Negro knows that his battle admits of no further compromise. The basis of the decision of the United States Supreme Court that segregation per se is discrimination, makes this implicit. That decision was itself only a recognition of the world's struggle for men's allegiances. Any doubt that the final contest for integration has been joined can be resolved by a visit to a Southern Negro church, such as the one in Lake City, South Carolina, which was burned to the ground by the blind and desperate mob. In this cultural center of the Negro one is likely to hear on any occasion the singing of "O Freedom!"

And before I'll be a slave
I'll be buried in my grave
And go home to my Lord
And be free!

Nor does the Negro stand alone in the arena of the fight. Small groups
of dedicated whites all over the South risk everything to stand by his
side, foreshadowing the ultimate reawakening of the disadvantaged
whites. The history of Populism and of native socialism in this region is
ample testimony of the revolutionary potential of the Southern masses.
Don West in Dalton, Georgia, the Bradens in Louisville, Charlie Jones
in Chapel Hill, Minter, Cox, and Editor Hazel Smith in Mississippi,
have but taken up the cause of their forbears.

The comfort of a middle-class Northern practice had tempted me for a
time. But, long before, when the Communist party tried to lure me into
abandoning law school, I sensed my efforts had to center on the law; and the
law was not so much a way to make a living as a weapon in the battle.

I returned to Louisville late in 1955. I was working on the civil portion of
the problem, while Louis Lusky, scion of a wealthy family, was handling
Carl's criminal appeal. His 335-page brief became a classic in civil liberties.

We were confident Carl would win his appeal, because the Supreme Court
in *Pennsylvania* v. *Nelson* had recently ruled that the enforcement of sedition
laws was the exclusive province of the federal government.

I also worked to bring as much publicity as possible to Carl's criminal case
appeal. No matter how clear the law was, judicial outrages still occurred,
and a good defense against them was an informed public.

There was dissension about supporting the civil case in which the bank
was trying to repossess the house. Some of my white friends felt that Carl
had bought the home with the intention of selling it to the Wades, although
why this should seem questionable in a capitalist society was beyond me. My
friend Ella Baker, of the old Workers' Education Project of WPA days,
accompanied me on visits to prominent liberals in order to form a committee
in the North to back the *Wade-Braden* cases, but we met with initial rebuffs.

The Bradens became active in the Southern Conference Education Fund,
and a small number of Northern liberals began to support that organization.
In discussing its program I had the pleasure of meeting Eleanor Roosevelt,
whose husband had not been one of my favorites during his lifetime.

By coincidence, I had just become the lawyer for the mysterious Madame

X, who had been the liaison between Franklin D. Roosevelt and the American Communist party during the wartime Russian alliance. Madame X was a member of the famous New England Adams family, and through her I became somewhat familiar with the complex character of the New Deal President.

The respectable brothers and sisters, cousins, nieces, and nephews of Madame X were very distressed by their relative's connections. My earliest task in her behalf was to prevent her incarceration in a mental institution. Nowadays, we are all plied with stories about the Soviet practice of shutting up dissidents in mental hospitals. Little has been said about a longstanding custom in the United States for wealthy people to hustle inconvenient members of their families into psychiatric confinement. This is done by using large sums of money to bribe psychiatrists to go before compliant judges, who piously sign incarcerating orders under the guise of protecting the hapless victim from himself or herself and society from his or her erratic behavior. Political nonconformity has long been recognized in every state as an abnormal, potentially dangerous aberration.

My tactic for Madame X was to threaten the authorities that I would blow up the whole maneuver in the media unless the efforts to confine her were dropped. Madame X was permitted to leave the state of New York and retire to the home of a cousin in Pennsylvania. I never heard from her again.

Mrs. Roosevelt never discussed Madame X with me, but she knew I was defending her. Early in 1956 the Spring Valley branch of the NAACP urged me to invite Mrs. Roosevelt to be the guest speaker at its annual celebration. To my surprise she accepted, but a problem arose in arranging adequate security in transporting her to Rockland County. She suggested that she ride alone with me in my Plymouth, and with some qualms I agreed this might afford the simplest solution to our dilemma. I drove by her residence in the East Sixties one afternoon and she laughingly got in the front seat. It must have seemed a lark to her. Amazed motorists gawked and waved.

We had an impressive attendance at the golf club the NAACP had secured for the gathering. It was one of the few occasions I had participated in where all classes of the community, black and white, joined in commemorating the *Brown* decision. It was my last appearance with respectable people in Rockland County. The Southern commitment was tying me irrevocably to the revolutionary left.

I continued to work on a brief to be filed in the action by South End Federal Savings and Loan Association to foreclose on the Wade house and return it to the all-white community. The tenor of the brief was that the U. S. Supreme

Court had outlawed enforcement of restrictive covenants in deeds—covenants that had been used throughout the country to bar blacks from owning homes. The bank was using its restrictive mortgage clause to achieve the same result.

I argued the motion in Louisville in the late fall of 1956. One man, Bishop Tucker, of black, white, and Indian stock, became so overwrought by the argument that I had to jump between him and the lawyer for the bank in order to avoid a fight.

A collateral matter arose. The Kentucky Commonwealth prosecutor sought to compel a Louisville radical, Henry Rhine, to give evidence in the *Braden-Wade* litigation before a grand jury. Rhine pleaded the Fifth Amendment and a lower-court judge ruled in his favor. The Commonwealth appealed to the Kentucky Supreme Court. Bill Zollinger, the Louisville lawyer secured for Rhine, was assisted by Rowland Watts of the Civil Liberties Union staff and by Leonard Boudin of the Emergency Civil Liberties Committee.

On February 8, 1957, our contention that the mortgage clause was being employed as a restrictive covenant was rejected. I thought it was an abominable ruling, but I was getting beyond the point of being surprised. We filed an immediate bill of exceptions preparatory to appeal.

Then, suddenly, everything started to mesh. A financial angel produced the ten thousand dollars necessary to pay off the mortgage and the home was saved for the Wades. The appeal was discontinued.

And the Kentucky Supreme Court reversed Carl Braden's conviction for violating the sedition statute. The court said the federal government had preempted for itself all prosecutions for attempts to overthrow the state.

We had won, but it was costly and time-consuming. The cases should never have appeared in a court.

As fantastic as the *Braden-Wade* cases were, they would seem the height of reason compared to two others that I had taken on in the meantime.

CHAPTER 11

Albizu Campos and
the Puerto Rican Dream

Alongside my concern about the denial of civil liberties and civil rights ran a parallel attention to the fate of the United States colonies. It struck me as inconsistent to be wrought up about Britain's oppression of its Caribbean holdings and not to be concerned about the treatment by the United States of its Caribbean colony—Puerto Rico. Ever since my debating days at Syracuse University, where I had espoused the cause of the Nicaraguan revolutionary Sandino, the heavy-handed dollar diplomacy of both Republican and Democratic administrations in their dealings with the neocolonies of Cuba and Haiti foreshadowed the program for Puerto Rico. In this colony, however, a vocal nationalist movement, led by the most charismatic personality I was ever to know, spelled trouble for the North American colossus.

Pedro Albizu Campos was very handsome. He had brown skin and large luminous eyes and —almost always—a warm, infectious smile. Albizu was unselfish, brave, deeply religious. And he was absolutely single-minded in pursuit of his lifelong goal—the total independence of Puerto Rico.

Pedro Albizu Campos had already been recognized as an important historical figure. He was the son of a wealthy Spanish-descended planter and a black woman. As a little boy he revealed exceptional intelligence, and his father hired capable tutors for him in Puerto Rico. Albizu entered the University of Vermont in his early teens; then, at age fifteen, he became the first Puerto Rican to attend Harvard. He was a superb student. He impressed his classmates so quickly that in his sophomore year he was chosen to deliver the student reply and appreciation to Rabindranath Tagore, the great Indian poet, who was that year's guest lecturer. The speech Albizu gave was considered so powerful that it has been preserved in the Harvard archives.

At age seventeen Albizu volunteered for combat in World War I; instead, he was sent to work with a black labor regiment in Panama. Years later he told me he would never forget the indignities visited upon the black troops by

North American racism: "I discovered that the United States had done the worst possible thing," he said. "They had divided the Puerto Rican troops into two regiments—of so-called colored men and so-called white men. Mine was supposed to be the colored regiment. It was a serious mistake. In Puerto Rico we don't have any serious racial issue."

After the war Albizu completed his studies at Harvard, graduating with a degree in chemical engineering. While at Harvard he met a young Peruvian descendant of Inca nobility, Laura de Meneses, who was a student at Radcliffe. They were married in 1922. Albizu went on to earn his law degree at the University of Puerto Rico.

Albizu rapidly won a reputation as an outstanding lawyer and his services were eagerly sought by American corporations. Instead he went into politics, soon rising to head the Nationalist party. Albizu possessed outstanding oratorical skills and a genuine love and respect for the Puerto Rican people, and he became known as Puerto Rico's greatest patriot. By 1930 he was the recognized and undisputed leader of the Nationalists. Also by 1930, as Byron Williams pointed out in his book *Puerto Rico, Commonwealth, State, or Nation?*, "Private corporations in the United States were the absentee owners of 60 percent of Puerto Rican banking and public utilities; 80 percent of the tobacco industry; 60 percent of the sugar industry; and 100 percent of the steamship lines that carried goods between Puerto Rico and the United States. Four absentee corporations owned 46 percent of all lands worked for sugar."

For a brief period the Nationalists participated in the elections, and their 1932 platform called for land redistribution, the development by Puerto Ricans of their natural resources, and the liberalization of trading rules. During this period Albizu changed. He felt that Puerto Rican elections were manipulated from the mainland and that the United States would never be peacefully persuaded to relinquish its rule. America, he believed, had too much at stake to permit Puerto Rican independence. Puerto Rico was the nearest Caribbean island to Europe and North Africa, it commanded the approaches to the United States from both the south and the east, and large American corporations—assured of a cheap and plentiful labor supply— were increasing their investments in the island. In addition, the United States had studded Puerto Rico with naval, army, and air bases, until it had become, after Okinawa, the most formidable outpost of American military power.

In February 1936, the chief of police of Puerto Rico, an American named E. Francis Riggs, was assassinated by two Nationalists, Elias Beauchamp and Hiram Rosado. The two Nationalists were beaten to death by the police, and there followed a period of intense repression. Nationalists were branded as outlaws, and long jail sentences were meted out. Some of the wives of the Nationalists were given sentences of four hundred years in prison. Their crime was that they had cooked meals for their husbands, thus aiding the Nationalist cause. Albizu Campos himself was arrested and convicted of conspiracy to overthrow the United States government in Puerto Rico. His prosecutor was an American named E. Cecil Snyder, and the judge was another North American, Robert A. Cooper. Albizu was sent to Atlanta Penitentiary.

There were cries of outrage all over Latin America. Albizu Campos was a figure of international renown, not a common criminal to be confined in a Georgia jail. A few years later, when the great Chilean poet Gabriela Mistral was presented the Nobel Prize for literature, she exclaimed, "This prize should be given to Don Pedro Albizu Campos, the greatest living Spanish American." Albizu represented not simply political opposition, but the highest ideals of Latin American culture.

On Palm Sunday, 1937, Puerto Rican friends of the Nationalists planned to parade to the old cathedral in Ponce to celebrate a Te Deum mass in memory of martyrs for Puerto Rican independence. Just before the procession was to begin, however, the American governor of Puerto Rico, Blanton Winship, canceled the parade permit. Then, when the crowd filled the street on the way to the cathedral, a detachment of American marines closed the street behind the people and opened fire. Twenty-three men, women, and children fell dead with the first volley. More than one hundred others were wounded. Professor Robert J. Hunter was commissioned by the U. S. government to investigate what had happened. "Most of the dead," Professor Hunter wrote, "were little more than children; none were armed; many were shot in the back while seeking refuge."

Blanton Winship blamed the bloodshed on a Nationalist riot. The United States Civil Liberties Union conducted a thorough investigation and branded it a "massacre." The Ponce Massacre is still mourned each Palm Sunday in Puerto Rico.

To cover their guilt, United States officials ordered the local prosecutor, Rafael Perez-Marchand, to apprehend and punish the leaders of the parade. Perez-Marchand refused and resigned his office. Years later, when I was defending Albizu Campos on another matter, Perez-Marchand and I became good friends.

Byron Williams described what life was like in Puerto Rico in 1940: "Life expectancy was forty-six years; infant mortality from pneumonia, influenza, and intestinal diseases was still very high. Wages had actually dropped during the 1930s, until farm workers were paid as little as six cents an hour. Skilled workers might make twenty-two cents an hour—if they could find work. Diets were poor, as might be expected in a country whose per capita income was $118 per year, and which had to import much of its foodstuffs from the United States at higher than stateside prices. Only half of Puerto Rico's children attended school; only three out of ten persons were literate.''

Albizu Campos was released from Atlanta Penitentiary in 1943 and moved to New York City. It was impossible not to admire him. He was the most completely selfless and humble man I had ever met. He loved the Puerto Rican people and called them his children. Often, tears would fill his eyes when he talked about their suffering. Albizu was very religious and his religion made him a revolutionary. ''You know, Conrad,'' he told me, ''God must suffer very much when he sees how the poor people are treated. God loves poor people and when he was on earth he tried to help them.''

It was during Albizu's stay in New York that noted American liberals and pacifists tried to turn him into a convert for nonviolence. While recovering at Columbus Hospital from the tuberculosis he had contracted in prison, Albizu was visited by such people as John Haynes Holmes, Roger Baldwin, Norman Thomas, J. Holmes Smith, and A. J. Muste. In public they referred to him as the Puerto Rican Gandhi, but their attempts to fasten such a sobriquet on the fiery leader of the Nationalists betrayed either an abysmal ignorance of his background or was a colossal exercise in deception.

Albizu Campos made a triumphal return to Puerto Rico in 1947. He was greeted at the docks by forty thousand cheering admirers and then by a gigantic rally at Sixto Escobar Stadium. He could have asked to be king and the people would have supported him. Instead he asked for democracy and independence. He set up his headquarters in a San Juan slum and proclaimed an intensification of the struggle for independence.

On April 14, 1948, Albizu was asked to speak at the University of Puerto Rico at a meeting in honor of José de Diego, an early advocate of independence. The meeting was declared illegal by American authorities and students who showed up were beaten by soldiers.

Albizu Campos was 5'9", a slender man with light brown skin and jet black hair. When he spoke, however, especially when he spoke in public, he became a giant, and it was impossible to listen to him and not be sympathetic to his cause. Puerto Rico had been a colony of Spain for four hundred years, and after that, since 1898, it had been dominated by the United States.

In the fall of 1948 the American Committee for Puerto Rican Independence sent Ruth Reynolds to Puerto Rico to investigate charges of political repression and brutality. Ruth was an avowed pacifist and a friend of Albizu Campos. She decided to hold hearings in the Ateneo, the public forum of San Juan. People were too frightened to show up, so Ruth interviewed them in their homes.

Meanwhile, Nationalist youths were being jailed by the hundreds by American officials for refusing to submit to U. S. military conscription. Some eighteen thousand Puerto Ricans served during World War I, and sixty-five thousand in World War II. Forty-three thousand would be sent to Korea. U. S. military bases occupied 13 percent of Puerto Rico's tillable land, and the island of Vieques would later be used for target practice in ship-to-shore shelling. It was clear in 1948 that events were building to an explosion.

My involvement with the Nationalists stemmed directly from the December 18, 1949, annual convention of the Nationalist party in Arecibo. Albizu Campos, filled with fire, addressed the delegates: "Stand up! All who are Nationalists—true Nationalists—those who are ready to give their lives and fortunes for this cause, stand up!"

Most of the people stood. Ruth Reynolds was present at the convention but said she did not stand.

On October 26, 1950, the Nationalists held a meeting at Fajardo in honor of General Valera, an advocate of independence. When the gathering broke up Ruth was offered a ride to San Juan with a friend, Burgos Fuentes. She accepted the ride.

The police stopped the car in Rio Piedras and searched it. In the trunk were dynamite bombs, molotov cocktails, rifles, and shotguns. The four men in the car were charged with illegal possession and transportation of firearms. Ruth Reynolds was questioned and released.

Four days later, on October 30, 1950, the Nationalists attacked. A small band invaded the Forteleza, built in 1533, which served as the governor's palace in San Juan. There were simultaneous uprisings in Arecibo, Utuado, Ponce, and Naranjito. The insurgents seized the mountain town of Jajuya; and only after it was flattened by American bombers was the government able to retake it.

On November 1, 1950, the entire world was shocked by the news from Washington. Two Puerto Rican Nationalists, Griselo Torresola and Oscar Collazo, attacked Blair House, where President Truman was living. In the summer of 1950, Truman had signed a bill that perpetuated the rule of the United States Congress over Puerto Rico. The bill was called Public Law

600, and it called for an election in Puerto Rico to see if the people wanted to draw up their own constitution: the Catch-22 was that Congress had to approve the constitution. During the attempt on President Truman's life, a guard was killed, as was Griselo Torresola, and Harry Truman himself narrowly escaped death. Oscar Collazo was sentenced to death, which was later reduced to life imprisonment.

The two Puerto Ricans, upon hearing of the revolt on the island, had tried to catch a plane to San Juan; but all flights were canceled because of the insurrection. On the spur of the moment the two men decided to assassinate the American president.

After the attack on Blair House, Pedro Albizu Campos and a small group of friends were arrested in the headquarters of their party at Cruz and Sol Streets in Old San Juan. They were charged with trying to overthrow the United States government in Puerto Rico by force and violence and with breaking Law 53, Puerto Rico's equivalent of the Smith Act, which made it a crime to advocate the overthrow of the U. S. government. Ruth Reynolds was arrested about the same time. She was charged with advocating the overthrow of the government by force, in violation of Law 53. Ruth talked with Albizu and then sent word to the States that they wanted me to handle their defense. They were aware that the symbol of a black lawyer defending a white pacifist woman and a brown-skinned Puerto Rican revolutionary would be highly significant.

I was thrilled by the opportunity to represent Ruth and Albizu. The Nationalists had been portrayed as terrorists and I knew my career would not be helped by the case; but I believed in the cause of Puerto Rican independence, and even before I passed the bar examination I had promised myself to handle cases in which social issues were involved.

Most members of the American Committee for Puerto Rican Independence opposed my retainer for political reasons. They were, in the main, Socialists and pacifists, and I was neither. A. J. Muste, pacifism's theoretician and a friend of the theoretician Paul Tillich, opposed my retainer. So did Roger Baldwin of the ACLU, who was no friend of Albizu's anyway: Baldwin was totally opposed to violence. Because of our wartime association, Norman Thomas leaned slightly in my favor. The matter was decided in my mind, however, when Ruth Reynolds sent a telegram demanding that the will of the defendants be honored.

I knew no Spanish and the nineteen pages of charges that arrived in the mail were in that language. Fortunately, a beautiful young friend and former nurse of Albizu Campos, Yolanda Moreno, translated the document. I had met Yolanda through Albizu and she was soon to become my wife. Yolanda was deeply attached to Don Pedro.

There were technical legal difficulties for me in representing Ruth and Albizu. Puerto Rican law was a combination of the Greco-Roman and Anglo-Saxon systems. The Anglo-Saxon system was by far the superior. For example, there was no presumption of innocence under Greco-Roman law. As a practical matter in the Ruth Reynolds case, Greco-Roman law ascribed a far greater significance to Ruth's presence in the car that carried the guns than did Anglo-Saxon law.

I flew to San Juan in December 1950, the first time I had ever been to Puerto Rico. In all, I would fly to Puerto Rico more than thirty times on these two cases. On this first visit I was met at the airport by Nationalist leaders Paulino Castro and Manolin Negron. Manolin Negron had recently been fired from his job as a teacher for refusing to recite the pledge of allegiance to the United States. The two men thought we had a strong legal case, but that politically we were in trouble. The authorities very much wanted convictions.

Within a few hours I was able to obtain permission from Attorney General Cordero to visit Ruth Reynolds in her cell at La Princesa, the forbidding old Spanish fortress that served as a prison for the Nationalists. All of them were being held without bail. I took a taxi to the gates of the jail and after being passed through a succession of iron-studded doors, I reached Ruth's cell. It was windowless, there was no bed, and an overflowing pail served as the latrine. The stench was horrible, not sharp and pungent like a stockyard but heavy and pervasive. There seemed to be no air to breathe.

The light was dim, and it took a while before I could see her sitting on the cold limestone floor. She was unable to stand up. She inched sideways on the stone bench, and as she came nearer the light of starvation was visible in her eyes. She reached out and touched my arm. "Go back to New York and tell them what you've seen," she said.

Her admonition was right, of course. If she and Albizu were going to win acquittal, it would be because of outside pressure, not because the authorities were determined to conduct a fair trial. American and Puerto Rican officials were enraged about the insurrection, not to mention the attempted assassination of President Truman, and they were determined to make the Nationalists pay.

I was not allowed to see Albizu. I was told that I was not his attorney of record; that he had retained Puerto Rican counsel. I became angry, pleaded, became angry again, but the authorities were determined that I would not see the famous leader of the Nationalists. The reason, I believe, was that they did not want me to see the conditions he was being forced to endure.

I stayed at the Palace Hotel in San Juan and people were constantly stopping by to thank me. I told them it was my honor, and it was. It was an honor to represent the man I felt was the world's greatest living orator. I was grateful that he used his skill for a just cause.

One day I was taking a taxi to visit a potential witness when the driver in the car behind us began to honk his horn. He was waving one arm and using the other to honk. I told the taxi driver to stop. The man behind us jumped out of his car and walked up to where I was sitting. "Mr. Lynn," he said, "I'm a judge in San Juan. I can't say this in public, but I want you to know I'm for you. Many people are pleased that a North American would care enough about out country to come and defend Albizu."

I familiarized myself as much as I could with the cases and hurried back to New York. It was of the utmost importance—because these were political trials—to alert the mainland to the prison ordeal of the Nationalists.

A defense committee was formed that included J. Holmes Smith, who had been a missionary in India and was a leading exponent of Gandhi in America; Ralph Templin, a professor of political science at Central State College in Ohio; and Thelma Mielke, the librarian at Long Island University. We held a public meeting at the Community church on Park Avenue and Thirty-fifth Street. I gave an emotional report, and the committee decided to send me on tour to raise funds for the defendants. I spoke at Columbia, Cornell, CCNY, the University of Wisconsin, the University of Minnesota, the University of Chicago, Antioch College, and at other schools. Very little was known about the independence movement in Puerto Rico; in fact, the regime of Governor Luis Munoz Marin had the support of the American liberal establishment.

I hammered hard at Luis Munoz Marin. Munoz Marin had lived for a time in Greenwich Village and was nominally a socialist. He sedulously cultivated American corporations, promising tax exemptions to any company that opened a factory in Puerto Rico. Munoz Marin painted the Nationalists as gunmen and crazy people, and some of the students I spoke to agreed with him. It was easier to evoke sympathy for the pacifist Ruth Reynolds, a Midwesterner, than for the Nationalists.

The trials did not begin until August 1951. Ruth's case was heard first. At the outset I insisted that the trial be conducted in English. The judge attempted to reconcile Spanish pride with fear of the North American overlord by ruling that the case would be conducted in both languages. In reality, it was conducted in Spanish, with interpretations in English at the court's discretion. I had anticipated that this would happen and had taken a crash course in Spanish from Yolanda, who was by then my wife. She was of Italian descent but had majored in Spanish at New York University.

The first day of the trial was spent debating the constitutionality of the Smith Act. At this time the Smith Act was being used extensively on the mainland to snare people who were considered dissidents. This was the heyday of Senator Joseph McCarthy, and his influence extended to Puerto Rico.

The main legal issue here was the constitutionality of Puerto Rico's "little Smith Act," Law 53. I pointed out that the Declaration of Independence said that under a certain circumstance—an unresponsive government—it was legal, indeed necessary, to overthrow the government, and I said that such a circumstance existed in Puerto Rico. I also quoted Oliver Wendell Holmes in the Gitlow decision, where he said that when the ideas of a revolutionary are held by the majority of the people, those ideas should be the law. I argued that Albizu's ideas were the sentiment of the majority. Finally I quoted William O. Douglas in the *United States* v. *Terminiello* (Terminiello was a fascist priest) where Douglas said that the purpose of free speech should be to incite people to anger against their oppressors.

The court ruled that Law 53 was legal, which was what I expected it would rule. A day would come when a more enlightened court would hold that such a law was an anachronism.

It was clear that the prosecution was using the trial of Ruth Reynolds as a rehearsal for the trial of the Nationalists, especially Albizu Campos. The prosecution's strategy was to show that Ruth had attended the meeting in Arecibo in December of 1949, and that she had stood when Albizu had asked the audience if they were willing to give their lives and fortunes for the cause of independence. Also, the prosecution placed Ruth in the car in which the explosives were found four days before the outbreak of the revolt. The defense conceded she had been in the car, but argued that she had not known what cargo it was carrying.

The testimony was completely contradictory. Witnesses for the defense said that Ruth did not stand. Witnesses for the prosecution, mainly paid police agents who had infiltrated the Nationalist party, said that she did. It was my job as Ruth's attorney to believe her, but even on a personal level I felt she was telling the truth. It was hard for me to believe that this woman, a bone-deep pacifist, was plotting to overthrow the U. S. government in Puerto Rico by force and violence. Her background argued against such a role: her father was a wealthy man who owned gold mines, but she had spurned his money to advocate the cause of nonviolence, a stand that led to her being disinherited. She was a member in good standing of the Fifth Avenue Presbyterian church. She even disliked swatting insects. Although it was probably not relevant, she did not look the part. She was a studious, sweet-faced, gentle woman in her early thirties. She was, as a matter of conscience, opposed to any form of violence.

A good deal of the defense's investigation had been spent on what should have been the irrelevant question of whether Ruth had been Albizu's lover. Albizu was happily married, but I knew the prosecution was going to devote a considerable amount of time to showing that Ruth's love for him had led her into the advocacy of violence, so I had to be able to counter that charge.

The prosecution decided to clinch its case by showing the jury the tragic aftermath of the fighting. The jury was told about the police and troops who were killed. Injured police were brought into court to exhibit their maimed limbs. Molotov cocktails, dynamite bombs fashioned out of beer cans, rifles, shotguns, all were put on display. I objected again and again, but the judge ruled that everything was material. I am not sure how much the prosecution profited from these displays. The jury was shocked, it is true, but so was Ruth Reynolds. Several times she broke down and cried when a particularly grisly piece of evidence was introduced.

Outside the courtroom Ralph Templin, the political science professor, was conducting a hunger strike. He went without food for the entire trial.

In addition to the witnesses we called, the defense comprised an appeal to the national spirit of independence. Each government witness was cross-examined about his knowledge of Puerto Rico's past. I stressed the long struggle for independence, dating back at least to 1868 when the *independistas* briefly took over the mountain community of Lares and including the opposition to American rule that began in 1898 with the Spanish-American War. Even the trial judge was moved. He asked one of his colleagues if it would be proper to invite me to his home for dinner.

The verdict, however, was foreordained. During a court recess I saw two of the jurors walking out of the prosecutor's office. The actual verdict, however, seemed to be a misreading of the judge's instructions. On the charge that Ruth promoted the revolt by her presence in the car that carried the explosives, she was acquitted. She was convicted of promoting the revolt by standing up during Albizu's speech in Arecibo.

I moved for arrest of judgment on the ground that the facts as determined did not amount to a violation of Law 53. The motion was denied. I also argued that Ruth was being mistreated in prison, and that it was likely she would die if sent back. The judge brushed this motion aside and gave Ruth a sentence of two to six years at hard labor.

It has often been the case in my career that my hardest work would come after the original verdict was rendered. I went on another speaking tour to raise the funds necessary for the appeal. On this particular tour I debated Bayard Rustin and James Farmer, two black pacifists who were hostile to the Nationalists. Rustin and Farmer were sincere pacifists. They would have given their lives rather than use violence.

The Albizu Campos trial began in late August 1951, amidst international furor. There were demonstrations in his behalf in all the communist countries, throughout Western Europe and Latin America, and in many cities in the United States. Prime Minister Nehru of India wrote a letter asking that the prosecution be stopped. Writers and humanists of world stature pleaded for Albizu's release. Religious leaders called for a day of prayer for justice.

Besides myself, Albizu's defense team consisted of Angel Cruz and Hernandez Vallé, two capable Puerto Rican attorneys with histories of representing political defendants. Hernandez Vallé was also a minister, and he was later charged with conspiring to overthrow the government. I represented him in that trial.

The three of us knew that the trial of Ruth Reynolds had been a practice run for the prosecution. The person whom the prosecution most wanted to convict was Albizu Campos. Albizu faced the death penalty, which made our responsibility awesome.

The court ruled—over defense objections—that no spectators would be permitted. The court was aware of Albizu's charismatic appeal, and they did not want the courtroom packed with fervent Nationalist supporters. Much more damaging to the defense was the jury selection, such as it was. The court, in effect, let the prosecution select the jurors. Five of the twelve were former Puerto Rican policemen.

Albizu's trial would have been an excellent political science seminar for high-school and university students. The case was almost completely political; very little law was involved.

The trial followed the format of the Ruth Reynolds case, a significant departure being the use of Albizu's public speeches to prove that he advocated the violent overthrow of American rule. The tactic backfired on the prosecution. In the courtroom there were large spaces in the wall instead of windows, to allow a freer circulation of air, and when a tape recording of one of Albizu's speeches was played it could be heard by the people who gathered outside each day to demonstrate support for the Nationalist leader.

It seemed that most of Puerto Rico was outside the courtroom that day, and soon they were cheering Albizu's words. It was impossible for that big crowd not to recognize the electrifying voice of this great orator. I tilted my head to the side and looked at him. He was almost skeleton thin, but a soft smile played on his lips, and he had large eyes that people swore could see the future.

The cheering outside grew louder and louder. The big courtroom with its dark gray walls seemed to rock with the sound. Even the hard-bitten jury was moved by Albizu's words. They could hear the crowd outside, and Albizu's voice, and for a moment I felt we might actually win the case.

Troops were called to disperse the crowd, and the sound of cheering changed to the ugly noises of street confrontation. Incredibly, the prosecution continued playing the tape. Finally the judge was impelled to stop it.

At the end of each day's session I rode in an open car with Albizu back to the jail in La Princesa. Each trip was a triumphal procession. Crowds packed the sidewalks and shouted allegiance to their hero.

The government had to find him guilty. He was too popular, too much of a threat. The judge sentenced him to seventy-nine years in prison, and that day there were angry riots all over Puerto Rico.

In 1953 I argued the appeal of Ruth Reynolds' conviction in the supreme court of Puerto Rico. Here we won a great victory. As I had predicted, the Smith Act was declared unconstitutional. A number of the justices on the supreme court had been former followers of Albizu, and although they had traded their beliefs for privilege they could still remember their younger, more idealistic years. Ruth Reynolds' conviction was reversed and she was released.

In November 1953, agitation for Albizu's release reached such heights that Munoz Marin agreed to free him if he would promise not to engage in further political activity. Albizu spurned the condition and refused to leave prison unless it was removed. Albizu also demanded that the other Nationalists be freed. The authorities had to physically eject him from prison.

During his last three years in prison, Albizu's physical condition had deteriorated badly. His friends were convinced that the authorities had experimented on his body with various rays. The charge remains a point of contention, although the matter has never been proved to my satisfaction one way or the other. In any event, my experiences with Pedro Albizu Campos and other Puerto Rican Nationalists were just beginning.

On March 1, 1954, four Puerto Rican Nationalists—Lolita Lebron, Irving

Flores, Rafael Cancel Miranda, and Andres Figueroa Cordero—traveled from New York City to Washington, D. C. They took up positions in the gallery of the House of Representatives and opened fire with guns they had smuggled in. When it was over, five congressmen were wounded.

The Nationalists made no attempt to get away. They *wanted* to be captured. Their objective was to compel Congress to place the independence of Puerto Rico on its agenda once again.

Lolita Lebron, a beautiful young poet, led the Nationalists. Lolita was a Catholic mystic and ardent Nationalist. I first met her when she came to my office to thank me for representing Albizu. Lolita was thirty years old in 1954. She had an oval face, lovely black eyes, and a stunning figure. She had a wonderfully elegant way of walking and was embarrassed by the attention men paid her. "They should not be interested in my body," she would say, "but in the body of Christ."

My wife and I counted Lolita among our closest friends. She had seen our son when he was born, even before I had. I was astounded when I heard the first reports of what she had done. It was natural that I would become her lawyer on the charges of felonious assault and attempted murder.

Lolita was a very proud woman. She had worked in New York's garment district but had been unemployed for more than a year before the shooting in the House of Representatives. Lolita would not accept public aid because she said she did not want anything from the United States except her country's independence. Lolita said she thought Albizu was the embodiment that God had chosen to work his will in Puerto Rico.

Five days after the violence in the House of Representatives, Pedro Albizu Campos was ordered reimprisoned by Governor Munoz Marin. Under the terms of Albizu's earlier release, the release he had protested, Munoz Marin had inserted the clause, "If Pedro Albizu Campos attempts or conspires against the public security, intending to subvert by violence or terror the constitutionally established order, . . ." then he could be reimprisoned. The pardon provided, however, that "on the summary revocation of the pardon, Pedro Albizu Campos may file in the courts of the country a petition for habeas corpus to question the determination of non-performance on his part of the conditions hereof."

I was close to Albizu and Lolita. I had met my wife, Yolanda, through Albizu. Our son Alexander was born in November 1952. His godfather was Albizu. His godmother was Lolita.

Lolita was tried in federal district court in Washington along with her confederates. I thought she had a chance, if only a slight one. The gun she had used was a .45 caliber. The police found all the bullets that had been fired during the raid, and each bullet that came from Lolita's gun had gone into the ceiling. I suggested that perhaps she had only intended to frighten the congressmen, but she scoffed at the idea. She said the gun had been too heavy for her and the recoil had forced her aim upward. On the stand she testified that she had intended to shoot the congressmen. She wanted to draw the world's attention to Puerto Rico's fight for freedom. God had called her to this mission and she was obeying his will.

Lolita was found guilty of assault with intent to commit murder and was sentenced to fifty-four years in prison. By now she may be the world's most famous political prisoner.

Nine months later, in 1955, Lolita was tried along with sixteen leaders of the Nationalist party from many parts of the United States and Puerto Rico in the federal court in Manhattan for conspiracy to murder the congressmen. Her beauty and poetic talent had already made her the most striking figure on trial. I represented eleven of the defendants, and my plan was to have Lolita testify at the climactic point of the defense.

I did not know, however, that the night before she was to testify, a priest had gained entry to her cell. He told her that her only son, age twelve, had drowned that afternoon in Puerto Rico. She said nothing to me before she took the stand. Then she quietly told the judge and jury of her tragedy, and asked the judge whether she could tell the jury about her son. He had the sensitivity to wave aside the objection of the prosecution, Lumbard.

Lolita related how she brought her son to Brooklyn when he was four. She could not find work and, as a Nationalist, could not accept welfare payments. One day she took the little boy on her shoulder and went looking for a dime in gutters so that she might buy him a little milk. Finally, she began to cry. "Don't worry, Mommy," her son said, "some day I'll turn myself into a bird and tuck you under my wing and we'll fly far, far away."

By this time the judge was blowing his nose, and the defense table and the jury were in tears. Lolita reminisced in her soft, liquid voice that entire court day and no one interrupted her. All the world's sorrow was summed up by Lolita Lebron, and I, for one, have never been the same since.

The defendants were found guilty at the end of a long trial. Lolita's sentence, however, was made to run concurrently with the one she had received in Washington.

Officials in Alderson, West Virginia, have telephoned my offIce to ask me to persuade Lolita to accept parole. This I refuse to do. The decision is Lolita's and only she can make it. As of this writing she is still in prison, and my family visits her whenever we can. She is very fond of her godson, Alexander.

Throughout the 1950s and early 1960s my efforts to free Albizu Campos (rearrested after the attack on the House of Representatives) were based on the constitutionality of the pardon document. His fellow Nationalists, his wife Dona Laura, and his children waged a ceaseless campaign for his freedom or, in lieu of that, for mitigation of the harsh conditions of his imprisonment: within a short period after his reimprisonment, he suffered three serious strokes and lost his ability to speak. Because their extralegal efforts were stymied, however, I remained convinced that the only way to free Albizu was through the courts. He had been put in jail without a trial, which violated the due process clause of the Fifth Amendment.

I first filed a petition in the federal court in Puerto Rico, but the court refused to accept jurisdiction. It referred the matter to the territorial courts and that raised what seemed to be an insurmountable problem. Albizu did not recognize the jurisdiction of the territorial courts. He considered them mere puppets of the United States. As a subject of the United States, however, he conceded power to the federal courts. Albizu was a man of great principle, and rather than violate a principle he preferred to remain in jail. That seemed to be that: the federal courts refused jurisdiction and Albizu would not allow me to go to the territorial courts. I disagreed with Albizu. I told him that I thought it was better to have some forum in which to present his ideas than none at all. But I could not persuade him.

Years went by. Technically I was still Albizu's attorney, but in reality there seemed little I could do. Finally, out of desperation, I tried a new tactic. In July 1962, my law interne, Don Gellers, went to Puerto Rico to prepare the groundwork for a habeas corpus application to the supreme court of Puerto Rico. We charged that Albizu had been jailed without a hearing. On September 18 we were ready to submit a writ of habeas corpus to be directed to Gerardo Delgado, warden at the Commonwealth Penitentiary at Rio Piedras. Actually, Albizu had for some time been confined as a prisoner to the Presbyterian hospital in Santurce, because of the many illnesses he was suffering.

The supreme court issued the writ on September 20 and ordered that a hearing be held on September 26 in superior court to determine if Albizu was being illegally detained. At the hearing the warden simply submitted Munoz Marin's reimprisonment order, with the comment that Albizu had subverted the established order by his conduct following the shooting in the House of Representatives. What Albizu had done was refuse to condemn Lolita

Lebron and her three friends. There had never been any evidence that Albizu had ordered or even known about their actions, but it was an established principle with him that he would never repudiate his followers. When asked to comment on what Lolita had done, he hailed it as an example "of the sublime heroism of a revolutionary woman." He would never have been jailed if he had said what the authorities wanted to hear.

My job at the hearing was not to get Albizu to repudiate his support for Lolita (something he was not going to do), but to stress the technical argument that Munoz Marin could not so condition a pardon as to deprive Albizu of a court hearing prior to reimprisonment. The supreme court had ordered that the hearing be held in superior court, and this court rejected our petition and dismissed the writ. I appealed to the supreme court, but there followed months of delay. I believed the supreme court was sympathetic to Albizu, but that they were afraid of provoking U. S. authorities.

It took almost a year to compel the clerk of the court to transmit the record to the supreme court. This clerk was no different from many others in the United States. He wanted a bribe before he did what was supposed to be his job. I will not pay bribes, although I know they can often facilitate the release of a client.

Meanwhile, I talked with various officials in Puerto Rico. Hiram Cancio, secretary of justice, expressed fear that if Albizu were released he might be whisked to Cuba by his followers. I spoke to his fears in a letter:

> Since speaking to you, I have carefully checked on the position of Albizu Campos about leaving Puerto Rico. You are, no doubt, familiar with the principle he has long espoused—no voluntary expatriation. One of the main reasons for the affection which his followers have for him is this refusal to leave the land of his birth. Now, I have sounded out the people who retained me . . . which include those who would have custody or care of Albizu Campos should he be released. I told them of Dr. Montilla's opinion that Albizu would survive only a few days if he were removed from familiar surroundings. . . .
>
> There is not the slightest likelihood that Pedro Albizu Campos would want to go to Cuba, and if any tried to carry him there in his dreadfully pitiful condition, to make propaganda, they would only arouse the horror of the peoples of Latin America.
>
> Finally, it must be apparent what public credit your government would gain if it released Albizu before any court order. Then, it would be an act of magnanimity which would grace well the executive power.

The secretary of justice did not act, so I went ahead with the appeal to the supreme court. The transcript of the record was finally filed on October 9, 1963. A hearing was held on February 12, 1964, but the solicitor general obtained permission to file a supplemental report, so a new hearing was scheduled for March 30. All this was quite irritating, and very unsettling for my law practice, but it had to be even more maddening for Albizu. Then the March 30 hearing was postponed.

On May 12 the supreme court vacated the order of the superior court and set a hearing on the merits for May 25, before the full bench of nine judges.

At last I felt there was reason for hope. I knew Albizu was gravely ill and I did not want him to spend his last days in prison. Millions of people felt the same way. Again there were demonstrations—in more than twenty countries—to exhort his freedom.

Yolanda went with me to Puerto Rico for the hearing. Alexander also came along. He had heard both of us talk about Lolita and Albizu, although of course he could remember nothing about either of them. The three of us visited Albizu and he was very weak and unable to enunciate clearly. Only in the brightness of his eyes could we detect the indomitable spirit.

It was slightly embarrassing for me to appear before the supreme court of Puerto Rico. Because of the many delays I had petitioned the United States Supreme Court for a writ of mandamus to compel the Puerto Rican court to decide the case. Now I had to face this same court.

Testimony lasted a full day, and the Puerto Rican supreme court reserved decision. No word came down all summer. Most of the fall passed.

I went back to the U. S. Supreme Court for the writ of mandamus. That did it! Whatever the U. S. Supreme Court decided would be embarrassing to Puerto Rican authorities, because it would show that the Puerto Rican supreme court was not really "supreme" at all, but subject to the will of the American high court. Munoz Marin ordered Albizu freed.

It was December 1964. Albizu was carried to a little cottage in a suburb of San Juan. During the remaining months of his life the cottage became a shrine for pilgrims all over Puerto Rico. In early May 1965, Albizu died in his sleep. Yolanda and I flew to Puerto Rico for his funeral.

No burial procession has affected me more than the sight of unending thousands of country people pouring into San Juan from all sections of the island. The woman walked by us barefooted, their arms piled high with loose flowers. On many faces I saw the curious mixture of sorrow and pride. After a while I had to sit down on the curb, overcome by a sense of irreplaceable loss.

As the huge crowd passed the edifice of the supreme court of Puerto Rico, students in a van raced to the dome of the capitol and hauled down the American flag and replaced it with the emblem of Puerto Rico. Ordinarily, such defiance would have caused brutal repression, but the government had carefully kept troops and police off the streets.

Finally the procession reached the cathedral. After a very brief ceremony the family and close friends gathered in the cemetery nearby. There, Albizu's widow and his political heirs vowed to carry on the struggle for liberty.

Obscure notices in the North American press expressed the hope and expectation that agitation for Puerto Rican independence would cease with the death of the Nationalist leader. An oppressor never learns that the death of a person does not kill an ideal.

CHAPTER 12

The Kissing Case

In Monroe, North Carolina, one afternoon in October 1958, two black children were walking their bicycles home from the segregated school they attended. The two children, Fuzzy Simpson, age seven, and Hanover Thompson, age nine, spotted a group of five white children, boys and girls, who asked them to stop and play. The game began as cops and robbers, but soon the two girls said they wanted to play something else. Six-year-old Sissy Marcus suggested they play house in one of the culverts by the side of the road. Nine-year-old Hanover Thompson climbed into the culvert and sat down as the daddy. Sissy, as the mommy, sat on Hanover's lap. Suddenly Sissy recognized him. Hanover had been her preschool playmate when his mother had worked as a housemaid for her mother. Sissy was so happy at seeing her friend that she kissed him on the cheek. Then she ran home to tell her mother the good news. Hanover Thompson and Fuzzy Simpson stayed behind, killing granddaddy spiders in the culvert.

Sissy Marcus told her mother about how she had met Hanover Thompson. When Bernice Marcus heard that Sissy had kissed Hanover, she grabbed the little girl, pulled her over to the sink, seized some brown soap and scrubbed out the child's mouth. All the while the horrified Bernice Marcus screamed about the dirty thing Sissy had done. Mrs. Marcus became more and more hysterical. Finally, she did what she considered her duty and called the police.

A patrol car picked up Hanover Thomson and Fuzzy Simpson before they even reached home. The two youngsters were locked in the county jail, an underground prison underneath the courthouse. The police notified the parents that the charge was rape, a crime that carried a possible death sentence.

The children were terrified. They did not know what a jail was, much less why they were in one. The incident with Sissy Marcus had seemed so trivial that they had forgotten it had taken place. It was Sissy Marcus who later testified that she had kissed Hanover Thompson.

The two boys were held incommunicado. Their mothers (the fathers had long since abandoned the families) sought information and were told their sons were being held in protective custody because angry white mobs might lynch them. This could have been true. It developed that certain men had heard about the incident and were as outraged as Mrs. Marcus. They became even more outraged when Robert Williams entered the case.

The mothers of Hanover Thompson and Fuzzy Simpson had gone to Robert Williams for help. Williams was president of the Union County (which included Monroe) NAACP. Williams was 32 years old, 5'11", and husky—he weighed 225 pounds—and he lived in Monroe on the street where he had been born. He was a former marine who had worked on an auto assembly line in Detroit before deciding he was needed in his hometown. That was in 1955 and Williams set about building a vigorous chapter of the NAACP. He first recruited a rising young black doctor, Albert Perry. Then he concentrated on the pool halls and beer parlors, which were filled with poor people, the unemployed and the casually employed, housemaids and janitors and porters. They each scraped up two dollars and joined the new NAACP that Williams had created.

In 1956 two black children drowned while swimming in a Monroe creek. Robert Williams alienated the whites in Monroe by asking the town council to allot one day a week for blacks to use the local swimming pool. The pool had been built with WPA funds and was maintained by local taxes. Blacks composed three-quarters of Monroe's population, but the town council refused, saying it was "a well-known fact that Negroes contaminated water" and deciding that it was too expensive to have to drain the pool every week.

The Ku Klux Klan should have considered this a victory, but they did not. The Klan blamed Dr. Albert Perry. They decided he was the "brains" behind what they considered an insult to the town. A Klan leader announced in the local newspaper that Dr. Perry's house would be burned to the ground.

The Klan nightriders came at midnight. Midnight was chosen because the Klan believed blacks were cowardly and afraid of ghosts. Robert Williams was ready for them. He had read in the newspaper what they intended to do and had assembled a group of young Monroe veterans. As the caravan of Klan cars wound up the country hill leading to Dr. Perry's home, the riflemen that Williams had stationed in trees and trenches opened fire. It was a Klan rule not to acknowledge casualties, so Williams never learned if any Klansmen were killed.

In 1958, however, Williams was aware from talking with Mrs. Thompson and Mrs. Simpson that the Klan would be very unhappy he had decided to intervene in what was soon to be known in many countries around the world as the Kissing Case.

Williams first contacted Kelly Alexander, a short, slender, light-complexioned black who was a millionaire mortician. Alexander was head of the North Carolina NAACP, and his money made him one of the most important people in the state. Alexander was proud of his connections with blacks (he was on a first-name basis with the Spauldings, the richest black family in America) and with the white Southern power structure. In my opinion he served on the NAACP chiefly to convince blacks whose funeral expenses were the source of his millions, that he was interested in their welfare. Alexander recoiled from the sexual implications of the Kissing Case and refused to help. He was a black man who had made good in the South, and he did not want the status quo disturbed by what might be a controversial and volatile case.

Williams then contacted Roy Wilkins at the national office of the NAACP. Wilkins was in no hurry to help, either. How did he know that the two black children were innocent? What civil liberties were involved? Interracial sex was an explosive issue, he said, and perhaps the NAACP, for the time being, ought to concern itself with other questions. Wilkins did hold out a form of help, however. He offered Robert Williams a job in the national office that paid a hefty salary. Williams was tempted. He was out of work and no one in Monroe was likely to hire him. Williams had a wife and two children and lived off the few dollars the poor people in Monroe could give him. But Williams recognized Wilkins's offer for what it was—a bribe to get him out of North Carolina—and turned it down.

My office has been called "the house of last resort"; it is because I have been willing to handle cases that were unpopular or dangerous. Williams called my office on November 2, 1958, a week after the "attempted rape" (the charge had been scaled down from actual rape). I had first met Williams when he asked me to litigate the question of whether blacks had the right to use the Monroe swimming pool, a case we won and, incidentally, one that led to the beautiful situation of little children of different colors overcoming the fear and prejudice that their parents held.

I would not have believed the case Robert Williams described had I not already been to Monroe. Two children were in jail without a reason that could make sense to civilized people.

"Conrad," Williams said, "I don't think we can pay you. I have a little money of my own, but it won't be nearly enough."

"This one's free," I said.

On November 4 I flew to Charlotte with George Weissman, a reporter for the *Nation*, and Robert Williams met us at the airport and drove us to Monroe. George Weissman made the trip on my promise that he would get a story straight out of the pre-Civil War South, and he was not disappointed.

As soon as we reached Monroe, before I contacted anyone else, I made an appointment with Juvenile Court Judge Hampton Price. Williams had told me that in the two days since he had called my office, Judge Price had held a "trial" and found the two boys guilty.

I went alone to meet Judge Price. One woman, a stenographer, was the only witness to the meeting, which took place in the judge's chambers, a cramped cubicle that smelled of mothballs and featured a Confederate flag hanging from an overhead light. Price was about fifty-five years old, short and red-faced, and I could see he was torn between conflicting emotions: he was pleased that he would be able to debate one of his decisions with a lawyer from New York; he was not happy that the lawyer was black.

Judge Price confirmed that he had sentenced the two boys. "Oh yes," he said, "we had a separate but equal hearing."

There was no point in becoming angry. I had seen too many judges in the South like Hampton Price. "What do you mean," I asked, "by a seperate but equal hearing?"

"Well, down here we do things a little different from you folks up there in New York. We feel we get along better if the white folks stay in their places and the niggers stay in theirs."

"Look!" I shouted, forgetting that I had just promised not to become angry. "I don't . . ."

"*You* look! We got contempt laws in this here court."

"We're not in court."

"I was tryin' to explain what happened. Now. On the mornin' I had the hearin', I called in the white parent, Mrs. Marcus, and her daughter. She told me in front of the same stenographer I have here now what happened to her child. I sent them home. Later I summoned the two nigger mothers and had the children brought up from the county jail. Since they just stood silent and didn't say nothin', I knew that was a confession of guilt. I gave the older nigger boy twelve years. The younger nigger got fourteen."

Unless America's system of justice had gone completely haywire, I was certain Hampton Price's decision would be overthrown on appeal. But that would cost money and take time, and I did not want the two boys languishing in jail. I was afraid the children might already have suffered serious mental harm. On Halloween night, "as a joke," three Monroe policemen broke into their cells. The police were wearing white sheets and said they were dressed as ghosts. The children screamed, which proved to the police that they were superstitious. What happened was that the two boys thought the Klan had come for them.

"Judge," I said, hoping that even this unfortunate example of the Southern legal system could be made to see logic, "assuming that Sissy Marcus did kiss Hanover Thompson, and it was only on the cheek as I understand, why did you sentence Fuzzy Simpson?"

"Sah! Don't you realize what that nigger boy witnessed? Don't you know what was planted in his mind? It'll take at least fourteen years to rehabilitate him."

"Judge, I'm sure you're a student of the United States Constitution. The Fourteenth Amendment of that Constitution says there must be a confrontation of witnesses at a trial. You admitted that no such confrontation occurred. The Marcuses weren't present when the defendants appeared."

Judge Price was not impressed by this argument. He advised me to go back to New York and stop interfering with local affairs.

A nine-year-old had been sentenced to twelve years in prison; a seven-year-old had received fourteen years. The best way to handle this case was to generate some publicity. I began calling every reporter I knew.

Ted Poston of the *New York Post* was the first to break the story. George Weissman's article appeared in the *Nation*. Still the NAACP refused to come into the case, but by this time there was great indignation among the rank and file against the leadership. Roy Wilkins stood firm. In the 1930s he had been a real champion of the underdog, but no more. I talked with Wilkins about the Kissing Case and he made a shocking remark. "Why," he asked, "do you want to represent those scum who are on welfare?"

On November 4, 1958, the day I arrived in Monroe, I met for the first time with the mothers of Hanover Thompson and Fuzzy Simpson. The women were nervous and frightened. Mrs. Thompson had three other children. Mrs. Simpson had four others. Both women earned fifteen dollars a week as domestic servants, and they received a few extra dollars each month from welfare to help feed their children. They were afraid they might lose the welfare if I pushed too hard for the release of Hanover and Fuzzy, but they were of course determined to go ahead. Mrs. Simpson, a shy woman, asked if I would also help her friend Martha Griffin. The landlord had just ordered

Mrs. Griffin and her four children out of the shack they lived in. I said I would do what I could.

The shack the Griffins lived in was owned by Chauncey Oglethorpe. Oglethorpe, who lived in an antebellum mansion, owned four full blocks of shacks in Monroe, all rented to black people, and I learned he was in the habit of dispossessing tenants whenever the mood struck him. I studied the dispossess notice Mrs. Griffin had received, and no reason was given for the eviction. Her rent was paid up-to-date.

The dispossess notice was illegal for two reasons: the Fourteenth Amendment made it unconstitutional to deprive a person of property, including rental property, without a reason, and the landlord-tenant laws of every state in the nation said precisely the same thing. I said I would handle the case, and the look in Mrs. Griffin's eyes made me want to cry. She had never thought that a black person would stand up to a man like Chauncey Oglethorpe.

I have often thought of moving to a small town like Monroe and practicing law. There is so much that could be done. I have been praised for handling cases like the Kissing Case, but the real heroes are people like Robert Williams and Dr. Albert Perry. It is one thing to go South and win a case. It is another to have to live in the South. When my job is finished I can return to the relative safety of New York. Williams and Perry had to stay and face the Klan and its hate-filled adherents. Neither of them earned much of a living. Williams survived because black people contributed a few pennies a week to "their" NAACP. Dr. Perry worked sixteen hours a day healing the sick and seldom thought of even submitting a bill. I never moved to the South. Perhaps I should have.

The hearing on the dispossess notice took place on November 6 in the court of the Honorable Hampton Price, whose duties seemed to encompass much more than matters affecting juveniles. The courtroom was small and paint was peeling from the walls. A Confederate flag hung next to the Stars and Stripes.

I had been staying at Robert Williams's home on Boyte Street. On the morning of the hearing, some 150 black people gathered outside. Then all of us walked to the courthouse. When we reached Hamlet, we walked in the street, not on the sidewalk, and I realized that these blacks had *never* walked on the sidewalk. There was no law against it. Walking in the street was simply part of their heritage, a heritage they never questioned.

"Mr. Lynn," Judge Price said, almost choking on the "Mister," "I observe that you did not heed my advice and return to New York."

"Judge Price," I said, almost choking on the "Judge," "I think the court will agree that a grave injustice will be visited on Mrs. Griffin if she is forced to leave her home."

"Injustice? Mr. Lynn, Mr. Oglethorpe is one of our leading citizens. He owns the property in question. He can do what he wants with it."

"No, he can't."

The courtroom was packed with black people. Many others were outside. Chauncey Oglethorpe was so confident of victory that he had not bothered to send an attorney to contest the case. But Oglethorpe had not calculated the apprehension that gripped Hampton Price at the sight of so many blacks. I presented the legal arguments, which would have been overwhelming in almost any other court in the country, and Price, whose face had developed a nervous tic, ruled in Mrs. Griffin's behalf. The blacks were astounded. I chuckled as I thought of the later meeting between Oglethorpe and Hampton Price. "You ruled *what*?" Oglethorpe would say.

The 150 who had come to the hearing began walking from Hamlet back to Robert Williams's house. "Why don't we walk on the sidewalk?" I asked, and stepped over the curb.

Robert Williams joined me. An old black woman came forward, her eyes agleam with defiance. Then they came in twos and threes, and finally all of them were on the sidewalk. By the time we reached Williams's home on Boyte Street we were singing the stirring words of a Negro spiritual. The spring in their steps and the bare glimmer of hope in their eyes revealed that those blacks had discovered a small measure of their humanity.

My main job was to secure the freedom of Hanover Thompson and Fuzzy Simpson. I had visited them in jail and was convinced they would suffer permanent scarring if they were not soon released. They were confined to separate cells which were filthy, and when they wanted to relieve themselves they had to do it in a bucket. It was chilly in North Carolina in November, but the bedding for each consisted of one soiled white linen sheet.

I decided that a writ of habeas corpus (forcing the state to produce the two boys in court on the ground that they had not received a fair trial) was the legal remedy. The right of habeas corpus dates back to the thirteenth century, but several North Carolina judges turned us down. The judges were reluctant to overrule their colleague Hampton Price. Finally, on November 10, I had to return to New York. I asked Williams to do research on North Carolina judges to see if he could find one who might be sympathetic.

In New York I worked to obtain as much publicity as possible, in the hope that popular pressure would force the authorities to relent. I also spoke in

Boston, and author Truman Nelson wrote a passage about the speech that I still treasure:

> Mr. Lynn is the only man left in these times with the oratorical power, the openness, compassion, and above all the innate sense of righteousness and prophecy that was the hallmark of the great abolitionists of the 1850s—Frederick Douglass, Garrison, Phillips, Charles Lenox Remond and Theodore Parker. In thirty years of constant communication with these last, not astrally but by an almost daily wrestling with and meditating over their words and their works, I have not encountered their like until I went one bitterly cold night to a small hall in Boston.
> . . .
> Mr. Lynn was the speaker and he laid a spell upon us all, a spell that only those with true oratorical power can evoke, in which the listener is swept out into a rushing stream of words, sensations, even passions, in which his own landscape vanishes and all is new around him, and he feels carried against his will and almost fearfully to some newness and change himself. He is swept over the dam of his own limitations and prejudices and can never get back or feel the same again. Perhaps I heard this because I have been listening for it so long; but I have heard him many times since, and he has never failed to take me up and fling me into new and instantaneous decisions of daring to be freer and open with other people . . . absolutely open with everyone, friend or enemy, as Lynn himself is.

The *New York Times* ran a story on the Kissing Case, but our big break came when the *London Observer* sent a reporter named Joyce Egginton to Monroe. She called me in New York before going to North Carolina and asked if the mothers were permitted to visit their children. I said they were not, but that she might be able to arrange such a meeting. Southern whites generally take pride in their British ancestry. They imagine themselves relatively uncontaminated by such immigrant strains as the Polish, the Portuguese, and the Italians. But they love the English.

Joyce Egginton was dark and pretty and very intelligent. Later she became a television newscaster in the United States. When she talked with the Monroe officials, they were delighted to accede to her every wish. She obtained permission for the two mothers to accompany her to the jail, hid a camera in a basket of fruit she was carrying, and snapped a picture of the tearful reunion of mothers and children. It appeared on the front page of the

London Observer on December 18, 1958, with a simple caption: "WHY?"

The next day there was a demonstration at the American embassy in London. A few days later there was another demonstration in Rotterdam. Then came demonstrations in Moscow, Peking, Rome, and Paris. North Carolina officials were not impressed. They dug in their heels and refused to budge, and the children spent Christmas in jail. At least the national office of the NAACP overcame its conservatism and agreed to pay for the appeals my office was preparing.

On January 4, 1959, Robert Williams called and said he thought he had found a judge who would issue the writ of habeas corpus. I flew to Charlotte the next day.

Williams, who was to meet me, had not yet arrived, so I sat in the lobby at the airport. Only white people were sitting there. A white woman looked at me and I looked back. The lobby was still as a tomb. Faces hardened. A foot scraped on the floor and the noise carried through the entire room. At that moment Robert Williams and Dr. Perry arrived. They took my arms and hurried me out of the airport. When we got to his car, I asked Williams what was wrong. "When you sit in the lobby of that airport," he said, "you're supposed to keep your eyes on the floor."

"I'll remember that next time," I said. *This* time, I did not want to become involved in any issue other than freeing Hanover and Fuzzy, who had already been in jail more than two months.

When we reached William's home a group of teenagers were waiting for us. People were always in and out of William's house—it served, for practical purposes, as a community meeting center—but these youngsters were excited and afraid. "Mr. Williams," one of them said, "we just heard three white men sayin' they were gonna kill you, shoot you down like a dog."

Williams asked where the men were. At the drugstore, he was told. Williams went into the house, and when he returned he was wearing a shoulder holster and a gun. "I guess I'd better have a talk with those three," he said.

"Let me come along," I said. There was a quiet anger about him and I knew there was no way I could stop him from going. I thought at least I could be a witness to what happened.

"I won't need help," William said.

Williams returned to the house thirty minutes later with a big smile on his face. He had gone to the drugstore, opened his coat so the three men could see his gun, and suggested they settle their quarrel right there. The men almost fell to their knees apologizing to Williams, who was not only a brave man but a clever psychologist. He knew the three men were mostly bluff, but if allowed to go unchallenged they might screw up their courage and actually commit the crime. The three were wise to have backed down. Williams, I had no doubt, would have been ready to kill. Growing up in Monroe had convinced him that no one was going to hand him his rights, that sitting back and waiting for justice invited injustice, and that only aggressiveness could force most Southern whites to leave him alone. Earlier, Williams had said nothing to the people in the Charlotte airport who were angry because I was not staring at the floor. He was brave but he was not suicidal. He did not know the people in the Charlotte airport. Monroe was his home, he did know the whites who lived there, and he knew how to deal with them.

In his living room that night, Williams explained why he thought he had found a judge who would issue the writ of habeas corpus. He pointed out that Southern judges who were about to retire often wanted to do something to salve their consciences after spending a lifetime dispensing unequal justice. Judge John Clarkson of Charlotte was seventy-two years old and had announced the date of his retirement. I agreed with Williams that Judge Clarkson would be just the man we were looking for; and in this particular case I would be happy to give him the chance to atone for whatever sins he had committed.

Williams drove me to Charlotte the next morning, January 6. Judge Clarkson turned out to be the very picture of a Southern plantation owner: tall, soft-spoken, paternalistic. He treated me with a certain deference. I was a nigger to him, but I was a lawyer and that made me better than other niggers. I felt a surge of hope when I walked into Clarkson's court and noted the absence of a Confederate flag.

Judge Clarkson did issue the writ. He said he knew his decision would be unpopular and he wanted it understood that in no way was he passing on the guilt or innocence of the two boys. Encouraged by this beginning, I suggested that Clarkson make the hearing on the writ returnable before him. If he did have an aching conscience, here was the opportunity to go all the way. Clarkson declined. He had already done more than his judicial sense dictated. He set the hearing for January 14 in the court of Judge Clarence Johnson, in the farming community of Wadesboro.

As Williams and I left the courtroom we were stopped by two reporters from the *Charlotte Observer.* There are many decent people in the South, and these were two of them. They said quite frankly that they thought the case was an outrage and asked if they could help. I suggested they call

Governor Luther Hodges. Hodges had the authority to free Hanover and Fuzzy immediately. One of the reporters did call, but Hodges brushed aside his questions and announced that he was directing Attorney General Malcolm Seawell, head of North Carolina's Department of Justice, to personally defend the decision of Juvenile Court Judge Hampton Price.

The state of North Carolina had gone mad. Or had it? The top law-enforcement official in the state had been personally assigned to make certain that two children remained behind bars. I knew the state had to feel very threatened. A way of life was being challenged, a way of life that said white authorities could do anything they wanted to black people. Perhaps the state felt that keeping Hanover and Fuzzy in jail would teach blacks a lesson. If this were true—and why else would Attorney General Seawell himself be handling the case—then more was at stake than the freedom of two young boys.

Hanover Thompson and Fuzzy Simpson· were the most talked about people in North Carolina. Most white residents of the state agreed they had received what they deserved. Surely, a nice little girl like Sissy Marcus would not have kissed Hanover Thompson unless he had made suggestive remarks. Fuzzy Simpson? After what he had seen (no matter that he could not remember the incident), he would become a dangerous sex pervert. Such was the thinking of many white people in North Carolina in 1959.

The night before the hearing in Wadesboro I visited Harry Golden, editor of a progressive newspaper called the *Carolina Israelite,* and a well-known author in his own right. I had already prepared my legal arguments and lined up witnesses, but I wanted more insight into the thinking of white Southerners. Golden was a short, stout man with black hair, and his favorite word was "amazing." He was more timid than his counterpart, I. F. Stone, but he seemed pleased that Williams and I were willing to challenge the established Southern order. He agreed that the state was using the case to determine just how much it could get away with. Golden's enthusiasm for our cause was tempered only by his fear of violence. He was a thoughtful man, and as we drank coffee in his newspaper office he described the intense racial and sexual feelings of the South: "Southerners are caught in the industrial revolution. It arrived here too late. Southern women have always been on a pedestal and now they want to come out of their little nooks and experience some freedom, the freedom their husbands have always had. They want jobs. They want other freedoms and this frightens the men. Parallel with this, Negroes are showing dissatisfaction with their sharecropper status. They also are looking for jobs. Southern white men, overdosed on fear and guilt, have decided there must be some reason why their women are getting restless at the same time as the Negroes. They have drawn the conclusion that a sexual relationship is involved."

On January 14 I rode to Wadesboro with Robert Williams. We arrived at 9:00 A.M. and the courthouse square was already filled with people. They were packed tight against one another and were spilling into the streets. Williams and I walked through a narrow corridor of space the crowd had cleared. We were flanked on each side by lanky white farmers, and the corridor was so narrow we could not walk side by side. "Keep your head up and look straight ahead," Williams said. I did what he advised but the saliva in my mouth had turned to sawdust.

Many of the farmers had pistols in their overalls. A few had shotguns which they held by the barrel with the butt resting on the ground. Up ahead the farmers were talking with one another, but as we came closer they grew still, motionless, their faces frozen. The corridor was perhaps thirty yards long and extended right to the courthouse door, but it seemed to me that it went on for a thousand miles and ended in eternity. It was good to get inside Judge Johnson's court, even though he had the largest Confederate flag I had yet seen in the South.

"Nothing to it," Williams said.

"Right," I answered, and collapsed on a bench reserved for spectators.

Attorney General Malcolm Seawell was already in the courtroom. He was tall and looked like an aristocrat, which he was. Seawell had pink skin and he wore a white suit. He was just doing what he considered his job, although in reality his job was to seek justice, not to keep innocent children in jail. Nevertheless, Seawell had great pride and he stuck to a set of principles, no matter how misguided they might be. He had some good qualities. I am sure he would not have sat back doing nothing while Kitty Genovese screamed for help. Nor, I am convinced, would he have backed down in front of Robert Williams, as those three in the drugstore did. I believe Seawell had courage and that there was a misdirected nobility about him: he would have been a Southern general in the Civil War.

Hanover Thompson and Fuzzy Simpson were being held in a big wire enclosure on the right front section of the courtroom. They were flanked on each side by two big deputy sheriffs with pearl-handled revolvers. Fuzzy was seven, but he looked no older than four. He was an alert, bright child with mischievous eyes and a flashing smile. Now he simply looked frightened. Hanover, age nine, was not as quick mentally as Fuzzy, but he was more responsible. He had helped his mother to do washing and sweeping and in a small way had tried to be a surrogate father for his younger brothers and sisters. Hanover's face was no older than nine, but behind that wire enclosure he reminded me of an old man who was hunched over.

Ours was the only case on the docket that day. I gave the defense argument first. Normally, I would have been sarcastic and filled with ridicule because the case was an affront to common intelligence, but in this town, in this courtroom, in front of this judge (Clarence Johnson appeared to have a terrible hangover and was in no mood for sarcasm), I decided I had better argue the law. It was plain, I said, that the children had been denied due process, because they had not been allowed to confront their accusers. At the risk of boring the judge, I cited more than twenty legal precedents for my argument, and told the court that if it desired I could bring in thousands more. Then I appealed to Judge Johnson's decency. How could he allow children who were not yet ten years old to be locked in jail, unable even to visit their mothers? I introduced letters that pleaded for the case to be dropped—from writers, actors, politicians, legal scholars, religious leaders, and university professors. When I concluded, Attorney General Seawell yawned.

Seawell stood up and pointed to where Bernice Marcus and her daughter Sissy were sitting. He said that Mrs. Marcus agreed with my argument that the punishment was unfair. Mrs. Marcus, he said, thought the punishment was too *lenient*! I looked back at this thin, nervous, pinch-faced woman, and she was nodding her head in vigorous agreement. She quickly dropped her eyes, however, when our glances met. I wanted to make myself feel sorry for all the Mrs. Marcuses in the world, but I could not.

Later I looked at Sissy. She was a pretty little girl with twinkling eyes. She had told the truth to Judge Hampton Price: it was she who had kissed Hanover. Sissy waved at me and I smiled back. I have often wondered what happened to her. She would be a grown woman now.

After Attorney General Seawell revealed that Mrs. Marcus thought the punishment was too lenient, he argued that the defense was trying to turn the case into a political matter, that we were trying to make the state of North Carolina look silly, and that what was involved was nothing less than the right of local people to enforce local customs.

I stood up and objected. "Your Honor, if the state of North Carolina has been made to look silly, it is because of its own actions. What the defense asks of this court is justice. Let these children go!"

"Sit down," said Judge Johnson.

"Yes," said Attorney General Seawell, "let them go. Let everything else go too. Our way of life. Our way of doing things, a way that has worked right well I might add. Let the outsiders like Lynn come in and tell us how to run our lives. But no!'' Seawell had been shouting. Now his voice was low, comforting, reasonable: "I say we dare not let these two go. Lynn and his ilk don't care about them. What they want is *revolution*. They want to spit in our faces and rip our sacred traditions to shreds.''

Seawell was carried away by his own rhetoric, but he could say what he wanted as far as I was concerned. What worried and frightened me was that the judge was clearly in sympathy. All the time Seawell spoke the judge nodded his head in agreement. I did not know whether it was a matter of conviction with Judge Johnson, or whether he was intimidated by Malcom Seawell. It was not often such a high official came to such a minor court. But there was much more involved than possible awe on the part of the judge. Most people in America do not realize that judges are not really independent. If they are federal judges, they work for the U. S. Justice Department, headed by the U. S. attorney general. If they are state judges, they are employed by the state Justice Department, and in this state the department was headed by Malcolm Seawell. In effect, Judge Johnson was going to rule on a case that his boss, Attorney General Seawell, obviously wanted to win. This is a situation that still exists in American jurisprudence, and it should be changed. Judges should be truly independent. They should not work for the Justice Department.

The arguments droned on and on. Seawell refused to be drawn into any discussion of law, and at times I was forced to follow his lead. I said that I had not "invaded" North Carolina, that I was a United States citizen and North Carolina was part of the United States, and furthermore that I was licensed to practice by the state itself. But that was not the issue, and I asked Judge Johnson to focus on what was—namely, that two young children were in jail. Robert Williams kept clenching and unclenching his fists, and I was afraid he might rush the deputy sheriffs, take the children in his arms, and try to carry them to safety through that crowd of menacing farmers. I went over to him and told him I was as angry as he was, and I asked him, please, "*Please* keep your composure.''

In the forty years I have practiced law I have never had a stronger legal case. Every judicial precedent for the past ninety years held that people accused of a crime had the right to confront their accusers in open court. It was basic. Otherwise we might as well go back to the Star Chamber, with its nameless charges and faceless accusers.

Judge Clarence Johnson did not see due process as the issue. He was outraged that his state had been held up to ridicule in the eyes of the world. He waved in the air the picture Joyce Egginton had taken and asked what the *London Observer* knew about North Carolina. At 3:00 P.M., almost six hours into the hearing, the mothers of Hanover and Fuzzy realized they were not going to win the case and they began to weep. Tiny Mrs. Simpson put her head on her knees and let out a groan that could have come from the throat of almost any black mother who had ever lived in the South. Gloster Current, the tough-minded director of branches for the NAACP, also began to cry. Attorney General Seawell asked for "decorum," and Judge Johnson told Gloster Current and the mothers to "shut up."

Jimmy Booker of the *Amsterdam News* was in the courtroom this day. His subsequent story about what passed for justice in North Carolina was one of the most moving pieces I have ever read. It would not have impressed Attorney General Seawell or Judge Johnson, however. Judge Johnson ruled that the children were guilty and ordered them back to jail. Seawell walked over to the defense table and offered me his hand. "A good try," he said. "You're a good lawyer, Lynn, and I enjoyed it." "I'll see you in hell before I shake your hand," I said.

I flew back to New York City the next day and our propaganda campaign moved into high gear. I had long been aware that, in certain instances, public speaking was at least as essential to criminal justice as was the preparation and trial of cases. I spoke to groups all around the country at forums organized by the NAACP which, after its receipt of Gloster Current's report on the hearing, had suddenly lost its conservative stance on the case. More important than the speeches, students in Rotterdam, Holland, circulated a petition calling for the release of Hanover Thompson and Fuzzy Simpson. After Rotterdam had been leveled by Nazi dive bombers during World War II, a high school had been built with American funds and named in honor of Franklin Delano Roosevelt. The students who were circulating the petition attended that school.

I telephoned Eleanor Roosevelt. I had met her several times in the past, and she had shown an admiration for the civil-rights-oriented practice I conducted. I knew Mrs. Roosevelt as an exceptional, brilliant, totally committed woman, the most truly democratic person I had ever met. She had supported an investigation I had conducted into the murder of Emmett Till, in Laurel, Mississippi. Till, fourteen years old, had allegedly whistled at a white woman. He was beaten, mutilated, castrated, and murdered, and his body had been thrown into a river. The investigation I conducted revealed the names of a number of his killers, but no one was ever tried.

Going to Mrs. Roosevelt was a last resort. She was a busy woman and I respected the many demands on her time. But Hanover Thompson and Fuzzy Simpson, two children, were in jail, and I knew I would never be able to concentrate on another case until theirs was resolved.

Mrs. Roosevelt and I had once spent several hours talking about socialism. She told me she felt it might be the only solution for a world that had such extremes between rich and poor. She said she hoped it was not, but that her mind was open on the subject.

I told Mrs. Roosevelt about the Kissing Case. I was too emotional, and my voice kept cracking when I talked about the two little boys and their frightened mothers. I told her I had pulled a sneaky trick on her; that I had arranged for her to receive—on Lincoln's Birthday—a petition from students at Franklin Delano Roosevelt High School in Rotterdam, which would call for her to intervene in the cases of Hanover Thompson and Fuzzy Simpson.

I was not happy that I had called her. I knew there were militant blacks who would say I was using my white connections to get justice. It was true, but this was a special case.

"Conrad," Mrs. Roosevelt said, "you did the wrong thing."

"I was afraid that I had," I said. I had misunderstood what she meant.

"No," she said. "I don't mean it that way. I mean about Hanover and Fuzzy. You should have told me before. Conrad, when is this country going to be fair?" And then Eleanor Roosevelt began to cry.

On Lincoln's Birthday, 1959, Mrs. Roosevelt received a petition signed by fifteen thousand students in Rotterdam. That same day she called President Dwight Eisenhower. She made him listen while she told him about the Kissing Case. "For God's sake," she concluded, "put a stop to this persecution."

Eisenhower called Governor Luther Hodges. He told Hodges he wanted the children released and their "criminal" records destroyed. It may not have been legal but it was effective. That day Hanover and Fuzzy were reunited with their mothers.

Their happiness that day filled me with great satisfaction, but their story does not have the happy ending I wish I could report. Young as they were, hope came too late in their lives, and they gradually sank back into the morass of poverty and indifference and racial scorn that was then, and is now, the lot of too many black people.

Hanover and Fuzzy grew up troubled and defiant and over the years had a number of brushes with the law, and their young adult lives have brought little happiness to them or to their families. The racists will nod and say they were right all along. While I can dismiss such bigoted and wrong-headed reactions, I am also human enough to wish that those young men whose lives I touched when they were children might have grown up strong and proud, might have passed on to others some of the love and concern they received. But what, after all, did they receive, but simple justice, and even that in the most grudging and backhanded way. Our great "victory" for them was in freeing them from a terrible danger that never should have arisen. Still, we do what we can, and hope it has some meaning and benefit, and then move on.

CHAPTER 13

Williams, the NAACP and the Klan

Robert Williams, president of the Union County, North Carolina, branch of the NAACP, sat in a courtroom in Monroe. It was May 1959, just three months after Eleanor Roosevelt's intervention in the Kissing Case. Williams was in the courtroom to document charges of judicial discrimination against blacks. He intended to present his evidence at that year's NAACP national convention.

Williams was in a bad mood. The night before, he had received a telephone threat against his life, and that, combined with the seemingly negligible pace of progress in Monroe, made him want to do something more physical than sit in court. What he was about to witness was not designed to calm him down.

The first case involved a twenty-year-old black who was an epileptic. He had been involved in an argument with a white woman over the use of a plow. In the course of the dispute he began twitching and touched the woman's wrist. He was charged with attempted rape.

This was pretty common fare in small Southern towns (Monroe was right on the South Carolina border). Because of the controversial cases I handled, and because of the press coverage they generated, I often received calls from Southern blacks who were faced with outrageous charges. My heart always went out to these people, but I just did not have the time to intervene in every instance. I did try to persuade local attorneys to help, and often they would.

The black epileptic did not have a lawyer and he was found guilty by the all-white jury. The judge said that because it was a first offense he was sentencing the epileptic to only five years. Robert Williams shifted his bulk on the spectators' bench and glared at the judge. The judge answered the look with a mild gaze.

A little later in the morning, there was the case of a white man accused of raping a black woman who was eight months pregnant. The same jury that heard the case against the epileptic sat on this case. A white woman testified that she had witnessed the assault, which took place in a cornfield. It seemed the man had not been satisfied with rape. He also beat the pregnant woman with a wrench. This time the jurors did not bother to rise from their seats to deliver the verdict: not guilty. The prosecutor shrugged and the judge looked at Williams with that same mild expression.

The third case that interested Williams involved a white male defendant. He had become annoyed because a black maid had been dusting in front of his door and had awakened him. He rushed out and kicked the maid down a flight of stairs, causing internal injuries so serious that she was hospitalized for six weeks. Again the jury did not even bother to leave its box to deliver the not-guilty verdict.

Robert Williams walked out of the courtroom into a blazing hot North Carolina sun. "I was thinking of revenge," he later told me.

Williams was standing in the bright sun when a stringer from UPI approached him. The stringer had seen what had gone on in court that day. "Williams," he said, "what do you think of what happened inside today?"

"This demonstration," said Robert Williams, "proves that the Negro in the South cannot expect justice in the courts. He must convict his attackers on the spot. He must meet violence with violence and lynching with lynching."

I was at home sick with the flu when I heard the news broadcast. Every thirty minutes radio station WOR repeated the scare line: "Negro leader in the South advocates meeting violence with violence."

Roy Wilkins was gripped with fear. Robert Williams was an official of the NAACP, and Roy Wilkins did not want to hear any talk about violence in his organization. Such talk would scare the liberals, and it was liberal money that made Wilkins' life comfortable. First, Wilkins suspended Robert Williams from the NAACP. *Then*, he called Williams and asked if he had made the statement. "I said it," Wilkins was told. Wilkins told Robert Williams that he was through.

Williams refused to step down, and black people in Monroe rallied to his support. He had defended their homes from attack by young white toughs, he had fought for them in court, he had stood up to the Klan, he had found food when they were hungry. Now they would stick by him.

When Roy Wilkins announced that he was taking the case before the national board, Williams called my office and asked if I would represent him. Of course I would. I knew Williams and admired his work. I knew Roy Wilkins too. I had known him when he was a fighter for justice. I knew him now, in 1959, when what was uppermost in his mind was maintaining his own position.

I received more than a dozen letters from black people in Monroe. The handwriting and grammar were pitiful, but the message, which was always the same, tugged at my heart: please don't let them take Mr. Williams away from us.

In 1959, two-thirds of the national board were white, and three-fourths of these were millionaires. Light years separated these people from Hanover Thompson and Fuzzy Simpson and that black epileptic and, yes, from Robert Williams, for whose murder the Klan had made a standing offer of five thousand dollars.

Williams flew to New York and stayed at my home. Each night after I returned from my office we discussed how we could best present the case to the national board. We knew Roy Wilkins would claim that the advocacy of violence automatically put Williams outside the avowed aims of the NAACP and, therefore, disqualified him from membership. This would be a powerful argument in the minds of the rich people who sat on the national board. They were basically decent whites who were genuinely appalled by conditions in the South, but they were not radicals. Their money gave them a stake in the system. They were reformers, and they could not understand a Robert Williams, who thought that the almost one hundred years that had passed since the Civil War was long enough to wait for equality.

I told Robert Williams he would win his case if he said what the national board wanted to hear—that he had made the statement about violence in the heat of the moment and that he was sorry. I pointed out that the national board would want to avoid a split in its ranks: the younger membership could be counted on to support Williams; older members would tend to side with Roy Wilkins.

I also told Williams he would probably lose if he did not disavow what he had said to that UPI stringer. This is the way I have always handled cases. I explain what defendants face, whichever way they decide to go, and leave the decision to them. I am generally in sympathy with what my clients are trying to accomplish, and therefore I can offer a competent and impassioned defense no matter which tactic they choose. In this case I was pleased that Robert Williams decided not to disavow what he had said. Basically, his statement amounted to the right of black people to self-defense.

Williams and I agreed that both of us should speak in front of the national board. Williams would describe conditions in Monroe, and I would argue the legal issues.

Williams could not have been more impressive. He told the national board what growing up in Monroe had been like. He told them about the Kissing

Case, and pointed out that Roy Wilkins had at first refused to help. He told them about the Klan. He told them about starvation in Monroe, and finally about that day he spent in court that led to his remark. He concluded, "You cannot put yourselves in my shoes. You have no right to try me because you don't know what I've been through."

I argued the legal issue. It was primarily an elementary lesson in constitutional law, explaining in effect that the right of self-defense was fundamental in a free society. These were intelligent people, so I quoted a number of legal precedents; and they were humane people, so I described how no black person had even walked on a sidewalk in Hamlet until November 1958. I said Robert Williams was a brave man who faced death every day because he worked for principles the national board advocated.

Daisy Bates, a heroic black woman who had fought for equality of education in Little Rock, supported Williams: "If they expel him, I don't see how I can stay in the NAACP."

The national board shied away from expelling Robert Williams. Instead it suspended him for six months. The board was wrong if it expected us to stand still for this compromise. We appealed to the national convention, which in 1959 was meeting in New York City.

The old guard was already having problems with the younger members. The NAACP policy of relying exclusively on legislation and the courts was clearly bankrupt as far as achieving full citizenship for blacks was concerned. But the entrenched leadership carried the overwhelming economic power and the NAACP's charter made basic change virtually impossible. The controversy over Robert Williams afforded a dramatic test of the power of the two factions. The debate took place on the convention floor. Before the debate, however, came the keynote speech.

The keynote speaker was Daisy Bates, and she broke our hearts: without turning a hair, she denounced Robert Williams. We had received no warning that she had deserted our side. We found out later that she had been given a job in the national office. It seemed a tragic compromise of principle for so slight a reward.

The old guard carried the day. The national convention voted to uphold the suspension of Robert Williams. I knew the decision would mainly hurt the black people of Monroe. They would be without the prestige and the funds of the NAACP. It would not make much difference to Robert Williams. He would continue doing what he could, as he had before.

Meanwhile, I had been gathering data about conditions in Monroe. Not only was justice there a cruel farce, but people were starving. It seemed to me that neither CORE nor the NAACP was willing to do the hard work necessary to bring genuine relief to Monroe. Their approach was legalistic—go slow, don't rock the boat. In this crisis a few of us, including Robert Williams, Professor Lonnie Cross from Atlanta University, the writer Julian Mayfield, historian John Hendrik Clark, and myself, formed the Coordinating Committee for Southern Relief.

We used our own money and contacted sympathetic friends for additional funds, and we sent relief caravans of food and clothing to the besieged areas in and around Monroe. This angered the authorities and they extracted a terrible vengeance. One of our chief supporters was Dr. Albert Perry, who was indefatigable in giving his services to what was one of the most impoverished communities in America. Dr. Perry was arrested and tried on a charge of committing an illegal abortion on a white woman. It was a blatant frame-up, but he was sentenced to a long prison term.

There was other harassment. The automobile insurance on Robert Willliams's car was canceled, and in North Carolina that meant he could not drive. I contacted Donald Shaffer, an insurance agent in Brooklyn, and he secured the necessary coverage. At about the same time, there were increasing threats against Williams's life. Local citizens were angry when he was reelected president of the Union County NAACP, despite his suspension.

That was the way matters stood when 1960 began. Early in February, in Greensboro, North Carolina, a group of black students sat in a lunchroom off campus and asked for service. Management refused, but the group decided to stay. They were savagely beaten by police and taken to jail. The climactic battle of the 1960s for civil rights had been joined.

A great deal of my time was spent organizing the food and clothing caravans, and not for the first time my law practice was disrupted. I had to tell prospective clients that I could not give their cases my full attention.

In March 1960, Robert Williams went to a drug store in Monroe and asked for a soda. He knew what he was going to get. Police clubbed him unconscious and carried him to jail. He was convicted of trespass and disorderly conduct.

That same month, Robert Williams and I were asked to speak at Yale. The crisis in Monroe made his appearance impossible, but I accepted the offer. It was the day after the Reverend William Sloane Coffin, Yale's popular chaplain, had been arrested in Anniston, Alabama, during the burning of a Freedom Bus by an angry white mob. The setting at Yale was perfect. It was only necessary for me to ride the wave of the students' emotion. It was probably the best speech I have ever given, and I don't remember a line of it.

Robert Williams, faced with an intransigent white power structure in Monroe, was becoming more militant. I had seen it happen before and it would happen many times again. Legitimate demands would be brushed aside, and then the demands would become more radical. Williams visited Cuba and came away from the experience believing that armed struggle was the answer to the problems of black people. Other black militants supported his position, which frightened not only the racist elements of Union County but liberal whites.

The racists lent fuel to Robert Williams's belief that change could not take place peacefully. The beatings, jail sentences, and murders meted out to Freedom Riders strengthened his convictions. I felt it would not be long before I would again be called upon to represent him. I was right, but no one could have anticipated the bizarre events that would lead up to that day.

On June 14, 1961, a number of us met with Robert Williams in New York City to discuss the growing armed violence against blacks in Union County. Black people had been wounded and killed by cowardly nightriders who fired into their homes from speeding cars.

The actor Ossie Davis was at the meeting. Ossie is a close friend of mine and has given a lot of money to progressive causes. Mae Mallory was at the meeting. She is a very physical woman, a block of granite. Once we were together on a demonstration at the United Nations when the police waded in swinging clubs. She took two policemen and cracked their heads together and knocked them unconscious. I represented her against the assault charge and we won. The police were too embarrassed to admit what a woman had done to them, and their case fell apart. Also at this meeting in New York City were Julian Mayfield, Ora Mobley, and Cal Hicks. I kept the minutes of the meeting:

> Julian Mayfield acted as chairman and submitted the agenda:
> 1. Integration or Separation.
> 2. Methods of protest coordination.
> 3. Economic aspects of struggle.
> 4. Propaganda and legal problems.
> Robert F. Williams presented the situation in the South. Afro-Americans are beginning to believe that the whites will never consent to integration. The tactic of nonviolence in sit-ins, freedom rides, etc., has proved useful but has to be backed up with forceful self-defense as in Charlotte, Jacksonville, Montgomery. . . . Martin L. King trying to derail revolutionary upsurge.

Ora Mobley urged that we not forget the international context. In forging their struggle, Afro-Americans must separate themselves from whites. Employment critical focus of fight.

Ossie Davis threw out the analysis that the economic dilemma was the heart of the American crisis.

Mae Mallory supports the view that we must hold ourselves separate for struggle. Muslims and black nationalists seek basic stake in economy. The role of unions.

Should have follow-up national conference. Cal Hicks proposes political party. Others say it should at first be limited to Afro-Americans.

During the summer of 1961 I made another visit to Monroe to check on the impact of our relief caravans. The town was divided into two armed camps.

Robert Williams took me to a revival meeting that was being held in a tent some five miles out of town. What struck me was the emotional power the black people expressed as they sang their spirituals. The imitations I had heard in the North paled in comparison. Previously I had dismissed the spirituals as a rationalization for the acceptance of oppression, but the experience Robert Williams allowed me to share changed my mind. The thrilling force and harmony I witnessed in that tent convinced me that religion and civil rights were blended together in the minds of black people into the same struggle for equality.

I stayed in Monroe for three weeks but had to leave in the middle of August. I wished I could have stayed a few weeks longer. Martin Luther King, Jr., had begun negotiations with Robert Williams over the possibility of using nonviolence to ease the tension in Monroe. Williams did not think it would work, but he agreed to give it a try.

On August 27, 1961, an interracial and sexually mixed group of twenty-five people arrived in Monroe. They announced that they would picket peacefully on the square block surrounding the Monroe courthouse. The night before this was to occur, segregationists ripped up the sidewalk with jackhammers, thus compelling the pickets to march in the street.

Martin Luther King's people did picket, but unforeeey the day they chose was one when most black residents were attending a revival meeting outside the town. Even more unfortunate was the fact that Robert Williams had promised to keep himself and his supporters away from Dr. King's pickets, in the hope that this would mollify the Klan enough to keep them from attacking.

The Klan made no similar promise to stay away. That morning, Klansmen visited white churches and suggested that now, when most blacks were out of town at a revival meeting, would be a good time to teach the "outsiders" a lesson.

At 2:00 P.M. a young black boy named Rorie Saunders came running down Boyte Street to report that the Klan was shooting at the pickets. Robert Williams asked that people be as calm as they could until the report was confirmed. Williams had sense—he was like a military commander—and he did not want to lead his people into a massacre. But the more militant blacks among them grabbed rifles and piled into cars and headed for the courthouse. When they arrived they found a mob of whites—from South Carolina according to their license plates—terrifying Dr. King's pickets by firing over their heads.

The black militants ushered a number of people to safety, including James Forman, who was Dr. King's personal emissary. His scalp had been split open by a policeman's billy. The police had stood around while the Klan was shooting, but when the carloads of blacks arrived they sprang into action.

The armed blacks guided their charges back to Boyte Street, where excited discussion took place. Some of the blacks wanted to shoot it out with the Klan and the police. They were willing to give their lives. Robert Williams wanted to survive and said that if they were going to fight they should wait for a day when the odds were more favorable.

Several hours later a car proceeded slowly down Boyte Street. The occupants were white. Robert Williams recognized them as the Steagall family, head of the Monroe chapter of the Ku Klux Klan. Other blacks recognized them too. The car was immediately encircled by a menacing crowd of black people. There were cries of "Kill them!" and "Shoot them!"

Robert Williams shouldered his way through the crowd. A number of blacks were not listening to him any more, but the majority still were. Williams invited the Steagalls into his home and said he would protect them, which he did. He had no admiration for these Klan members, but he did not want to encourage retaliation by letting them be killed. Blacks threatened to break in and get the Steagalls. Williams stood firm.

State police threw a cordon around the black community. They claimed Williams had kidnapped the Steagalls. The Steagalls had already been released but were unavailable for comment to the press. The state police said that unless Williams surrendered, they would come in shooting. A number of blacks did not want their leader to surrender. They said they would stay with him, that they would fight to the death. Obviously, they felt strongly about the issue, but they also knew that an entire nation would learn about their sacrifice. In addition, they did not believe Robert Williams stood a chance in North Carolina of fighting a kidnap charge.

About 10:00 P.M. Robert Williams called me at my home. My advice was that he surrender, with a group of black ministers and educators as witnesses that he had done so peacefully. He said he thought even that precaution would not guarantee his safety. I asked him to stall for as much time as possible, and he said he would.

I called the attorney general's office in Washington and was told they "would look into it." I called the White House and asked to speak to President Kennedy. I was given an aide who also promised to look into it. I began calling foreign embassies. I knew a small-scale civil war might break out at any moment in Monroe.

The next morning the state police invaded Monroe's black community. They encountered no resistance. They also did not find Robert Williams. The blacks closest to him had taken a vote the previous night: whether to fight it out, or whether to get Williams out of Monroe. The moderates carried the day. Robert Williams, with the help of his friends, slipped out of the black community and out of the lynch-mob atmosphere in Monroe.

That same morning, in a glimmer of honesty, Mrs. Steagall, chairwoman of the Women's Auxiliary of the Monroe Ku Klux Klan, admitted to a reporter that Robert Williams had saved her family's life. Later she changed her story.

That afternoon the FBI called to warn me that Robert Williams could not escape. The agent said he had a tip that Robert Williams was headed south, and he told me that the FBI had posted "four hundred agents on the Mexican border." He said if I knew where Williams was, I should tell him. I told him he should investigate civil-rights violations in North Carolina. Then I hung up.

Robert Williams escaped into Canada. He later went to Cuba and to China. He returned to Detroit in 1969 and there fought a long battle against extradition to North Carolina. In January 1976, Harold Steagall, head of the Monroe Klan, died. He had been a Baptist minister, and both he and his wife were very religious people. Mrs. Steagall said she interpreted her husband's death as a sign that God did not want her to testify against Robert Williams. Without Mrs. Steagall's testimony there was no case, and the prosecution dropped the charges.

In February 1976, Robert Williams returned to Monroe.

CHAPTER 14

A Visit to Cuba

While in Puerto Rico in 1960 on behalf of Albizu Campos, I decided to take my wife, Yolanda, and our three children, Suzanne, Alexander, and Gabrielle, to Cuba. Relations had not yet been broken with Fidel's government, but considerable harassment attended the way of anyone trying to visit the new country. It was not until I had called officials who knew me in Puerto Rico that we were permitted to board a plane via Haiti to Cuba.

The stopover in Haiti was dreadfully depressing. It was the only place I ever visited where little beggar children sought alms in three languages: French, Spanish, and English. It was not understandable to me how Americans could take pleasure jaunts to Haiti. No more damning indictment of American "protection" can be found anywhere in the world.

At last we stepped off the plane in Havana! Visitors were greeted by an orchestra playing Latin tunes and everyone seemed to be celebrating. It was the euphoria of the revolution.

We stayed in a house in the Miramar section of Havana, and on the second day we went for a trolley ride. I looked for a fare collector after the five of us were on the bus, but there was none. We took our seats in confusion. At length a young man tapped me on the shoulder and said in English, "If you want to contribute anything, there's a man in the corner." I thanked him, walked over to the host, and gave him some money.

About a week later our two younger children returned from Varadero Beach looking upset. It seemed that Cuban children had formed a ring around them on the beach and chanted, "Yanqui go home! Yanqui go home!" It was our first experience with an alien nationalism. Many times after that we found the children playing "bad Americans" in a mock war against the good Cubans.

It was apparent that ordinary people in Cuba enjoyed unaccustomed comforts and an amplified diet, thanks to the confiscation of foreign-owned holdings. We asked ourselves only one question when we left: how long can it last?

Back in the United States the tempo of change had accelerated. The government was clashing with people at home and abroad. The Congo had achieved its independence, and economic war would soon be declared on Cuba.

Ben Davis asked if I would represent the Communist party in an application for the release of Henry Winston, chairman of their national commission, before the parole board in Washington. I agreed.

As I got out of a taxi in the capital and placed my briefcase on the ground, preparatory to fishing for a tip, the case was snatched away and I never even obtained a glimpse of the thief. I was sure, however, that he was in the employ of the FBI.

All the records of Winston's case had been in that briefcase, so my efforts before the parole board were seriously impaired. Also, Winston was going blind and was on the verge of complete paralysis. He was one of the last Smith Act defendants still in prison, and his application for parole was cruelly rejected.

Not long after this, Fidel Castro decided to visit the United Nations, which soon permitted me to perform an act of which I have always been proud. Fidel and his entourage put up briefly in the Shellburne Hotel, where a hostile news media accused him of plucking live chickens. Needless to relate, his stay at the Shellburne was highly unpleasant for him.

Two days before Castro arrived in the city, Bob Tabor of the Fair Play for Cuba Committee telephoned me and said he was anticipating difficulties at the downtown hotel. We were casting about for another place when my next-door neighbor, Jim Dickerson, had the happy inspiration to suggest that I call the Hotel Theresa in Harlem to ask about accommodations for the Cuban delegation. Love Woods, the manager of the Theresa, was hesitant. He demanded nine hundred dollars in cash in advance. It was a Saturday night.

It came to me that gamblers would have that kind of money on a weekend. We contracted a sympathetic gambler, the money was paid, and the Cuban delegation moved from the downtown hotel to Harlem.

The black community's celebration was immense and spontaneous, and Castro had scored a master stroke. Leaders of Third World and socialist nations called at the hotel to pay homage to him as the symbol of world revolt. Gamal Abdul Nasser, keenly aware of the rise of the Black Muslims, was the first to visit and be photographed. Nikita Khrushchev came to Harlem to visit Fidel. American officials could not help but realize they had suffered a big propaganda defeat. What U.S. leader would visit a foreign nation and live among its poorest citizens? The lesson was not lost on other peoples.

I met Fidel at a reception at the Theresa, and also Juan Almeida, the black chief of staff of the Cuban armed forces. Harlem took pride in the tandem of black officials who labored in Cuba's revolutionary movement.

Crowds of black people stood outside the Theresa night and day, and when members of the delegation walked the streets of the ghetto they were followed by admiring throngs. Blacks on the street absorbed more political education on these occasions than they had from any lesson since the Great Depression.

White liberals responded with great bitterness, villifying the Cubans with every snide remark imaginable, and black lickspittles echoed them slavishly. Writing in the Amsterdam News, October 1, 1960, James Booker noted: "The Baptist Ministers' Conference of Greater New York and Vicinity representing five hundred clergymen and over 100,000 Baptists, the largest in Harlem, deplores and condemns any attempts by Fideral Castro to make the Harlem community a battleground for his doctrine of hate and greed, and importing anti–U.S. agitators who have by their riotous actions brought discredit upon our community."

Louis Goldberg, a WPA comrade of mine who had since become an official in the New York State Labor Department, was typical of the liberal who reacted most antagonistically to any hint that there was an identity of interests between oppressed black Americans and Cuban revolutionaries. When we returned from Cuba he invited me and Yolanda to dinner at his fashionable home in Jamaica Estates, Queens and he politely trotted out every canard then current about the evils of the "Castro dictatorship."

Meanwhile, John F. Kennedy was elected president with the promise of a progressive term, but I wanted to see his maneuvers toward Cuba. I busied myself with political cases and representing poorer citizens, taking only enough civil cases to maintain myself and my family in a degree of comfort. Yolanda was always supportive, as were the children when they grew older, and in that I was a truly fortunate individual.

I was not popular in Rockland County where we were living, but neither were people really unfriendly. The case that caused the most community division revolved around our backyard neighbor, Ruth Best, a pacifist and a Quaker. To protest against war preparations, Ruth refused to obey a civil air-defense drill and sat down in the middle of a street instead. This was pretty tame stuff, but the good citizens of Haverstraw, where the incident occurred, were so irate that a mob gathered outside the courthouse on the day her trial was to begin. The mob became so menacing that the judge had to adjourn the trial for a week. The Haverstraw Presbyterian minister led the community's clergy in pleading for calm. The next week the courtroom was crowded but orderly. Ruth gave a moving statement detailing the pacifist position, then pleaded guilty and and paid a twenty-five dollar fine.

My opponents in Rockland County had their opportunity early in 1961. The senior class at Suffern High School asked me to address them on the civil-rights struggle. The invitation was tendered by the school athletic director.

On the night of the program the athletic director introduced me to a man named Romerstein, and asked whether I would mind if Romerstein followed my talk with a few remarks of his own. I readily agreed, although I was a little puzzled. My talk was well received, and then Romerstein stood up.

"I'm going to tell you," he said, "just how the red rat you have just heard crawled out of the woodwork."

Romerstein dramatically removed some notes he had been carrying in his pocket and began talking about my first induction into the Young Communist League and my first arrests, and he made hair-raising innuendos about my representing various Communists and about the purpose of our trip to Cuba. Romerstein was so loud and so fanatic that some of the students began to laugh. Then he singled out the Jewish students among them: he said they should be ashamed to be listening to a Communist, and that as a Jew he personally wanted to atone for the dreadful tendency of his people to lean toward the Reds.

In any case, Romerstein was so belligerent and so insulting that the best tactic I could use was to let him go on.

The United States invaded Cuba at the Bay of Pigs in April 1961, and a number of black militants were open in their praise of Castro's victory. For more than a year I had been engaging first James Farmer, then Bayard Rustin, in debates before liberal groups on the necessity of armed struggle as opposed to Martin Luther King's program of nonviolence. The savage beatings, murders, and court sentences being meted out to the Freedom Riders did not make their task any easier.

Following the Bay of Pigs, many black militants throughout the country became alarmed over the possibility that Kennedy might launch an all-out offensive against Cuba to wipe out the revolution. We hastily issued a manifesto warning the government that any attempt to overthrow the Cuban regime by force of arms would mean that we would launch an armed struggle in the United States to aid our Cuban brothers and sisters. About thirty of us signed the manifesto, including Julian Mayfield, John H. Clarke, William Worthy, James Boggs, Mae Mallory, Ossie Davis, Ora Mobley, Calvin Hicks, and myself.

The manifesto began: "Because we have known oppression, because we have suffered more than other Americans, because we are still fighting for our own liberation from tyranny, we Afro-Americans have the right and duty to raise our voices in protest against the forces of oppression that now seek to crush a free people linked to us by bonds of blood and a common heritage."

The liberals responded by calling us black fascists and reverse racists. Of course, the liberals did not use such language to describe the savage Southern murderers who were decimating the Freedom Riders.

The Socialists were no better than the liberals, but they were consistent. They had long argued, that blacks had no special problems, that when the liberation of workers took place, Afro-Americans would also be free. The thousands of lynchings of black people since the Civil War, the endemic discrimination against them in unions and by employers, the everyday events in Alabama and Mississippi and all over the South, these and much more revealed the inanity of the Socialist position and the position of the liberals as well.

In any case, calling us fascists and racists when we were merely defending ourselves against those who truly deserved the names was not much different from the position of Governor Patterson of Alabama when he said the Freedom Riders were being beaten because they were "provocative."

Still I did not sever all ties to the liberals. In the spring of 1961 I helped sponsor a reception at the One Fifth Avenue Hotel in New York City for Mrs. Gabrielle of New Orleans. She had courageously escorted her children through threatening, vicious crowds of whites in order achieve integration of a school in her home town, and as a consequence she was physically attacked and her husband lost his job.

The respectable site of the affair proved irresistible to the liberals. Pan Stone came from Cedar Crest; the Holliday sisters came in from Great Neck; Lorraine Hansberry's white husband showed up; Miriam Eversley and other members of the Negro Establishment put in appearances; and the Clark Foremans and the Mayfields represented the left.

I presented an award to Mrs. Gabrielle on behalf of the Long Island

Committee for Brotherhood, and award I had been given the previous year.

In December 1961, I reluctantly accepted membership on the Executive Committee of the National Council of the Emergency Civil Liberties Committee. I hesitated because of the hectic nature of my schedule. As I mentioned, I had to process enough civil cases to support my family, yet the cases I was really interested in paid only nominal fees at best and were financial burdens. In 1955 I moved my office from Harlem to 141 Broadway, near Wall Street, so I could save some time by being near the courts.

Early in 1962 a North Carolina judge granted an order authorizing me to take interrogatories from Robert Williams in Cuba to be used in defense of other militants still awaiting trial for kidnapping. All diplomatic relations had been broken with Cuba and it was necessary for me to use my contacts in the Socialist Workers party to secure a visa through the Cuban consul in Toronto. I had no difficulty acquiring a passport after exhibiting the order from the North Carolina judge.

The quickest way to Cuba at the time was by way of Miami. I took Eastern Airlines to Florida, and en route I struck up a conversation with an Eastern vice-president. When he discovered where I was going, he asked about other cases I was handling. This led to a discussion of the entire civil-rights scene, and then the vice-president pulled a real surprise.

"Why not desegregate the International Hotel before you go to Cuba?" he asked.

Why not? I thought. The International Hotel was located on airport property, and I thought I might as well spend the night there was anywhere else.

When the plane landed, the vice-president hurried on ahead. I picked up my baggage and went to the International Hotel. There was a long line of people waiting to secure rooms and I joined them. When I reached the cashier, I asked for a single room as casually as I could. He hesitated, looked at me, hesitated again, then, making up his mind, shoved the register in front of me. He charged eighteen dollars, which seemed high, but in a sense it was worth much more.

The Cuban bellhop who took my bags to the elevator was unhappy. He was a refugee and had quickly acquired one custom to accelerate his Americanization: a hatred of niggers.

A few more eyebrows were raised when I sat in the hotel dining room that night. The vice-president I had met on the plane strolled over.

"The hotel is desegregated," I said.

He smiled and then laughed, a good, hearty laugh.

The next morning at eight there was pounding on my door. There were two of them and they were from the FBI.

"Mr. Lynn?"

"Yes."

"We have instructions to search your briefcase. Of course, we will not do this without your consent."

"Why do you want to search my briefcase?"

"To be frank, we've already searched your other luggage. We did it last night in the baggage room. We could not look at your briefcase because you were carrying it."

I was not overly surprised by this information. I invited the gentlemen in and handed them the briefcase. The only item that interested them was a small phonograph record.

"Are you taking this record to anyone in Cuba, Mr. Lynn?"

"Yes. To Robert Williams. A friend of his in Canada asked me to deliver it."

"Do you mind if we play the record?"

"The record is not mine."

"Do you know what it's about?"

"No, I don't."

"Do you object to us playing it?"

"Yes, I do. It is not my property and you have taken it out of the briefcase of a lawyer on the way to interview his client. You are affecting the confidential relation of a lawyer with his client, and that client's constitutional rights are involved."

"Does Williams know you are bringing this record?"

"No, he does not."

"Well, Mr. Lynn," one of them said in that tone of voice that indicates the nice-guy part of the interview is over, "you are going to have to make up your mind. You are not going to board any flight for Cuba until we have heard this record."

I had to think quickly. I realized that Williams's friend in Toronto was discreet and would not endanger me or Williams by sending a secret or seditious message.

"Go ahead," I said. "Play the record."

They went to a music shop in the airport and cleared out everyone, including the proprietor. Because the record had been in my possession, I was allowed to stay.

They placed the record on a phonograph and a mournful sort of blues song filled the air. The words were those of a slave lamenting and then resolving to be free. The back of the neck of the agent nearer to me began to redden, and I wanted to laugh. He stopped the record before it finished and returned it to me.

I arrived in Havana on February 1, 1962, and the orchestra, enthusiastic as ever, was still there to greet people. While customs was processing me somewhat laboriously, Robert Williams arrived. After that, things speeded up and we were soon on our way to the Hotel Riviera.

Fortunately, I had arrived in time for the Second Declaration of Havana, which was to be Castro's answer to the plan Kennedy announced at Punta del Este: a program of massive economic aid to the South and Central American regimes he approved of, to forestall the growth of communism in the hemisphere. Neither Kennedy nor any of his advisers had the insight into Latin America that men like Waldo Frank possessed, and I knew the projected investments could have only short-term influence.

I sat up late that night with Robert Williams and his wife Mabel discussing our mutual friends in Monroe. Mabel was already active in the women's trade-union federation in Cuba and had become proficient in Spanish.

Earlier in the evening we had gone swimming in the hotel's magnificent pool. The Cubans wore scanty bathing suits: obviously, the puritan phase of the revolution had not yet set in, but I had no doubt that it would, since all revolutions seemed to pass through parallel phases.

The next morning there was a massive demonstration. A number of cars were lined up in front of the hotel, and Robert Williams and Mabel were seated in the first one. I was in the third from the front. The cortege followed Williams's car, which was driven slowly through the narrow streets of Old Havana. On each side of the streets were dense throngs, and as Williams's car came into view the cry would go up, "Robert Williams! Robert Williams!" in staccato accents.

The reception dumbfounded me. I was thoroughly unprepared for it. Black people stood on corners wiping tears from their eyes. North Carolina wanted Williams in jail, but in Cuba he seemed to be the most popular person next to Castro.

More than a million people filled the square that day. Williams began to introduce me to other guests on the podium and I soon realized that this was perhaps the largest gathering of revolutionary leaders in history. Certainly I could not recall reading about any similar gathering after the Russian and French revolutions.

I saw Pedrito, son of Pedro Albizu Campos, and he introduced me to Juliao, the diminutive Brazilian militant of whom we expected great things. I was introduced to Salvador Allende, the left-wing Socialist who had been a candidate for president of Chile. They had come, from all over Latin America, united in the belief that their countries should be independent.

Fidel began his intransigent answer to John Kennedy, and it lasted three hours. A master of the Marxist dialectic, Castro threw the whole travail of the Latin America revolution into stark relief. Kennedy dispensed dollars and military might; Castro called on the spirit and will of the people to fight on until liberation of the hemisphere had been achieved. The North American press described the speech as a harangue. Those who heard it called it thrilling.

Later in the week I was able to talk with members of delegations from all the noncapitalist countries. The Chinese always ate alone. I never saw them fraternizing, even with the Cubans. It was only with citizens of small countries that I found ready rapport.

I secured a duly authorized Cuban notary and took the interrogatories of Robert and Mabel Williams. I could stay only one week, so I did not make extensive tours of the countryside. I did visit some small, impressive housing cooperatives and a few state farms that were being cultivated with machinery.

I was most impressed with the élan evident in the bearing of the young black women who were attending school for the first time. In the afternoons I watched them as they marched out of the schools with tools slung over their shoulders. The buoyancy of their songs was unmistakable.

Another impressive development was the great advance in elementary education. Some of the schools used audio-visual techniques that foreshadowed later innovations in the United States. Quite obviously the revolution was placing its faith in the young. The American economic boycott had forced the government to depend solely on Russia for critical economic items, and there were elated crowds whenever a Russian tanker pulled into Havana harbor.

A problem arose about my return to the mainland. Just a little more than a week before, William Worthy made his return trip by hopping a plane to Miami. Federal officials seized him at the airport, contending that his passport had not been validated for travel to Cuba, and he was turned over to the Miami police who promptly jailed him. We were worried for his life since it was by no means uncommon for a black prisoner in a Southern jail to be beaten to death. Fortunately, William Worthy had too many influential friends for this tactic to be feasible, and he remained alive for the legal proceedings which finally freed him.

Cuban officials strongly advised against my returning by way of Miami, so I boarded a plane for Gander, Newfoundland. On my way through customs my passport was seized by a Canadian police official.

"I have instructions," he said, "not to permit you to continue back to the United States."

This was an amazing statement. I asked if I had violated Canadian law, and he hemmed and hawed. It seemed that the State Department in Washington had passed these instructions along, and Canadian officials were obeying them as if they were employees of the U.S. government.

I telephoned Yolanda and asked that she contact Leonard Boudin, general counsel for the Emergency Civil Liberties Committee. Boudin called the Passport Office and threatened legal action, and forty-eight hours later I was on a Canadian Airlines plane bound for New York via Montreal. There was another hassle in Montreal while customs officials, whose U.S. citizenship I shared, debated over my passport. It had been validated for Cuba, so there was no legitimate reason for their hesitation. I was not enlightened on this point until a year later when I received a subpoena from the Committee on Un-American Activities of the U.S. House of Representatives.

CHAPTER 15

Confrontation with HUAC

Soon after returning from Cuba I leased a suite at 401 Broadway and formed a limited partnership with George Spitz. He was much younger than I and had a remarkably retentive memory for obscure legal data, which he combined with excellent analytical skills. He concentrated on negligence cases, but occasionally he collaborated with me on a civil-liberties or serious criminal case.

Our secretary was married to Fred Hampton, one of Adam Clayton Powell's accountants. When Powell was indicted and stood trial for income-tax evasion, Fred Hampton was one of his loyal followers who took the rap for him. I never heard that Mrs. Hampton received any aid from the Harlem congressman as a result of her husband's jail sentence sacrifice.

I gave numerous speeches to black groups. In one that was particularly well received, in Detroit, I told about my impressions of Cuba:

> I saw Robert Williams. He is the guest of the Cuban government, and I want to tell you why that is. The story is never told to the people, but you would know why if you were ever privileged to be in the Senate and hear Senator Eastland of Mississippi or Senator Strom Thurmond of South Carolina or Senator Smathers from Florida making a speech on Cuba. It never gets into the papers, but it is in the Congressional Record. These men say in their speeches that "we have to knock out the government of Castro, because the niggers have too much power." The chief of staff, says Senator Thurmond, is a nigger. And Senator Thurmond is right. I found that out. His name is Juan Almeida. As the *New York Times* says, the real power in the Foreign Office of Cuba is Carlos Olivares. He is a black man. I found that to be true too.
>
> When I went out to the countryside, I found all these black people. Cuba was one of the islands where there was very little intermixture of the races. So in the countryside you find all these people of straight African descent. They are about one-third of the population and they

have been the submerged part. When you talk to the American tourists and the gangsters who used to go to Havana in the winter, they never tell you anything about these black people. They never really saw them. But when Castro's revolutionary army fought for power, the first thing it did was afford liberty to the black peasant. These black peasants formed the core of Castro's army. Now these black women in the countryside, who never knew how to read and write and could never do anything but the most menial tasks, go to school in the country. I saw them going to school, with their banners on their shoulders, singing, marching in ranks. I also saw those black militiawomen. I am not going to apologize for them. They were carrying Czech submachine guns that fire seven hundred bullets a minute. I want to tell you that no one is going to overturn their government. This is the government which freed them.

I went into the city of Havana and into its beautiful suburbs, Vedado and Miramar. Havana is probably the most beautiful city in the Western world. In these suburbs are the mansions where the wealthy, the American sugar millionaries and gangsters, used to live. Now Castro's government has taken these women and brought them into Havana to teach them about modern hygiene and modern plumbing. They put fifteen or twenty of these women in one of these mansions with a house mother and they learn to read and write. They learn to be free!

In the early fall of 1962 our firm added a new partner and became Lynn, Spitz and Condon. Gene Ann Condon had been an attorney in the corporation counsel's office for the city of New York, but she was drawn to the type of work I was doing. She was a very able trial lawyer and highly intelligent.

Our work attracted a number of student civil-rights activists, in and out of law school, who came and performed voluntary work for varying periods in the summer. One of these was a Columbia Law School graduate named Don Gellers. For a considerable period, beginning in 1961, he handled the various legal efforts to free Albizu Campos from prison, and he also made a number of trips with me to Puerto Rico in pursuit of that objective. Later, this dedicated lawyer went to Passamaquoddy, Maine, and took up the cause of the American Indians.

My chief regret was my lack of contact with black college students. The NAACP, often in no hurry to fight racism, was very efficient in spreading the work that I was a communist and that it was enough of a handicap to be black.

In 1962 my attention was drawn more and more to the activity of American "advisers" in Vietnam and Laos. The victory of the Vietnamese against the French in 1954 had heartened all the anticolonialists, and now it seemed that the Americans were going to take over where the French left off.

It was not possible for me to concentrate on Vietnam or anything else, however, because on April 19, 1963, I was handed a "Greeting" from Chairman Francis E. Walter of the Commitee on Un-American Activities of the U.S. House of Representatives. This was 1963, but the right-wingers had still not stopped trying to harass people.

The subpoena was unexpected but not surprising. The radicalization of the civil-rights movement was becoming a major concern to the government. John Kennedy was still hesitating over whether to include blacks in his "New Frontier," and the survival of the Cuban revolutionary regime was making a profound impression upon the militants of the black vanguard. Broadcasts by Robert Williams over Radio Free Dixie in Havana, in which he called for armed revolt by the black masses, were having an unsettling effect on the Establishment. I was the most vocal spokesman for this point of view, and efforts by private citizens, mostly black, to have me disbarred were increased and received enthusiastic encouragement from prominent members of the bar.

Confronted with a witch hunt, I wrote to Whitney North Seymour, Jr., chairman of the Civil Liberties Committee of the New York County Lawyers Association. The association was the largest organization of judges and lawyers in the world, and I had been a dues-paying member for many years. The primary obligation of the association was to protect its members, but Seymour would not even answer my letter. Phone calls evoked no response. It became clear to me that the committee was interested only in defending the civil liberties of those it considered safe, and that radicals would have to sink or swim on their own.

A call to the ACLU evoked a different response. Melvin Wulf, the general counsel, told me he was assigning David Shapiro of Washington, D.C., to defend me. This was heartening news. I had known Shapiro for years. He was a friend of my partner, George Spitz, and had acquired a reputation as a top antitrust lawyer. In our first conference, Shapiro dissipated any doubts I had about his expertise in civil liberties. He said he was assigning his staff to make a meticulous study of each member of the House Committee on Un-American Activities. He was pleased when I said I would not invoke the Fifth Amendment, that I had nothing to hide. He agreed that we should take the offensive.

As an attorney, I frequently had clients who employed the Fifth Amendment. Often it served to protect innocent third parties. The Supreme Court, however, in the *Dennis* case, had ruled that the Communist party was an arm of a hostile foreign power and that this justified suspending constitutional guarantees. More than any other factor, this ruling created the Silent Generation of the fifties. Perceptive minds who might have spoken out against the direction of American imperialism were reduced to the study of minutia and the advocacy of trivia, and former trade-union theoreticians scurried to the safety of university teaching positions.

I felt that the House committee, in trying to suppress dissent, had made a mistake in ordering me to appear. I was certainly not going to make the mistake others had made. Many people had been destroyed morally and economically by being compelled to take the Fifth Amendment. The committee, with the willing cooperation of the press, implied that these people had something to hide, when really they were refusing to "rat" on friends. My friends were not members of the Communist party, and I intended to confront my inquisitors, not bow and scrape in front of them.

My friends were not idle. Gwen Mallett, chairman of the Independent Negro Committee to End Racism and Ban the Bomb, sent a detailed letter of protest to HUAC. Kathleeen Aberle and Truman Nelson also sent letters. The Emergency Civil Liberties Committee issued a protest. The New York Council to Abolish HUAC assembled an impressive list of public figures who issued a joint statement condemning the inquisition.

For the same hearing, HUAC also called my friend Leo Huberman, editor with Paul Sweezy of the Monthly Review; J. P. Murray, New York University professor; Jesus Colon, columnist for the Daily Worker; and Freddie Jerome, son of the Communist party theoretician, V. J. Jerome. Freddie Jerome was far to the left of his father.

Elizabeth Geismar, youngest daughter of my close friends Max and Anne Geismar, was one of my secretaries, and she went to Washington ahead of me to handle the preliminaries. She was a recent graduate of Sarah Lawrence, highly intelligent and very attractive. I could not help but compare the youth generation of the sixties, so different from the uninvolved youth of the fifties, with the young radicals I knew in the twenties and thirties.

The joust began on May 6 in a small, crowded hearing room. Freddie Jerome invoked the Fifth Amendment many times to avoid naming his associates in the Progressive Labor Committee. My turn came.

"Are you a member of the Communist party?" asked Edwin Willis of Louisiana.

I told this Southern congressman that I had been a member of the Communist party, but that I was no longer. Then Willis made a mistake. He read into the record a letter he had received from Pan Stone:

> You are not my representative in Congress but we are neighbors in a sense and I admire the stand you have taken in Congress on numerous occasions. . . . I have known Mr. Lynn since the early 1930s when he was a student at Syracuse University College of Law at the time I was teaching in the School of Citizenship there. His past affiliation with the Young Communist League and later with the Communist party are known to me as well as to the FBI. He discussed with me that the time his reasons for breaking with the YCL and why he was expelled from the Communist party. In both instances the cause, basically, was his dedication to civil liberties and the American Bill of Rights. It is this same dedication to American justice and due process of law that has prompted him to defend Robert Williams. It is hardly necessary for me to add that I have no use for Robert Williams. And I condemn the support he is giving the Castro regime in Cuba.
>
> What I don't understand is why the KKK leaders and those of the White Citizen's Councils as well as organizations like the John Birch Society whose activities are flagrantly un-American are not regarded as security risks and a threat to the American way of life.
>
> I can well imagine the propaganda advantage it will give the Kremlin and the Cuban communists when it is learned that on May 6 Mr. Lynn was called before HUAC for his defense of Robert Williams. On the other hand, it presents the HUAC with a unique opportunity to demonstrate the fact that lawyers in America are to be protected, as well as respected, in discharging their obligation to uphold the principles of justice and due process of law."

Pan Stone was the niece of a Supreme Court justice and could hardly be called unpatriotic. She may have misinterpreted my motives, but the construction she put on my activities made them more palatable to the hurrah boys on the committee.

I took the offense against HUAC, using David Shapiro's research material. Every member of the committee except one was from the South, and I cited injustice after injustice that had been visited upon black people in each congressman's district. This unsettled the congressmen, who were more accustomed to harrassing and attacking than having their own motives questioned.

The New York Times summarized my testimony the next day: "Mr. Lynn did not refuse to answer questions. He said he joined the Communist Party in 1934 and was expelled in 1937. He denied he had 'knowingly and willfully' supported Communist propaganda . . . 'I object to this being characterized as Communist propaganda,' he said, 'I am definitely on the left. I don't happen to be satisfied with a government that permits brutalization of the Negroes in Birmingham.' At this the audience of about seventy-five applauded vigorously."

The committee was holding the hearing at the wrong time. Only the day before, in Birmingham, Alabama, one thousand black people demonstrating for their elementary rights had been jailed. Hundreds had been beaten. Hundreds had been bitten and maimed by police dogs. Hundreds had been tortured with water streams and cattle prods. And HUAC was saying that I was the un-American!

The *Times* indicated in its story that Chairman Edwin Willis had asked if I had helped Robert Williams escape from the country. I was quoted as saying, "We reconstituted the Underground Railroad and he got out through Canada." I did indeed make the statement, and I could have been charged with aiding a fugitive to escape. But it would have been politically disastrous to indict me, and I was confirmed in a basic belief: white reactionaries have difficulty attacking a Negro when his basic thrust seems to be the succor of black people.

In excusing me from further testimony, Edwin Willis revealed that I was a member of the international Communist conspiracy. Childish reasoning such as this would be laughable were it not taken seriously by rightist zealots. Willis also said I was the first "honest" Communist he had met. This dubious praise failed to impress me.

I. F. Stone covered the proceedings and praised my conduct in his newsletter. Paul Cowan wrote a wonderful story for the *Harvard Crimson*. I did not notice that I lost any business as a result of the hearing.

The Negro press treated the matter gingerly. The editors did not want to appear too openly supportive of my stand because it might make them suspect. Also, many of them were resentful of my frequent, harsh criticisms, of the traditional spinelessness of black editors and their unwillingness to take a stand.

On June 15, 1963, the *New Yorker* magazine published an article about the formation of a new political party:

At Harlem Square, on the corner of Seventh Avenue, a meeting was in progress. . . .

William Worthy was speaking when we arrived. He suggested the formation, by Negroes, of a Freedom Now party, to propose Negro candidates for public offices. "Think about it," he said. "Talk about it. Kick the idea around. We may not win many offices, but with one out of ten Americans a Negro . . . we can make our voice heard in the land."

There was applause with Mr. Worthy sat down, and he rose again to say a few more words. "Do you know what would happen if Fidel Castro were President of the United States instead of John F. Kennedy?" Mr. Worthy said.

"Bull Connor would be given a fair trial and then shot. Ninety-five percent of the police would have to flee to South Africa for political asylum. J. Edgar Hoover would be thrown into an integrated jail. If that didn't cure him, he would be left there for life."

The crowd laughed and applauded.

Just then we spotted a friend in the crowd, a young Negro woman who has lived in Harlem all her life . . .

"There's going to be trouble," our friend said. . . . "On a hot summer night, it wouldn't take much to set off a riot—not isolated violence but a kind of revolution. Five years ago, it was still a problem for social workers—jobs, education, housing in which children wouldn't wake up to find rats in their beds. Now something will have to be done on an enormous scale or there's going to be murder."

A few more speakers addressed the assemblage, including myself, and we followed through on the formation of the Freedom Now party. Just at this time John Kennedy had finally spoken out forthrightly on civil rights, and Martin Luther King was planning a massive march on Washington. I was skeptical of the further use of this tactic, but decided to attend. If we felt no viable program was enunciated, we would issue a call for our new party.

The most active elements preparing for the march, the students and labor people, made it known that they were going to stage sit-ins and other non-violent actions in Washington. Bayard Rustin and Walter Reuther moved quickly to squelch such developments, and at the march itself John Lewis of SNCC was compelled to jettison the more angry sections of his speech. Dr. King made his famous "I Have a Dream" delivery and most people left for home in a euphoria of religious exaltation and brotherly love (in retrospect, it is clear that the nonviolent strategy and tactics of Martin Luther King were the best available weapons for the black people in the period of the sixties. Martin Luther King showed, by his strong stand against the Vietnam war and his final alliance with the union garbagemen of Memphis showed that he was capable of growth into the most significant leader the black people have had in this century. Therefore, it was necessary to the Establishment that Martin Luther King be assassinated.)

The radicals repaired to the Park Sheraton Hotel to prepare our manifesto for a Freedom Now party. After a five-hour meeting we agreed to form a committee for a Freedom Now party with myself as acting chairman. The main disagreement at the meeting was between the separatists and the integrationists. A shaky compromise was reached: all candidates for public office would be black, but individuals of whatever color were free to join. In this way we hoped to have a party primarily devoted to the interests of blacks.

The black press published stories of our meeting without comment. The *New York Times,* however, was quick to condemn, denouncing our project as "racism in politics." I wrote a letter to the *Times*, published on October 26, 1963, which was adopted as the definitive defense of our party's position:

> Your recent editorial "Racism in Politics" commenting adversely on the launching of the Freedom Now Party, is a good example of the socially ingenuous and complacent liberalism which has hobbled the Negro civil rights movement. . . .
>
> The Negro does indeed seek "full equality" in American life. His goal, however, is not simply the attainment of an overdue right, but the use of that right as a means for changing and bettering a society which has created the deprivation in which he has spent his life. . . .
>
> To call a party organized by Negroes racist in the light of the facts is to ignore sociological reality and merely bandy labels. Rather such a party can become a beacon for all who are conscious of the corruption and decay in our society. . . .
>
> The *Times* decries the Freedom Now Party's belief in the efficacy of black political action because American Negroes, unlike African blacks, are a small minority. But is not the overriding strength of the democratic process exactly the outlet it provides for minority action? If the Negro can initiate and maintain a real party, unified in aim and action throughout the country, such a minority group can well turn the

balance of power by swinging its members out of one or other of the established old-line parties. Such processes of "bargaining power" are well known to the partisan politics of the United States.

Lastly, the leadership which such a party would provide should not be underestimated. The Negro is tremendously involved, spiritually and emotionally, in his great movement towards full equality in a better society. Nothing gives him more powerful motivation than a political party he has formed in which he will work with that sense of total belonging which alone brings complete dedication and which he has never before been offered. In no way do we bar whites from supporting us, physically, morally, intellectually and financially in a party with an all-inclusive definition of freedom and justice.

While fending off the white liberals with one hand, it was necessary to use the other to hold back the separatists. Many blacks made it crystal clear they wanted no truck with white people. They were particularly concerned that certain white radical parties not obtain a manipulating influence in our councils. For instance, the Socialist Workers party had played a major role in the events in Monroe, North Carolina. Also, the SWP had begun to see the revolutionary implications of the Black Muslim movement with the rise of its latest spokesman, Malcolm X. Jim Boggs wrote me a sharp letter:

I wrote that I did not believe the party should be under any kind of umbrella. If you want to know what I mean by an umbrella, I mean that it should not be under the auspices of any radical group. And if you want me to be more concrete, I am under the impression that the people you have in Detroit and Cleveland are people whom you were given by the SWP. Are they or are they not? And isn't this true of other places?

The other point I want to get home very clearly and very sharply. If white radicals are saying that they must be in the party in order for it to be a party, then I am against the damn party. Because I don't believe that they have any prerogative to be in the party. . . . There are going to have to be some choices here. Are you going to have some Muslims or are you going to have some whites and no Muslims? Because you are not going to have the two. I don't see how you can have, particularly in the South, the concept of black political power and have some white people deciding about that power.

For instance, Grace, my wife, hasn't got a damn bit of business in the black political party unless they label her a Negro in this country.

In this letter Jim Boggs posed all the questions that bedevil an all-black party in the United States. Despite the singular oppression visited upon the black person in this country, his activities at all levels have almost always been inextricably intertwined with whites or other races. One of the great pleasures I have always had has been the association with the most diverse kinds of human beings, and such contact is one of the great merits of American urban life. Grace Boggs herself was of Chinese origin.

An exclusivist black political movement was long overdue, but the truth was that every black movement since Marcus Garvey had significant white participation. It was even true of the Muslims when they became important.

The Freedom Now party ran Mayoral candidates in 1963 with results that were mildly encouraging. A number of radical groups that were predominantly white were critical of our efforts because we were siphoning off potential recruits to their ranks.

Later, the Freedom Now party ran candidates for offices at every level, including the presidency. Massive police infiltration attested to our potential and, alas, was a major cause in our failure to accomplish more. The most impressive campaign was waged by Albert Cleage of Detroit who received thirty-nine thousand votes for governor of Michigan, in November 1964.

CHAPTER 16

Malcolm X and the Fight against the War

The Freedom Now party was bedeviled and finally scuttled by its inability to decide whether it should remain an all-black entity or aim for eventual integration into the general social structure. But there was one movement which had settled that question for itself—the Black Muslims.

It was Malcolm X, that singular graduate of the ghetto, who first made me examine the role of the Black Muslims in big cities. I had been acutely aware that the irrational, emotional escape often provided by a new sect could effectively deflect social unrest into harmless channels. It was not until I saw the results the Muslims achieved with black drug-addicts and alcoholics in the prisons that I began to study the movement without hostility.

The lost souls in jail caused a certain esthetic revulsion in me. The fact that I could rationally surmise what had caused their plight did not affect this reaction. But the Muslims turned so many derelicts into heroes that my distaste for lowly "criminals" evaporated. I was proud to join them on the picket lines.

I never asked the leader of the fighting arm of the Nation of Islam his name, but I believe we achieved a complete understanding with each other. By the autumn of 1964 almost half my time was taken up defending Black Muslims.

Malcolm had returned from Africa and the Middle East in 1964 with a mature revolutionary philosophy. He had not changed his belief that blacks must take the lead in tearing down the institutions of a rotting society, but now he devoted a great deal of time to explaining that blacks must welcome allies in the Third World and even from the majority population in America. As long as he had presented all white people as devils and forecast a mystical apocalypse for them, the newspapers, radio, and television played up his every word. When he took the classic road of the revolutionary, the media attempted to ignore him.

I appeared on the same platform with Malcolm in Greenwich Village and later at the Audubon Ballroom with one of the United Nations representatives from Tanzania. At this later meeting Malcolm talked with me about the Socialist Workers party. He was grateful that its paper, the *Militant*, was printing his speeches in full because his message was at least being circulated. But he noticed, and I did too, that a strong nonviolent tendency was beginning to show itself in the SWP. This would seem laughable if an individual examined only the group's rhetoric, but it was nonetheless true. The SWP could no more escape the influence of the pervading psychology than most other groups. Only the hungry barbarians at the gates incessantly see their salvation in war.

Malcolm was the most moving black orator of his time. His sardonic barbs gave a lift and inspiration to his audiences that no other orator could match. Adam Powell at the zenith of his powers in the late 1930s stirred his listeners in a very direct fashion, but Malcolm's delivery enjoined thought as well as passion. Elijah Mohammed could not abide such a disciple. The Allah-intoxicated head of the faith had been relegated to a secondary role.

Malcolm's final, unforgivable act was his founding of the Organization of Afro-American Unity, a strictly political group. Malcolm could no longer accept Elijah as the head of the religion, ostensibly because of certain of the old man's peccadilloes that had come to light. I could not believe, however, that these minor delinquencies could cause such a profound schism in the movement. A more important cause, I thought, was that Elijah's peculiar stance made his denunciations of society highly ambiguous. I could not understand, for example, how at a meeting in a stadium in Washington, Elijah could accept twenty-five dollars from George Lincoln Rockwell, leader of the American Nazi party. It reminded me of Marcus Garvey's acceptance of support from Bilbo in the 1920s.

I was unable to attend the meeting on February 21, 1965. My friend Mary Kochiyama was sitting in the front row of the auditorium when Malcolm walked out alone. Suddenly there was a moment's distraction—someone began a loud quarrel in the center of the room—and then Mary saw the three gunmen get up and begin to shoot. She pushed her son under a seat and raced to the platform, arriving just in time to cradle the head of the fallen hero in her arms.

Few of us believed the line peddled in the daily press that Malcolm's death was the product of Muslim rivalry.

Malcolm's loss was incalculable. The government knew this as well as the millions of black people who mourned him. As the embattled segregationists like Lester Maddox with his ax handles and Bull Connor with his cattle prods beat back the advance of the black people, Martin Luther King began to lose his appeal for the young, and a yawning gap grew between the races. When Malcolm was murdered, the apocalyptic predictions of Elijah Mohammed that the white race would be destroyed in some vaguely defined Armageddon in 1973 seemed for many in the ghetto the only hope to which they could cling.

Also, just two weeks before Malcolm's assassination, Lyndon Johnson ordered the bombing of North Vietnam. Liberals and radicals reacted with dismay. Johnson had been elected as a peace candidate, but the wily rascal had secured a blank check from the Senate in August 1964, the "Tonkin Gulf Resolution," which he used as an excuse to dramatically escalate the war. Draft calls increased and the country was placed on a basis of semimobilization. Johnson shrewdly did not ask for a declaration of war.

I probably handled more draft-resistance cases than any other lawyer. Among my earliest clients was David Mitchell, a graduate of Brown University and the son of New England WASPs. Mitchell had organized a group called End the Draft, an interesting combination of revolutionaries and liberals. Mitchell was internationalist in outlook and came to me because he wanted to build his case around the Nuremberg Convention and the United Nations Charter.

Mitchell's draft board, in New Canaan, Connecticut, tried to induce him to send it data on his draft qualifications as early as August 1961. At that time, however, he was in jail as a result of an act of civil disobedience against the deployment of nuclear-armed Polaris submarines. When he learned of the board's inquiry, he wrote that he was disaffiliating himself from the conscription system. After a further exchange of letters, the board fell silent for two years. Then, in January 1964, the board sent Mitchell a brochure explaining that he could exercise various options to apply for a deferment. Mitchell replied:

> I realize that I could employ means to gain exemption from induction, but this does not interest me. My purpose is not to be classified within the draft system, but rather to oppose the draft. While classification might suit some sort of individual "convenience" my acceptance of classification would be a negation of my social responsibility.
>
> I oppose the draft, not as something wrong for just me or wrong for only certain people, but as something wrong for the peace and survival of the world. Selective Service is the criminal in this case

as can be judged by American militarism throughout the world—from Cuba to Panama to South Vietnam and by our basing of policies on nuclear war. I refuse to cooperate in any way which would support the continuance of such activities.

The draft board ordered Mitchell to appear for induction on June 10, 1964. Shortly after that I notified the board that I represented Mitchell, but the board continued to correspond with the "delinquent." It was apparent that its upper-middle-class members were reluctant to prosecute one of their own kind. Finally, when Mitchell ignored yet another order to report for induction, the matter was turned over to the grand jury in New Haven.

Mitchell's End the Draft Committee drummed up public support throughout the summer of 1965 (his trial was set for September 13). The left wing of the Quakers came to the committee's aid and planned to picket in front of the courthouse. I was asked if this sort of pressure was legal. I said the picket line might be dispersed by the police on the ground that it exercised illegal influence on the court.

Every effort to build a campaign against the draft and the war in black communities met indifference and, occasionally, hostility. Part of the reason could be found in Daniel P. Moynihan's *The Negro Family—The Case for National Action*. Moynihan, a sociologist of the Glazer-Reisman school, had been commissioned by the United States Department of Labor to study the black minority. The Great Depression, Moynihan pointed out, created entire communities of black people in major cities. They existed largely on welfare payments and menial jobs. It was easier for the black women to find work than it was for the men. Unable to support their families, these men often left their households, because under welfare rules it was frequently possible to obtain welfare payments more quickly when the man was not around. This served to denigrate still further the image of the black man in his neighborhood, and the matrifocal family became commonplace.

Unemployment for black youth in many cities reached more than 50 percent. These were the shock troops of rebellion, but Moynihan figured he had the solution to their mollification. Since the government was moving toward a massive involvment in Vietnam, the ranks of the infantry could be swelled by drafting young blacks. Such a policy would decrease the ranks of the unemployed in the ghetto tinderboxes and would enable the government to discipline and subdue these blacks through the army. The drill sergeant was the ideal father figure, and best of all they would be fighting for the very system they had begun to rebel against at home. This last conclusion was never explicitly expressed by Moynihan, but it was implicit in the entire purpose of his work. He prescribed a remedy that could be, and was, immediately applied, but it was a short-run answer: like most American pragmatists, he would face the result of his prescription when it appeared.

With the Mitchell case I faced the same problems I'd had with many other cases and would increasingly have as I represented more and more draft resisters. The organizations backing the cases gave high priority to their organizational and propaganda needs and low priority to paying the lawyer. If I'd had financial resources in the form of personal wealth or well-heeled clients, it would have been possible to carry on without adequate fees, but I had neither.

It was a rainy September morning when I arrived in New Haven for David Mitchell's trial. The picket line was already functioning. I approached a white-haired lady carrying a placard and asked what she would do if a policeman told her she had no right to picket. "I will tell him," she said, "that the Lord told me to do this."

That was all I needed to hear. I was prepared with an answer if the judge complained about the picket line.

The first day of the Mitchell trial was devoted to arguing my motion to dismiss the indictment on grounds of constitutional and international law. I tried to show that the use of the draft in an undeclared war, ten thousand miles from our shores, was unconstitutional as a violation of the war powers entrusted to Congress in the country's basic charter. The frequent resort to undeclared armed interventions had become characteristic of the cold war.

I reminded the court that the United States had ratified the United Nations Charter as a treaty. By sponsoring resolution (2) (95) of the United Nations General Assembly on December 11, 1946, we had adopted the principles of the Nuremberg Judgment. Those principles rendered individuals of offending nations at war responsible for any war crimes they committed. No longer could people hide behind the rubric that they were only following orders. Therefore, I argued, it was essential that every American called to duty in this war search his conscience to determine whether he might be called upon to commit war crimes. The fact that the war was illegal might by itself indicate that any killing might be judged a war crime.

Finally, I described actual war crimes that the United States was perpetrating on Vietnamese soil, in violation of our professed adherence to the revolutionary rights of peoples. I told the court we were substituting our own imperialist rule for that of the French, who had been compelled to abandon Vietnam after Dien Bien Phu. I quoted Lyndon Johnson talking to a group of American students and saying that he "would like to see them develop as much fanaticism about the U.S. political system as young Nazis did about their system during the war." I also quoted Nguyen Van Ky of South Vietnam who, when asked to name his heroes, replied, "I have only one—Hitler."

Before concluding my argument, I called the court's attention to the documented list of atrocities committed by American troops in Vietnam, and I said that David Mitchell had every right to point out the violations of U.S. treaty obligations and to use them as a reason to refuse to serve in the armed forces.

The U.S. attorney did not dispute my account of treaty violations and atrocities, but said my argument was devoted to political questions that were beyond the jurisdiction of the court to examine. The court reserved decision.

At the end of the day David Mitchell expressed great unhappiness at my approach to his case. He felt that I had been too legalistic. I tried in vain to explain to him that the framework of a trial precluded a strictly moral exhortation. Unless his position could be presented as a defense, it would not be heard at all.

The next day I received a phone call from the judge, who stated that David Mitchell no longer wanted me as his lawyer. Nevertheless, he ordered me to be present in a week's time when the trial resumed.

During that week I pointed out to Mitchell and his committee that I had never been paid a fee in his case. The nominal sums sent to me from time to time barely covered printing and other expenses. I asked them to have a payment of one thousand dollars on the resumption of the trial, since I anticipated having to stay in a hotel in New Haven for the duration of the controversy.

When the trial resumed, the court took the precaution of appointing a former United States attorney to assist me. The judge refused to excuse me, even though Mitchell had made it clear that he would not permit me or the appointed attorney to act for him.

The problems raised by the Mitchell case have, no doubt, plagued many other lawyers. Prior to this they had not caused me concern, because I was as much a political activist as I was a trial lawyer. It was not difficult for me to guide the legal battle in a direction that would achieve the political objective. Arthur Garfield Hays, in accordance with Clarence Darrow's technique, had taught me how to do this in the early 1940s, and I honed the tactic in the first Freedom Ride case in 1947, in the Puerto Rican Nationalist trials, and in the Kissing case.

But the Mitchell case was more intractable because I was dealing with a splinter political group. Such groups are made up of people with very stubborn nonconformist veiws. They wish to use the courts as forums and are impatient with rules of court procedure and evidence. As a young communist in the 1920s reading about the Sacco and Vanzetti case, I was also contemptuous of common-law trial rules. It seemed to me at the time that lawyers were by and large tricksters, who would be gotten rid of in the society of my dreams. But the experience of the years tempered that judgment. The coming of socialism would not, in and of itself, eliminate human dispute.

At the end of another day in the Mitchell case I implored the judge to excuse me from further attendance, and he reluctantly assented. Mitchell continued to interrupt and disrupt the proceedings as much as possible. The jury returned a verdict of guilty and the judge gave Mitchell the maximum sentence, five years.

There is a certain logic, it seems to me, in disrupting a trial if one has determined that no justice can be gotten in a capitalist court. But I believe disruption should be subordinated to taking every opportunity to win converts to the dissident's point of view, which is seldom accomplished by obstructing or flouting the court. Numerous examples of famous political trials come to mind: the Haymarket trials, Bill Haywood's trial, the Tom Mooney case, the Sacco and Vanzetti case—in all these the victims of state prosecution won converts and a place in history by using the state's machinery to deliver their messages.

The United States Court of Appeals for the Second Circuit reversed David Mitchell's conviction on the ground that he had not been given sufficient opportunity to secure counsel of his own choice after he had discharged me.

The End the Draft Committee was able to obtain the services of Fyke Farmer, a friend of mine from Nashville, Tennessee, and a redoubtable legal opponent of the Korean and Vietnam wars. But Farmer found that he could not persuade the defendant to frame his case within permissible canons, and he bowed out.

Mitchell obtained William Kunstler. The new trial was held in Hartford, and Kunstler followed his client's instructions. Two witnesses who had been in North Vietnam offered to testify on what they had observed of the effects of American bombing. They were refused permission to testify. The defense asked for the issuance of subpoenas to two dissident Green Berets who were being held in confinement by the army. The request was denied. The defendant moved to take depositions abroad from one American and several Vietnamese about the bombing and gassing of civilians. That request was also denied. The judge sentenced David Mitchell to five years in prison.

I handled many draft-refusal cases in the 1960s and early 1970s, but none was more important than the case of Guy Gillette, a 6′5″, 240-pound Texas cowboy, then living in Yonkers. Gillette was good looking, had a touch of patriotism, and was very honest. He said he would not fight in Vietnam because the war was immoral. He said he was an atheist and would not claim exemption on religious grounds.

Our position was that an individual who had profound political or philo-sophical objections to a war should have the same rights as a person with religious objections. This was an extremely important distinction in the minds of radicals and was the logical culmination of principled objections to war. There were many cases throughout the country in the courts on just this point, but it was the Guy Gillette case that the U.S. Supreme Court agreed to hear.

Almost immediately, thirty-nine other law firms joined the case as friends of the court or participants in the brief. Argument was set for December 1970, and when I arrived at the Supreme Court building I was greeted by former Attorney General Ramsey Clark, who had joined our litigation as a friend of the court. Clark talked to me about the case and emphasized its importance. No one really thought we could win this case, but *something* might be salvaged.

The Supreme Court was packed that day. My old nemesis on the Winfred Lynn case, Thurgood Marshall, kept glancing away when I looked at him.

Lawyers can be torn apart when they appear in front of the justices of the Supreme Court. The justices, rather than being lazy, stupid representatives of the ruling class, as some radicals simplistically believed, are extremely bright men who inevitably are well-versed on any matter that appears before them. Most have first-rate minds, and all benefit greatly from top researchers and assistants. Seldom have I worked as hard on a case as I did on Gillette's.

Nevertheless, I had barely begun my argument when I was interrupted by a barrage of hostile questions. Only Justice William O. Douglas seemed sympathetic.

Back and forth we parried. Regardless of the court's hostility, I had a strong case and would not be intimidated. I pointed out that to punish Guy

Gillette would be to do so simply because he was honest. He could have objected to conscription on religious grounds and avoided the war, and certainly his true objections were as strong as any religious person's.

The Supreme Court announced its decision in January 1971. Thurgood Marshall wrote the majority opinion that found against Gillette. It was an eight-to-one decision, with Justice Douglas on our side. His opinion, although a minority of one, may herald that bright future day when thoughtful people turn away in revulsion from the horrors of an immoral war. Even as his physical strength was ebbing Douglas showed that for the rational and compassionate man the light of the mind does not dim. Because of the opinion he placed on the record, some future client and his lawyer have the opportunity to take up the fight we waged unsuccessfully during the Vietnam war.

CHAPTER 17

To the War Zone

David Mitchell's End the Draft Committee sold thousands of copies of the brief I had prepared for his trial in the Federal District Court for the Eastern District of Connecticut. That gave me the idea of writing a paperback manual for draft resisters. Grove Press insisted on titling it, *How to Stay Out of the Army*. It was published in 1966 and sold well.

The era of the Vietnam war found me restless and not getting any younger. I had not had the opportunity to be in the theater of action in the Spanish civil war. Army Intelligence had yanked me out of a combat until just as I was getting ready to sail for Italy in 1943. How could I get to the war zone now?

Early in 1967 I was visited by Leonard Liggio, a representative of Bertrand Russell's proposed War Crimes Commission. The great English philosopher felt that action was required to demonstrate for world opinion the ghastly devastation and horrible murders being committed by U.S. forces in Vietnam in callous disregard of developed rules of international law. These included principles that America had sponsored for adoption upon the founding of the United Nations.

Liggio proposed that I become a member of the War Crimes Commission and go to Europe to help set up a tribunal to take testimony. I did not give an immediate answer because I had a number of pressing cases, and the trip would necessitate being separated from my family for a considerable period, but the idea excited me. In early March 1967, it did seem possible for me to take a month off.

I arranged with my partners for the transfer of certain cases, and we were able to obtain postponements on others.

I flew directly to Paris and was met by Deirdre Griswold, an eloquent young organizer for Youth Against War and Fascism. She had arranged for me to stay at a small hotel within walking distance of the Cathedral of Notre Dame. As soon as I was settled at the hotel I called Ellen Wright, the widow of Richard Wright. On the spur of the moment she decided to throw a dinner party.

Deirdre Griswold had informed me that I had been selected as chairman of the fourth investigating committee of the War Crimes Tribunal, and that I would be going to Southeast Asia! It was thought best that I proceed to Rome and join Professor Basso from the University of Rome's Law School, who was also going to Indochina.

A complication arose. An American lawyer named Boardman had been scheduled to go to Southeast Asia, but decided not to make the trip. His round-trip ticket to Phnom Penh, Cambodia, had cost $1,323, and it seemed the airline was unwilling to refund the money. I consented to pose as Mr. Boardman. However, since he was tall and white and I was short and black, it did not seem that I could go all the way to Cambodia and back—with approximately ten stopovers—without being detected. It was necessary to trust to luck.

Our first stop was Rome. The law school professor had already gone on to Hanoi, so I had no choice except to follow alone.

The next stop was Tel Aviv. The Israeli city had intrigued me for several years, ever since I had begun to study the kibbutzim. Martin Buber was one of my favorite contemporary philosophers, and I was eager to see how his ideas were being put into practice. But I was not in Tel Aviv long enough to do so, although the place did remind me of a bustling American city set down upon a somewhat arid land. In the airport I was struck by the number of African women who seemed to be domestic servants. This was common in New York, but it had not occurred to me that the practice would be imported by Israel.

We also stopped in Teheran, New Delhi, and finally Bangkok. New Delhi was terribly depressing. Gandhi's homeland was the favorite topic of pacifists in America. It was a subcontinent, they rhapsodized, that had won its independence by nonviolent methods. What rubbish! The sight of the emaciated mendicants stretched out on the ground did not shock me so much as the aplomb and insouciance of the Indian ladies in rustling silk saris who stepped over them. It may be that those poor beggars had a philosophy (although they were so oppressed I doubted if they could even think) that the exhibition of extreme deprivation has a cathartic effect on the beholder. It only enveloped me in gloom.

Bangkok was a city occupied by the United States army and air force, and it did not seem wise to wander around much. I was traveling on someone else's ticket, and U.S. authorities might put two and two together and realize that I was the lawyer who had represented hundreds of draft resisters and dissident soldiers.

When our craft next soared into the skies, it was the last leg to Cambodia. The flight had been remarkably smooth all the way. The stewardesses on Air France were solicitous of my comfort after I discreetly conveyed to them that I was bitterly opposed to America's aggression in former French Indochina.

The plane settled down at Phnom Penh airport in the haze of a humid afternoon. Wilfred Burchett, the Australian journalist barred from his own country because it was alleged he was a Communist, was supposed to meet me at the Norodom Hotel, but when I arrived, there was a note saying he had seized an opportunity to take his wife and children to the seashore for a rare holiday. He promised to see me the next day.

Dinner was delicious. The Cambodians are noted for their cuisine, and I did not hesitate to enjoy it. That night I realized I was homesick and wrote a letter to Yolanda.

Wilfred Burchett was waiting for me in the lobby the next morning. He had bursting spirits, hair beginning to turn white, and an air that was unquestionably Australian. He gave me a number of books—one written by himself—about Cambodia, and I resolved to give myself a cram course.

For years I had heard people talk about Wilfred Burchett, and I knew his writings as an excellent source of anti-imperialist fact. If he was a Communist, he was the most undoctrinaire Communist I had ever met. He struck me more as a very dedicated anti-imperialist.

Burchett told me he had considerable admiration for the Cambodian chief of state, Prince Norodom Sihanouk. Sihanouk was the descendant of a royal line that had ruled Cambodia for centuries, and he could hardly be classified as a socialist. Yet his antagonism to the imperialist powers who exercised dominion in his area during the years of his rule—the French, Japanese, English, and Americans—had become legendary. Burchett was convinced that despite Sihanouk's brief flirtations with Western powers, in the end his commitment would be to the social revolution.

Sihanouk was a character and the Cambodian people loved him. He wrote plays and acted in them. He competed in literary contests and, not unexpectedly, won first prizes. Sihanouk's scale of living did not rival Bao Dai's, but he was no ascetic.

Burchett told me that the only way for me to travel to Hanoi would be by the International Control Commission plane that was expected within four or five days. That night in the hotel I was unable to sleep, and I switched on the little radio I had brought from the United States. Suddenly I heard the strains of an inspiring melody, sung by a women's choir from Chungking:

> Arise ye prisoners of starvation
> Arise ye wretched of the earth
> For justice thunders condemnation
> A better world's in birth

It was a thrilling and most appropriate message for the part of the world in which I found myself. I missed Yolanda and my three teenage children, but I was glad I had come.

The next day I met a Foreign Office functionary who involved me in discussions of the boundary disputes that plagued the government. The British and French had drawn the boundary lines of the many states of Southeast Asia, which had never been fully accepted by the peoples involved. My dim view of the British and French presumption in fixing lines between the countries struck a responsive chord among my hosts.

I took many walks about the city. The huge Olympic market in Phnom Penh fascinated me with its strange smells and (for me) incomprehensible cacophony. Since I had heard so much about the preoccupation of the people of the Far East with religion, I was eager to visit temples in Phnom Penh. I learned that the Ministry of Water Supply had taken over a large Catholic cathedral to use for national supervision of crop production. This seemed an advance and a commentary on the regard that the people held for their former "protectors." Within easy walking distance of the cathedral was a Buddhist pagoda where silent monks were meditating. A group of schoolchildren had climbed the hill to the pagoda, and their laughing gestures at the monks did not indicate juvenile piety.

Before I left Cambodia, Burchett took me to his home in a quiet, modern area of the city. His wife Vessa was a vivacious gray-haired woman who spoke Italian, French, Khmer, Chinese, and English, in addition to her native Bulgarian. Her three young children spoke Italian and Khmer, but no English, which was of little practical use in their locale.

I explained to Burchett that I might have my passport taken away from me if I used it to enter North Vietnam, which the U.S. government regarded as an enemy country. Burchett went into conference at the Foreign Office and emerged with a document that identified me as a diplomatic aide of the Cambodian government.

The International Control Commission plane left Phnom Penh with the Czech ambassador to North Vietnam aboard, plus the French ambassador and his wife, a detachment of Indian soldiers, a young Quaker from Chicago, and myself. We cruised in a propeller-driven plane in clear sunshine along the Cambodian border, and then went up the Laotian border to Vientiane. Laotian officials questioned my provisional diplomatic status but did not pursue the matter. The plane remained in Vientiane until dark, then we loaded in again and headed for Hanoi. A young woman met us at the airport in Hanoi and deposited a big bouquet of flowers in my arms. The vice-chief of the army drove me to a hotel. We talked through a translator.

The descent into Hanoi at 2:00 A.M. had a dreamlike quality about it. The city was lighted with what appeared to be thousands of twinkling diamonds. It was incredible to me that any city in a war zone, subject to the dreadful bombing of the U.S. air force, would dare be so casually lighted at night. Later I learned of the enormously efficient North Vietnamese antiaircraft defenses and realized they were not merely exhibiting bravado.

I checked into the Reunification Hotel, and later in the morning I set out to meet my fellow members of the Bertrand Russell War Crimes Commission. The first people I saw were two American blacks: Julius Lester from Georgia and Charlie Cobb from Philadelphia. Both were veterans of the civil-rights movement, and in the ensuing days we became fast friends.

At the noon meal I met the remaining members of the fourth investigating committee who were in Hanoi. They were Professor Basso of Rome; Dr. Martin Birnstingle, an English physician from St. Bartholomew's Hospital who was attached to the University of London; and Dr. Fischer, a Paris physician. Felix Greene joined us at the table. He was an English writer and photographer who had lived for many years in the United States, and I had great admiration for his work. Greene's sense of humor matched that of my SNCC friends.

That afternoon we had our first briefing on the war and Vietnam at the National University. Our instructors confined themselves to the French language, although many Vietnamese intellectuals spoke English. I knew that Ho Chi Minh spoke English. He had spent some time in the United States a number of decades earlier and was impressed by the democratic dogma developed by our founding fathers. In the first constitution of the Democratic Republic of Vietnam, 1946, the imperishable tenets of the inalienable rights of man which were in our Declaration of Independence were incorporated almost word for word.

Evidence of Chinese cultural influence was everywhere in Hanoi, so it surprised me to see that the Vietnamese, like the Cambodians, used Cyrillic characters in their writings. After listening to accounts of how the Vietnamese had fought off Chinese and Mongol invaders for a period of more than a thousand years, I could understand their fierce national pride and their will for distinctive national invividuality. Because the Vietnamese had always been outnumbered by their enemies, they maintained a high level of military proficiency, and the Communist party had added to this an unrivaled knowledge of the use of propaganda.

By the end of the second day in Hanoi the two SNCC members of our party were pressing to obtain permission to go into the countryside. In particular, Julius Lester was asking the government to give him a rifle so that he could go south with the guerrillas to fight his white fellow countrymen from the United States. Julius was the most bitter black man I had ever known, and he was particularly bitter in his rejoinders to white people. I hoped that as time went on he would begin to make distinctions among whites. All of us did agree, however, that we could not do the job we were assigned unless we got into the provinces, where United States planes were sowing destruction.

The government yielded to our wishes. Felix Greene was on excellent terms with many Vietnamese officials, and he played a major role in gaining permission for us to proceed to Thanh Hoa province, which was almost due south of Hanoi in the delta of the great Red River, and whose capital was a seaport of the Gulf of Tonkin.

We traveled by jeep, automobile, and truck. Our destination was 130 miles from Hanoi and it took a night to get there. At night we were relatively safe from the U.S. airmen who were flying from carriers stationed in the Gulf of Tonkin and from bases in South Vietnam and Thailand.

We were thrilled by the calm resolution of our North Vietnamese companions and ashamed of any trepidation. The North Vietnamese had been living under the bombing for years and nowhere could we detect signs of defeatism or fear.

From time to time during the night we would stop on the banks of a stream where the bridges had been knocked out. We always found pontoons over which we could cross. I was greatly impressed by the ingenuity in adversity that our hosts displayed: with simple materials they exhibited limitless imagination.

In the morning we bedded down in a tiny thatched-hut village. I rested a few hours and then ventured outside. Almost immediately I encountered a woman Vietnamese doctor who had been assigned to us in Hanoi. A rather painful boil had developed on my upper right thigh, and she was intent on inspecting it. I was embarrassed to have to take my pants down at her command, and my embarrassment worsened when she called over some other women. I hesitated to raise a protest and imagined it was the custom of Vietnamese women to be so casual while observing a man's genitalia. But the women were interested in my legs. I was built rather heavily from the waist down, and they seemed to marvel at the size of my calves and thighs. Someone translated what they were saying, which was "peasant, peasant." I was told that lawyers in that part of the world traditionally came from the upper sedentary classes, yet I had the legs of a sturdy peasant. It was an anomaly at which they continued to wonder.

We inspected sites where the bombing had been the heaviest. The largest leprosarium in the Far East had been turned into charred, broken walls of brick. With macabre dedication the U.S. flyers had followed hospital units, broken down in size to escape notice, and bombed them wherever they stopped. In this case the purpose seemed to be to compel the lepers to flee and disperse themselves among the general population to spur infection.

A little later we visited the tiny hamlet of Dan Loi. It consisted of small thatched houses set in rice paddies. It had no military significance, unless the prospect of small farmers tending their fields, or little children leading oxen out to pasture, was intolerable to the American high command. Two weeks earlier the village had been attacked by a squadron of fighterbombers, and direct hits had been scored on some of the huts. Nine villagers were killed: three women and six children. No soldiers were killed because none were there. Twelve houses were demolished and many animals disemboweled. In this manner a great victory had been achieved and a number of Vietnamese were spared the horrors of communism.

We dug the casings of fragmentation bombs out of the ground. Hundreds of little steel pellets, slightly larger than BB ammunition, had flown out in all directions, tearing into the bodies of human beings and animals within a hundred-foot radius. Other jagged iron pieces tore gaping holes in their victims.

None of us slept very well that night, and we jumped out of bed the next morning to the roar of antiaircraft artillery some miles away. We traveled about five miles by jeep to another little cluster of what had been houses. The peasants were still putting out the flames. The small community had been bombed and napalmed. I saw a mother sitting on the ground, screaming, holding the burned remains of a little baby.

Later I saw the grandfather of the dead child talking with the mother. A Vietnamese captain translated a vow the mother was making. She had one son left, fourteen years old. She promised that he would be raised to join the army and avenge the death of his baby sister.

By this time I had begun to mourn with the villagers. North Vietnam was becoming unbearable, and the thought of being an American filled me with an unshakable sense of guilt.

That afternoon we visited a convent for nuns. It had been blasted with bombs and virtually destroyed. The craters were very large, indicating the use of thousand-pound bombs. Not far from the convent was the site of an eighteenth-century pagoda that had been completely demolished. The only point of bombing these architectural monuments was to obliterate the country's culture. Even the Nazis during and just before World War II made some pretense of preserving historical artifacts. Clearly we were in the historical stage, predicted by Spengler, of wars of total annihilation.

The next day we were in Toan Phuc hamlet and we enjoyed a communal meal. It was a welcome respite from the evening before when we witnessed a pitched battle between a U.S. plane and an antiaircraft battery and were probably close to becoming casualties of the war we were reporting. After eating, I went over in my mind the scenes of carnage I had witnessed, and a pattern began to emerge. The United States high command was deliberately trying to destroy all vestiges of advances in health, agriculture, water purification, and every other evidence of scientific progress this small Asian nation had achieved since its independence as a socialist country in 1946. There was dreadful method in my country's madness. It fitted well with the deep-rooted convictions of white supremacy and Western superiority. If North Vietnam's collective achievements could be destroyed, the American public would be easily convinced that they had never existed. The mass media in the United States was slavish in its unquestioning obedience to governmental suggestion of what should be released to the people.

The question of socialism as the solution to the problems of the inner cities in America, as the solution to the problem of running a high-employment economy without depending on armaments and war, as the solution to race and religious hatreds, could not be forever adjourned on the U.S. agenda. But the administration, by destroying the evidence of a humane solution in

North Vietnam, was undercutting the program of the progressive forces in America at the same time it was attempting to sow despair in any country that tried a noncapitalist solution to its problems.

The United States dared not carry out the logic of its program in China or the Soviet Union. That would entail the probable destruction of its own industrial-military complex. The high command struck its heroic pose in blasting tiny countries like North Vietnam, or holding on to its military bases: Guantanamo, for example, in the small country of Cuba, or Chagarramas in minuscule Trinidad. But it was less than courageous when attempting to impose its latter-day "final solution" in socialist countries of any size.

The North Vietnamese government was concerned about our safety, so when it was time to return to Hanoi the trip was made in slow stages. The Vietnamese captain who had accompanied us told me there had been reservations in sections of the government about whether we should be allowed to visit areas that were under active bombardment.

Before we began our return journey we were treated to a puppet show. It portrayed the great air-battle that had taken place at Ham Rong. Local militia manned the antiaircraft nests, but "manned" was not quite the right word, because I had witnessed the local militia when it was drilling and most of the members were women. I had seen them march out to the fields each day with agricultural tools in their hands and rifles slung over their shoulders, and I was reminded of the dauntless Cuban women.

The heroine of the battle at Ham Rong had been a Catholic nun who volunteered to carry water to the soldiers. Throughout the long and terrible bombing she ministered to her sisters and brothers operating the guns. This nun's activity was the central theme of the puppet play.

The U.S. government constantly played up the argument that when Ho Chi Minh came to power in the North, hundreds of thousands of Catholics fled to South Vietnam. It was necessary for the government to take this line, because it was quite aware that the Catholic hierarchy in America was the most dependable source of reaction. Long before, I had come to the conclusion that if the Catholic rank and file could be won to socialism, capitalism could not long survive. Only the Catholics have a dogma which in its fervor matches that of the communists and socialists, and the Catholics are the last repository of capitalist faith. The inbred skepticism of Protestants makes them ill-suited to oppose social change on rational grounds, and the logic for the revolutionary overthrow of traditional institutions can only be stayed by a fanatical mystique.

When we arrived in Hanoi we began to prepare reports on our findings.

The conclusions of our medical experts on the objective evidence were most convincing in revealing the true intentions of the U.S. military.

The bombing of Hanoi began and it was impossible for the government to tell us when a plane would be available to take us out. I became adept at leaping into shelters and pulling the concrete cover over my head.

One evening at the Reunification Hotel I was approached by Quakers who had sailed into the port of Haiphong in their little vessel, the *Phoenix*, with medical supplies for the North Vietnamese. I noticed these Quakers had gained the ears of major officials in the Hanoi government, who I suspected felt that the Quakers could be useful in mobilizing American opinion to stop the war or, at least, to stop the bombing of North Vietnam. Several Quakers suggested that I try to impress on the Vietnamese the immense military might of the United States and emphasize to them that they had no chance to win a military showdown. I listened politely but wanted to laugh out loud. The North Vietnamese well knew the terrible power of the United States, but they knew also that the wide-flung interests of America's ruling circles precluded a solution consisting purely of blood and iron. Curtis LeMay could rant all he wanted about bombing North Vietnam "back to the Stone Age," but the government, with obligations in NATO, worried about rising tensions in the Middle East, and concerned about the fury of the antiwar forces in the U.S., was not free to do everything it wanted.

I later raised this subject with the Vietnamese captain who had been assigned to us. He smiled slightly. Later that night, about 1:00 A.M., he woke me. Felix Greene was with him. The captain told me he thought I might want to watch a shift of equipment the North Vietnamese were making.

We drove to a major crossroads about five miles outside the city, and it was not long before I heard the rumble of tanks. They came to the intersection and made a 180-degree turn and moved off to our left. The tanks came on and on, and I stood there spellbound. Then came heavy artillery and antiaircraft batteries, supplied by China, and they too moved in a seemingly endless line. Then came giant platforms, carrying what I assumed to be huge rockets. Next came light and heavy artillery. The concentration of artillery reminded me of the doctrine of Voronov, the master of the heavy guns at Stalingrad. We stood for some three hours, and when we left the procession was still passing. The captain had nothing to say, but great pride shone in his eyes.

Felix Greene told me that the North Vietnamese had never committed their regular army to battle. It was largely concentrated between Hanoi and the Chinese border. My conviction was unshaken that the United States could not win the war short of an atomic holocaust, and that could mean the end of humankind. China was manufacturing nuclear weapons, and it would not welcome the United States incinerating its southeastern neighbors with impunity. Nor could Soviet Russia stand by and see a socialist country treated to the "final solution"; that had become clear in the stand-off over Cuba.

I hinted to the Quakers that there was not the slightest chance North Vietnam would surrender, and I suggested they try to persuade the United States to back off. I knew they were exerting what pressure they could on Johnson and I sympathized with their dilemma.

But I was given no time to contemplate the discomfiture of the Quakers.

On my way to North Vietnam, on the plane at Teheran, a young Persian businessman had sat beside me. He surprised me with his command of English and he told me he was on the way to Japan, and English was the language of commerce used in that country.

Then he asked me brightly, had I heard the news that Adam Clayton Powell was going to defy the government powers that had been hounding him. Powell was preparing to return from his retreat on the island of Bimini to New York City. He had gotten into difficulty in Congress and was under a contempt citation in New York. One circumstance I had learned on my long odyssey to Southeast Asia was that Adam Powell, with his defiant statements against the largely white ruling establishments everywhere, had become a symbol of assertiveness to the nonwhite oppressed masses all over the world.

My husky brown-skinned pedicab operator in Phnom Penh had been certain that Powell would return to New York City. But on this Tuesday morning in the Reunification Hotel in Hanoi the answer could no longer be avoided.

The dining room was filled with Europeans, a few Afro-Cubans, American Quakers, and our fourth investigating team. One of the Quakers had raised the insistent question: "Had Congressmen Powell returned to New York City to defy his persecutors?"

An English diplomat excused himself, saying he wanted to listen to his short-wave radio in his room. In a few moments he had returned. To the dining room he announced in a subtly amused voice:

"Mr. Powell saw fit not to return."

Every nonwhite in that room sat stunned—Cubans, Vietnamese, West Indians, Africans, and black Americans. Then Julius Lester stood up.

"The nigger was chicken." And he stalked out of the room.

In this last gathering Julius had not become noticeably more mellow toward white people, but he had acquired a reluctant attachment to Felix Greene. Felix simply did not have the unconscious hang-ups of 99 percent of English people and Americans when it came to associating with or even thinking of black people.

Finally, on April 1, 1967, I began the long return journey home. My Cambodian *aide mémoire* stood me in good stead. French doctors at Orly airfield generously gave me the vaccinations that enabled me to go through U.S. customs. It was wonderful to be back home again.

CHAPTER 18

The Black Panthers

For a few years I enjoyed the relative pleasure of fulfilling speaking engagements on the Vietnam war. Then in the early spring of 1970 I was assigned by the appellate division of the supreme court in New York to defend one of three Black Panthers. The three were accused of attempted murder and robbery in an alleged plot to replenish the treasury of the Panther party with the fruits of their forceful activity. It was a welcome assignment, since the Black Panthers ordinarily did not retain black lawyers. Charles Garry, when he was in New York City at the opening of the case of the Panther 21, explained to me that in 1966 Panther leaders Huey Newton and Bobby Seale approached well-heeled Negro lawyers in California for legal aid and were spurned disdainfully. They had put down all Black lawyers since, with the exception of those approved by the National Lawyers Guild. That is why in middle-class circles of Negroes the Panthers were considered to be ultimately under the control of the Communist party. The National Lawyers Guild in the Negro public mind, at least in the New York City area, was considered to be dominated by old-line Communists. It seemed to me that the relationship must have been ambivalent, since the Panthers in their program and activity were far to the left of the American Communist party.

The particular Panther I was assigned to defend was Jerome West, a moody, withdrawn youth of nineteen. He was a little miffed that I had not visited him in the Rikers Island prison before the trial, but my overcrowded schedule would not permit it. But it wasn't long into the pretrial proceedings before he realized a close rapport with me. The two other assigned lawyers were Elliot Taikheff, a fine and somewhat flamboyant trial lawyer, and Paul Chevigny, sworn enemy of the cops, author of the widely hailed volume *Police Power*. Lawyers are not noted for working well together, but our collaboration was an exception. Where one of us was weak, the other was strong, and we had real affection for each other. Elliot represented Ricardo DeLeon, the oldest and most political of the accused, and Paul represented Alfred Cain.

The defendants were all Brooklyn residents who had joined a unit of the Panther party. The police had succeeded in insinuating an agent into this unit, named Wilbert Thomas. With the three accused he worked out a plan to obtain sawed-off shotguns and pistols and a car, and to drive from Brooklyn to Harlem to hold up a seedy Lenox Avenue hotel for the purpose of obtaining funds to replenish the treasury of the party. Just as the car in which they were riding was leaving the West Side Highway in New York City, at 125th Street, they were halted by a large company of heavily armed policemen. The charges against them were attempted murder, conspiracy to commit murder, conspiracy to commit robbery, attempted assault, attempted robbery, grand larceny, possession of a sawed-off shotgun, and possession of a canister of lachrymating gas.

The automobile had been purchased by the agent for the crime, and one of the guns was that of the agent.

The effort to pick the jury, in late April 1970, made us all revise our concepts of the state of mind of the average American. The government had waged a relentless campaign to exterminate the Panthers. Attorney General Mitchell in the spring of 1969 had likened them to mad dogs who must be eliminated. On the slightest pretexts, police all over the nation had raided Panther meetings with an eagerness to use their guns. In less than two years, twenty-eight Panthers had been murdered by the cops.

The Panthers were afflicted or blessed with foolhardy courage. Unceasingly, in public, they advised black people to get guns and defend themselves "by any means necessary." Recollecting readings of the Russian Revolution, I had always assumed that at a certain juncture it would be essential for the revolutionary forces to go underground. Some of the more nearly erudite Panthers paid lip service to this axiom, but their actions belied their words. It seemed almost as if they were prepared to commit suicide.

Then the "pigs" made a serious error. One early morning in Chicago they burst into the home of Fred Hampton, a twenty-year-old charismatic orator of the Panthers, and his friends. Hampton's body was riddled with bullets before he could rise from his bed. Other occupants of the house were wounded. The Panthers had the presence of mind to invite the press and TV media into the home where the police claimed a dreadful gun battle had taken place. From the condition of the walls, the doors, and the floors it was evident that the police had made an unprovoked and murderous assault. The left gave solid and vocal support to the Panthers in this situation. Even the NAACP and the Urban League in Chicago condemned the murder. A coroner's jury absolved the cops. This only confirmed in the minds of people of independent thought that all law-interpreting as well as law-enforcing agencies were engaged in a vendetta against the Black Panthers. In Hollywood, actors and actresses gave benefits for the Panthers. In the posh New York apartment of Leonard Bernstein, the conductor, the Panthers and their friends were entertained.

The extreme alienation of many of the young black generation from all white people had benefited the government. The Panthers, too, were emotionally anti-white, and anti-Semitic, but their spokespeople felt it necessary to maintain some kind of Marxist line, so they welcomed white allies—a development dooming the strategy of divide and rule. Even more than the blacks, the white left and the left-wing liberals knew that facism could come to America only if the races remained irrevocably split. Overtures on the part of these middle and upper-class whites, however, would not bridge the gap for the Establishment had working for it a whole corps of militant sounding Toms and provacateurs who constantly beat the drums of hatred for whitey. And in a period of recession, the bulk of organized labor remained hostile to the black workers as a way of preserving their jobs.

But the economic downturn had other effects, as well. The mail carriers were long known as the most docile group of American workers. A large proportion of them were blacks or of other minority groups. Next to the porters, they were considered the most faithful servants of the boss class. But inflation was making it more and more difficult for them to sustain their families on their meager wages. They struck, nationwide, in many instances against the will of their official union leaders. This event was an eyeopener to young black militants: evidently, these were sections of the working class with revolutionary potential. When Nixon called out units of the army to keep the communication system of the mail alive, black dissidents learned what true working-class power meant. And the mailmen began to reflect on the causes of inflation. Capitalism could no longer be taken for granted as the best of all possible ways of life; and on the picket lines, black and white workers began to fraternize. Possibly, their class interests superseded even racial bias.

For all these reasons, the selection of the jury in the Black Panther trial to which I had been assigned, marked a turning point for me in my appraisal of the average middle-class American. Fortunately, in New York procedure, the lawyers are permitted to select jurors for a trial. On either side of a case they can reject prospective jurors for "cause." That means if it is revealed by questioning that a person has a basic predilection for either side before evidence is presented, he or she is excused from service as a juror by the judge upon the motion of a lawyer. In addition, each side of the case in a felony prosecution has twenty peremptory challenges. This means that the lawyer may strike a juror from the jury box for no stated reason at all.

Throughout the country, the peremptory challenge is the primary means for keeping black people and other minority groups from sitting on trial juries. The district attorney does not want to admit to open prejudice, but he is convinced that black people will be less inclined to convict black defendants than will white people. That may be true today, but in years past it has not been true. The middle-class Negro called to jury service is very anxious to show that blacks can be as respectable as whites. So he or she leans over backward to be harsh in judgment of black people caught "out of line." They have far less willingness to see extenuating circumstances than the white middle-class juror, who may know why black people have less opportunity for gainful pursuits and are therefore more likely to commit crimes. At times he will show mercy to assuage his conscience.

In the Black Panther case, Assistant District Attorney Fine proceeded diligently to use his peremptory challenges to exclude every Negro chosen for the box. But he didn't anticipate the backlash from the whites. At the beginning of the second day of jury selection a tiny white woman in her twenties indicated that she wanted to speak to the judge out of hearing of the courtroom. The lawyers and the court stenographers huddled with her at the bench. Our judge was Harold Birns, former building commissioner of the city of New York and already known as the fairest supreme court criminal term trial judge in the city. The prospective juror, Mary Wills, her lips trembling, told the judge that from what she had seen in his court she would not vote for conviction of the accused Panthers even if they were proved guilty beyond a reasonable doubt. She further admitted that she had discussed her opinion with others in the box. The judge solemnly warned her that he could sentence her for contempt. She acknowledged that she knew this, but she firmly insisted that she would never convict the Panthers. She was excused from service.

Her action opened the floodgates. One after another, seven more jurors filed before the judge and told him they could not serve. One or two admitted to prejudice about the Panthers: one was a black man who said he had a conviction that the Panthers were being persecuted by the government, and therefore he could not fairly consider the evidence of the prosecution.

Day after day, therefore, this process was repeated. The debate about the

Black Panthers in both the black and white community had become so impassioned that it was almost impossible to find someone who did not have a fixed conviction. One middle-aged Negro woman whose air was of the utmost respectability troubled us. Our clients were adamant in insisting that we strike her from the box; but we didn't want to use our peremptory challenges in a way that was as bigoted as the prosecution's. Then I had an idea.

"Mrs. Harris, you live on St. Nicholas Terrace?" I asked.

"Yes, I do."

"How far uptown is that?"

"That is near 128th Street."

"That is in the heart of Harlem, isn't it Mrs. Harris?"

Her answer was yes, but she had gotten the signal. She went up before the judge and quietly asked him to excuse her because she felt her life might be in danger if she found any of these defendants guilty. The judge excused her from service. Finally, we obtained a jury of seven whites and five blacks. Our defense tactics were well coordinated. At every opportunity we would show the jury that the defendants were the dupes of the police through the agent in their midst. On the other hand, the prosecution would constantly point up the terrifying potentialities to the public peace of men and women committed to armed depredations on law-abiding citizens, black and white.

After seven weeks of trial the case was submitted to the jury. The jurors, after sustained deliberation, indicated to Judge Birns that they had arrived at a verdict of acquittal on the charges of attempted murder, conspiracy to murder, conspiracy to rob, and attempted assault; but they were deadlocked over the other charges. The judge refused our motions to have the defendants declared acquitted of the charges on which the jury had reached a verdict. He insisted that they had to reach a verdict on all charges before he would make any determination. This was clearly in violation of the law which requires that when a jury has reached a verdict on any count, that verdict must be accepted for that count.

Finally, two of the jurors became ill, and Judge Birns declared a mistrial. A new trial was ordered to begin in the summer.

Just as the second trial of our three Black Panthers began in August, a prison riot broke out in the Tombs. Most of the imprisoned men were, like our defendants, awaiting trial. Some, like the Harlem Six, had been expecting trial for two years; so that the presumption of innocence which is supposed to attach to accused persons in American society was revealed as a travesty.

The second trial of the three Panthers began haltingly before Judge James Leff. Judge Birns had just rendered an opinion rejecting our arguments that he should have acknowledged the verdicts of acquittal on major counts against Alfred Cain and Jerome West. He claimed that these verdicts were never fully consummated and Judge Leff refused to disturb these conclusions.

In spite of the turmoil about the occupation of the Tombs by rebellious prisoners, our selection of the jury once again revealed that white middle-class citizens in New York City could not be relied upon by the authorities to be biased against the Black Panthers—quite the contrary, was the experience of the trial lawyers. It took two-and-a-half weeks to pick this second jury, mainly because so many prospective jurors asserted that they believed the Panthers were the subject of governmental persecution. And most of the people with this opinion were white. Finally, we were able to pick a jury consisting of a white woman, four white men, three black women, and four black men. It was the first jury I had ever appeared before, of which the majority membership was black.

The press and radio sedulously avoided mentioning the trial. It was becoming apparent that the growing polarization of American society made this case unique. The Black Panther party had expelled our defendants from membership. It felt that any show of interest in the case might implicate the party in the alleged conspiracies. The rest of the left slavishly followed the Panther lead. None of the better known Left organs, such as the *Guardian,* printed any articles on the case. The underground press avoided it. It might have been assumed that the center would be pleased at the show of impartiality on the part of so many prospective middle-class jurors but it, too, kept silent. The right avoided the case as if it were a plague. The Negro press and reporters, afraid of being tarred with the Panther brush, also kept silent.

Judge James Leff ran an even-handed court without fanfare and without preening himself on his virtures. Occasionally, DeLeon or Cain would make a brief black-power outburst, but he ignored them. In the entire seven weeks of the trial the defendants were not reproved once by the judge. The corrections department underlings, however, resorted to all kinds of harassing byplay to provoke the defendants—without success. My client, Jerome West, was placed in solitary confinement at Riker's Island, for supposed "sassiness" to this guards. On occasion he was deprived of his underwear, so that he would have to appear in a solvenly manner before the jury. Sometimes it was necessary for his mother, who attended the trial faithfully, to send out for a shirt for him to wear.

Mrs. Melvina Cain, mother of defendant Alfred Cain, was also a daily spectator. She had acquired a considerable background in the Marxist analysis of society and was more of a conscious revolutionary than her son.

In the opening address to the jury I again stressed that the state had constructed a criminal scene through an astute *agent provocateur*. If the jury came to the conclusion in the following weeks that the sequence of events in which the defendants participated was a product of the Bureau of Special Services—the Red Squad of the New York Police Department—then it was duty bound to acquit the defendants of the conspiracy counts. It seemed to the defense lawyers that the additional possessory counts regarding a sawed-off shotgun, a rifle, and a so-called canister of a macelike substance would also fail, since they were adjuncts in the whole scheme.

The differences in defence technique pointed up the difference in background among the trial lawyers. Paul Chevigny exhaustively questioned the state's witnesses during cross-examination. He was able to bring out that the chief witness for the district attorney, Wilbert Thomas, the police informer, had altered his official reports to his superiors in one crucial particular. In his typewritten report of one day's activities, he had not mentioned Jerome West. In his handwritten report, from which the typewritten matter had been copied, he had inserted "Jerome West" above the line. The question immediately in the minds of the jurors was whether this insertion had been made between trials. We kept hammering away at the probability that Thomas had retained his handwritten notes between trials and thus could make the alteration in the record. But he had been unable to change the typewritten record, beause that was in the safe at the Bureau of Special Services.

Elliott Taikheff had been a scientist before he became a lawyer. His facility was in cross-examining the expert witnesses for the government on their technical competence and on the soundness of their conclusions. Both my colleagues were products of what I call the Warren School of criminal law. They were painstakingly determined in their use of all the new aids to the defense lawyer afforded by the Warren Court's concern for the rights of the individual. They were particularly adept in exploring the limits of disclosure of sources required of the government. Because the New York legislature had recently extended defence on the ground of entrapment, the frame-up could be made to boomerang against the prosecuter.

Six weeks after the trial had begun we were able to sum up to the jury. Throughout the trial I had been concerned with not antagonizing the jury by prolix procedures. My colleagues most emphatically did not share this concern. Paul's summation lasted two-and-and-a-half hours. Elliot outdid him by twenty minutes. Since my theory of the case caused me to concentrate on describing the trial as a scenario of the prosecution, it was possible for me to limit my summation to thirty-five minutes. As usual, it was an extemporaneous effort, but the court stenographer caught most of it.

At the outset I apologized to the jury:

> Mr. Fine at the beginning of this whole matter many weeks ago pointed out to you that above all you should not let sympathy interfere with your deliberations. However, it is appropriate that at this time I express my sympathy for the jury because in a sense you are a captive audience. You can't get up and walk out any time you want to. And all of you have been here for a very long time.
>
> You realize that it is your obligation. You act at this time as an organ of the government, and, perhaps, your role is the chief vindication for the type of government we live under. If there is any hope for the future, it lies in the calm consideration of people such as you, who recognize that you have the fate of people in your hands and your results reflect the level at which we have arrived. . . .
>
> All lawyers, by this time I'm sure you are aware, are examples of great egos. Otherwise you never become a lawyer, and, so, you wonder why in hell do we have to have three people summing up in the same case? The reason is, first, that each of us represents an individual defendant. . . . The second reason is that the human mind and imagination has infinite variety . . . on the same circumstances each individual has a specific point of view; not quite the same as anyone else . . . so my only justification for being before you and speaking is because my view of what took place . . . has a slightly different angle. . . .

After trying to win the friendly attention of the jury in this manner I repeated my theory of the case:

> I said to you in the very beginning, when I opened to the jury, I said that it is my understanding of this whole matter that it was a police trap. It was a setup. It was like a gigantic play, very dramatic circumstances to it, and it was all set up by the police.

Therefore, when I look at this thing, I see it as a matter that has certain facets which must fit into place. Now, Mr. Fine, in opening to the jury said—he warned you: "My children are growing up here." He is talking about the city of New York—"my children."

And what his implication is, of course, is that we want to make the streets safe for them. And so right away, right away, I have no hesitation about saying this, he is appealing to a prejudice. "Our children may not be safe because these people are not yet convicted of a crime."

I say that this whole trial became more and more instinct as it went along; as the district attorney pressed harder and harder, there was an appeal to class prejudice, the difference in the status of the people, the discription of the circumstances in which they live. The appeal to political prejudice, if you remember, the constant throwing out about, "Did you get the stuff from Communist China?" Does each individual member of the jury look under his bed at night to see whether a dirty communist with whiskers and all is lurking underneath there. . . .

Captain Kissane let the cat out of the bag. The Bureau of Special Services had the job of planning. Wilbert Thomas only worked for the Bureau of Special Services. He had his job to perform. He worked under a Sergeant Lowla. . . .

After exploring some of the evidence at the trial, I tackled the key proof of the so-called conspiracy, which was a tape recording of a conversation between DeLeon and Wilbert Thomas, received by Thomas on his home telephone:

. . . Finally, in order to convince you that they really had the goods on these young men, they played one tape recording of one conversation that took place between DeLeon and Wilbert Thomas over the telephone.

Now, we concede that that was the voice of DeLeon on this phone.

They want you to know or feel that this language here was really Aesopian language—it didn't mean what it actually says; that it was really a sort of code language . . . what they were really doing was planning this conspiracy to rob. . . .

Now, I submit to you, from what you learned already about the development of these defendants—I submit to you that this means what it says. The district attorney introduced it. It means what it says. . . . This comes from people who live on the level that Gray meant when he wrote "Elegy in a Country Churchyard"—the short and simple annals of the poor. They speak directly. They're not playing around. They're talking about what they really mean.

And I suggest to you that if you just read this straight, what DeLeon and Thomas were talking about was a date with some women. This boy expresses what satisfaction he had got in enjoying some woman's body. He doesn't talk in the romantic terms of the French troubadours, but he speaks to you in language—and you are the jury. The jury has to take some pretty rough stuff, so I'm going to have to read to you a little of the language, and I submit to you he meant what he said. He didn't mean something else. He meant what he said. . . .

"Yeah right! But I had to relate to some pussy, man, shit, Dan. Hey dig it! I couldn't relate to it too tough because I was just trying to get there." Then there was a little, hardly audible giggle.

"Mother fucking meeting was over. I had to put up with that jive."

He's talking about some women and how he is satisfied, or lack of satisfaction with what he experienced in a night with that woman.

And you keep on reading down the line here: "Yeah, well did you relate to that other big, fine bitch up there man. Hey, listen I'm gonna run. . . ."

. . . Obviously what he's talking about are their individual dates. He knew that he couldn't talk too openly about it. He talked openly enough for me. I understood it. But after all, Thomas did have a wife. So, maybe, it was a little shaded in that respect. But it seems to me that this is quite clear. They're talking about a date with some women.

Now, you remember Wilbert Thomas talking about that girl Vickie. Remember, Vickie—up there on 142nd Street? She was a junkie, and he was going to shake her down for some money; she liked him and he liked her. He admitted that on the stand. He got frightened for a few minutes up there, and he admitted it. You saw that smile on his face when he talked about Vickie. Vickie was one of these women. I don't know which one the other was. . . . "He did this relate to the bitch quick, you know." That means something to people who are living on that level.

I submit to you that . . . what this tape recording is, is the talking over between DeLeon and Thomas about two women that they were going to have some sexual relations with, and they were talking about the influence of the sexual relations before.

We don't need to be squeamish about this, because the liberty of these boys is at stake. I want you to take this and consider it on that level. Don't consider it on some other level.

I don't want to elevate these boys somewhere where they're not, and I don't want you to assume that if you are to have a reasonable doubt, and, therefore, must acquit, that they are lily pure. We're not saying that.

We're saying that what the district attorney had done is try to construct an elaborate plot to put three Panthers away; and Wilbert Thomas, his agent, was a little too eager to set the thing up. The trap exploded in his face becuause it was so obvious that he took the initiative at every point.

I believe that as difficult as the times that we live in are, and we cannot expect you to be oblivious to what is happening every day, nevertheless, by your consideration and understanding—I am not asking you for sympathy, but you are not to be deprived of your understanding—I am convinced that when you understand this matter, by your verdict you will indicate that our trust in you is vindicated.

After this summation the court was recessed until the next morning. Then, the district attorney summed up for three hours and the judge made a five-hour charge to the jury. The jury began its deliberations on Wednesday, September 23. None the lawyers was quite as happy with this jury as we had been with the first jury in the spring. With the first, we were certain of, at the least, a hung jury—we knew the hippies would not let us down. But the majority of this jury consisted of middle-class Negroes. They related to my idiom very well, but they also had on their minds the proper image of the Negro. They would not be as forgiving of delinquency on the part of angry black men as would liberal or radical whites. We had concluded during the long trial that three white jurors were in our corner. By Friday afternoon the tension was beginning to get to me.

Since my office was only a five-minute run from the court, I had taken the chance of returning there to try to clear up some work while waiting for the jury. About two o'clock in the afternoon I received a phone call that the jury was about to come in. I ran over to the court, only to find that the doors were locked. The judge had maintained very tight security throughout the trial, fearing violence from any source. It was quite annoying to me, however, to be barred from entering the courtroom even though the judge had sent for me.

At this juncture a young white man, to whom I had spoken briefly during the morning, attempted to quiet me by saying that we'd all be let in shortly. In uncontrolled irritation I threw a right-hand blow at him which glanced off his shoulder. It was the first time I had struck a man in anger in more than forty years. He understood and backed away, but I was embarrassed. The court opened about five minutes later and I told the judge that he should have told the attendants to keep the door open for me. In any event, the jurors were simply anxious to receive answers to certain questions on conspiracy and were not yet ready with a verdict.

On Saturday afternoon my wife and I went to visit the Reneks in Pound Ridge, in Westchester County. Playing tennis with Ethel and her friend relaxed me and I almost forgot about the case. Just as we finished dinner, however, the phone rang. Judge Leff was calling to say that the jury expected to reach a verdict that night. This surprised me, because I had figured that the jury would spend the weekend at the expense of the government, eating fine meals and enjoying their luxury accommodations. I had only a tennis shirt and shorts and had brought no change in clothing. I talked to Paul Chevigny on the phone he promised to find a friend my size in New York City who would lend me a suit of clothes. After a ninety-minute drive into the city I found Paul with a gray suit, which fitted me reasonably well. He had also had the prescience to bring a tie.

We walked into court and met our clients for the first time in four days. About 9:30 at night the jury came in. Under the guidance of Court Clerk O'Brien it began to announce its verdicts. All the defendants were acquitted on the main charge of conspiracy to commit armed robbery. Of the original counts, those of attempted murder, assault in the first and second degree, and conspiracy to commit murder had been dismissed by the judge before the case was given to the jury. Alfred Cain was convicted of possession of a sawed-off shotgun, defacement of a weapon, and possession of the macelike canister. Ricardo DeLeon was convicted of possession of the sawed-off shotgun and possession of the canister. My client, Jerome West, was convicted of possession of the sawed-off shotgun alone. Under the circumstances, we could not be too disappointed. Of course, we all felt that possession of weapons without illegal intent to use them was not a crime: when the jury found that the men were not conspiring illegally, then we believed such finding eliminated criminal intent.

The judge did not pronounce sentence until October 22. He announced that the probation report on Alfred Cain was incomplete, so he adjourned sentence on him for a later date. He gave Ricardo DeLeon the maximum sentence, not less than seven years in the penitentiary. He gave Jerome West up to three years imprisonment. I was disappointed. In my plea for clemency I had asked that the judge sentence Jerome to the time he had already served in prison, fourteen months. Later I learned that, that very morning in the same building, a white man, who had been found guilty of possession without a license of a loaded pistol, had been sentenced to pay a fine of $250—period. In Marin County, California, during the shoot out with the Panthers in the early fall of 1970, a judge had been murdered. After that, aside even from the usual bias against black men, judges had now begun to carry a fear of Panthers that was quite irrational.

CHAPTER 19

The ZANU Guerrillas

It seemed that now a year never went by that failed to produce a case that was controversial and intriguing. There was one, however, of particular interest because of the political affiliation of the defendants: the two men were representatives of the Zimbabwe African National Union (ZANU), an organization of guerrillas fighting to overthrow the white apartheid regime of Rhodesia.

One of the men was Tapson Mawere, who for years had been ZANU's official spokesman—with observer status—at the United Nations. The other man was Synos Mangazva, also a member of ZANU and a professor at one of the colleges of the City University of New York. They were on a Trailways bus from New York City to Norfolk, Virginia, on June 7, 1975, when the bus broke down in the small southern Delaware town of Harrington. The two Africans, both big and husky, followed other passengers into a nearby restaurant. They could have had no idea that they would soon be embroiled in a trial that would receive international coverage and earn the attention of then–Secretary of State Henry Kissinger.

Dr. Emma C. Durazzo, president of the Wilmington, Delaware, NAACP, described in the *Delaware Spectator* what happened after Mawere and Mangazva walked into the Harrington restaurant:

> Mawere ordered a cup of coffee and was served. But Mangazva asked for a menu to order some food. He was not served. . . . To the surprise of the two men, in a few moments a man appeared who was later discovered to be a plainclothes policeman. He tried to seize Mangazva, apparently to put him under arrest, but made no explanation. Mangazva refused to go with the plainclothesman, and Mawere joined the protest. . . . In a few moments another plainclothes policeman and four uniformed police of the Harrington force arrived. A scuffle began as the police attempted to drag Mangazva out of the restaurant into an unmarked car. During this scuffle, Mangazva was

221

thrown through the glass door of the restaurant, cutting his shoulder severely. Mawere, in trying to stop the beating and the kicking of his friend, was also being treated roughly. There was never any explanation as to why Mangazva was the focal point of the action.

As the police were dragging Mangazva into the car, Mawere tried to stop them. The end result was that both were pushed into the car and taken to the local police station.

Mawere and Mangazva spent the night in Smyrna prison. Mawere was charged with disorderly conduct and obstructing the police, and Mangazva with assault, resisting arrest, intoxication, and disorderly conduct.

The case was first referred to me by my long-time friend, George Houser, executive secretary of the American Committee on Africa. I was extremely pressed at the time, so I contacted Louis Redding, a prominent black civil-rights lawyer in Wilmington, and asked him to represent the Africans.

Louis Redding advised the two men to plead guilty with the probability that he could obtain suspended sentences. Mawere and Mangazva were indignant at this proposal and wondered aloud whether I had consented to it. It seemed to them that they were victims of a racist or a political frame-up and had fought such frame-ups in Southern Africa. Why, they wondered, should they do less in America?

I hurried to Dover, where the case was to be tried, and succeeded in winning a postponement of the trial. At the same time, Judge Merrill C. Trader of the court of common pleas made it clear that I would not be permitted to try the case without a Delaware associate. In this situation the DuPont law firm of Richard, Layton and Finger of Wilmington allowed their young black associate, James H. Gilliam, Jr., to come to our aid. He agreed to work with me throughout the trial, and I never enjoyed a more harmonious and cooperative legal association. Despite Gilliam's attachment to the giant DuPont interests, he had gained the confidence of most black activists in Delaware.

Gilliam introduced me to Wilbert Cooper, president of the Dover chapter of the NAACP. Cooper invited me to speak to his group.

Houser's group and some other interested Americans concerned about the international image of the country alerted the U.S. State Department about the upcoming trial. The deputy assistant secretary for African affairs, Charles A. Hames, wrote Governor Sherman Tribbett of Delaware that his department was concerned about "isolated incidents" that distort the image of America and do not serve American interests.

Of course, what Hames at the State Department was anticipating were demonstrations in other countries for the two accused ZANU representatives—demonstrations that did indeed take place. But the Delaware governor, involved in lesser affairs, saw matters differently. He was affronted by the State Department's "interference" in the case and said, "I have no reason whatsoever to believe that any person anywhere in the world is not going to receive a fair hearing under our judicial system."

When Judge Trader heard that I intended to speak to the Dover NAACP, he sent me a comprehensive gag order on July 22, 1975, which read, in part: "During the time that the above captioned criminal actions are pending before this court, no lawyer associated with the prosecution or defense shall give or authorize any extrajudicial statement or interview relating to the trial, or the parties or the issues in the trial for dissemination by any means of public communication."

I replied on July 25: "I know your directive on pretrial statements is not intended to inhibit the constitutional rights of anyone involved in this matter."

I gave a lengthy report on the case to the Dover NAACP on July 29, and radio stations in Delaware carried the gist of my remarks that same evening. Judge Trader sent me a letter on August 1:

> It has been noted that the Delaware Code of Professional Responsibility prohibits counsel from making extrajudicial statements relating to the guilt or innocence of the accused. It has been brought to my attention that it was reported in the Tuesday, July 29, 1975, edition of the *Delaware State News* that Mr. Lynn discussed the merits of the cases before the court at a meeting of the Central Delaware Branch of the N.A.A.C.P. It was further reported . . . that at the same meeting Mr. Lynn indicated that he would not follow the directive of the court relating to extrajudicial statements. I am requesting that Mr. Lynn advise me if the report of his remarks in the *Delaware State News* was accurate, and also whether he made any statements on the cases before the court relating to the merits of the case or expressed an opinion on the guilt or innocence of the accused and further whether he indicated he would not follow the court's directive concerning extrajudicial statements. I would expect to receive Mr. Lynn's reply on or before Friday, August 8, 1975.

I sent the judge my reply on August 4:

As I said before the Kent County branch of the National Association for the Advancement of Colored People on the night before the hearing on the motions in this case, poor people can never secure a fair trial in a civil-rights matter if they are barred from bringing to the attention of the public their plight prior to trial. There are a number of cogent reasons why they must have this right as an integral part of due process:

1. A poor person needs to have funds raised for his defense. The defendants, Mawere and Mangazva, as representatives of ZANU, the independence movement of the black people of Southern Rhodesia, are in very straitened circumstances and would be unable to afford an adequate defense without an appeal to the public. An adequate defense is necessary because their first counsel in Delaware suggested that they plead guilty to public intoxication.

2. In a democracy the court performs an educational role for the people. The information I have is that the Civil Rights Act granting full citizenship to Negroes is disregarded in southern Delaware where this incident occurred. Even more important then my role as counsel is my obligation to help teach black people in benighted sections of this country that they are entitled to the respect and dignity accorded to human beings.

I also mentioned to Judge Trader that the U.S. Supreme Court in *Sheppard* v. *Maxwell* had said, after pointing out that it was concerned about the great amount of publicity in the case. "The principle that justice cannot survive behind walls of silence has long been reflected in the Anglo-American distrust for secret trials."

My reply was concluded by expressing "surprise" that his letter to me had been a carbon copy and that the original had gone to the deputy attorney general.

On August 5, 1975, I appeared on Delaware's only TV station and was interviewed by a courageous young black woman named Marilyn Darling. She had done her research and reminded me of that confrontation with white youths outside Wilmington in the 1940s on our march to Washington. I remembered that lowly road worker who came to our aid, and remembering almost overwhelmed me.

The *New York Times* and *Washington Post* were covering the case. The defendants were not two isolated men facing Southern justice, but representatives of a group with international standing. Mawere was on personal terms with numerous African leaders, including the presidents of several countries. The implications of the case were enormous, and the cause of Mawere and Mangazva was just: the overthrow of the racist Rhodesian government headed by white supremacist Ian Smith. Why, then, were the two ZANU men being tried? Had Mangazva really been drunk and disorderly in a southern Delaware town? Was Mawere really disorderly? Or, as their supporters suspected, had they unknowingly walked into a whites-only restaurant and been beaten because of it.

Henry Kissinger held a press conference in early August, during which the situation was brought up:

Q. Mr. Secretary, did the somewhat unprecedented intervention of your African desk with the governor of Delaware on behalf of two members of ZANU—an African terrorist group without U.N. credentials—did this have anything to do with the widely reported resignation of Ambassador Nathaniel Davis?

A. No, because I don't even know what you're talking about.

Q. It's been reported on page one of the *Star* and *Post,* Mr. Secretary.

A. Well . . .

Q. You don't read those papers, or . . .

A. I don't want to offend the press, but I regret to say that I am not familiar with this particular incident; but I will be within fifteen minutes of leaving here.

A black Wilmington city councilman introduced a motion to have the case dropped by the attorney general of Delaware. The motion was defeated.

It was perhaps the biggest case of civil-rights nature that tiny Delaware had ever witnessed, but the state was not about to back down. Much of the world seemed to have passed Delaware by. Until recently, the whipping post had been used in Delaware, and gift shops were still selling a postcard for a dime that depicted a black man being flogged. In the 1950s Delaware had indicted a woman for witchcraft!

When I arrived in Dover on September 2 to try the case, I was greeted by a loud and determined picket line in front of the courthouse. Each person in the line bore a placard calling for an end to the prosecution of the two African leaders and demanding an end to Delaware's "racist justice."

Judge Trader called me to the bench and asked if I had anything to do with assembling the pickets. I assured him that their appearance was as much a surprise to me as it was to him. He suggested that I tell them to disperse so as not to disturb the even-handed progress of the trial. This I declined to do, and Judge Trader made no further mention of the matter. Occasionally, as the days went by and the chants of the pickets became clearly audible in the courtroom, a deputy sheriff would try to persuade the pickets to soften their demonstration.

The jury was selected on the first day. Judge Trader was the only person allowed to question the jury, and after its selection (four men, eight women, two of the women black) we went straight into the trial. The courtroom was packed, mostly with supporters of the ZANU defendants, but there were plenty of newspeople on hand too.

Prosecutor Abraham began by portraying the defendants as oversized drunken Africans who did not understand the civilized ways of Delaware. He insisted that the police had tried to guide them courteously to a proper attitude in the restaurant but had been rebuffed and attacked in belligerent fashion.

I responded with my opening remarks in a subdued fashion, asking the jury to determine for themselves who was telling the truth. This seemed to surprise some of the jurors, who undoubtedly had read some of the reports in the press that had described me as a militant hard nose.

Prosecutor Abraham began what seemed an endless parade of witnesses. Two demure waitresses testified that they were frightened by the brusque orders of the two big black men whose language they could barely understand. Police and restaurant patrons followed to relate a story of such unrestrained belligerence on the part of the accused that only the application of minimum force prevented lasting physical and human damage to the community. About twenty witnesses were called. One of them, a policeman, tesified that Synos Mangazva, a university professor, had told him, "Me no understand."

The testimony of that cop spoke worlds to the ZANU supporters. Had Synos Mangazva, with his measured, clipped, perfect English, really said, "Me no understand"? Or had the cop imagined that all black people spoke that way?

The result of the trial really hinged on who the jury would believe. Would they believe the twenty assorted witnesses called by the prosecution, or would they accept the word of the defendants? The testimony of the local residents and cops was totally different from that given by the defendants.

The ZANU men tesified in their own behalf. They told, in calm, faultless English, how they had been assaulted in the restaurant. They said that uniformed police had thrown Mangazva through the glass door. This was a crucial discrepancy in the testimony presented by the two sides. The prosecution insisted that only one uniformed policeman had been present when the men had been ejected from the restaurant.

We had no other eyewitnesses. Any blacks who might have been on that Trailways bus either had not witnessed the incident or were too intimidated to testify.

But we did have three character witnesses. William Johnston, a white, president of the Episcopal Churchmen for South Africa, took the stand to say that the defendants were of the highest moral character; as did Davis M'Gabe, a professor at City University and fellow countryman of the defendants. M'Gabe testified in similar glowing terms of the excellent reputations of the defendants. Third was Acting New York Supreme Court Judge William Booth, whose qualifications as a jurist had to impress Judge Trader. Booth vouched for the integrity and unstinting reputations for honesty of the ZANU defendants.

Then Judge Booth did something that was rare, perhaps unique. He left the witness stand and joined the picket line outside the courthouse!

Now the prosecution, in rebuttal, sprang its ace witness: James Watson, the first black the prosecution had called. Watson was a bus driver for Trailways, and he said he had witnessed much of what had taken place. He also said he had seen *three* uniformed cops *inside* the restaurant as Mangazva was being thrown through the door. None of the prosecution's witnesses had said any such thing.

This was the prosecution's witness, and he was saying what we had been contending all along! At a signal from the prosecutor the judge declared a recess. The prosecutor went into the hall and I heard him tell Watson, the bus driver, to change his story.

Back in the court I told Judge Trader what I had overheard. The prosecutor did not dispute me. "Your Honor," I said, "if you permit the deputy attorney general to put this witness on the stand again, I will have to request an investigation."

I think the judge knew I was referring to him. Whatever the case, Watson was not permitted to take the stand again.

Judge Trader's charge to the jury was careful and unemotional, and while he was giving it I decided on my summation. The jurors, it seemed to me, had a Deep South psychology, that is, they were deeply religious. In asking them to believe the black defendants, I appealed to their consciences. I asked them to search their hearts for a decision they knew to be right, and I finished by quoting the great poem of the abolitionist poet James Russell Lowell, on the execution of John Brown:

> Truth's forever on the Scaffold
> Wrong's forever on the Throne
> Yet that Scaffold sways the future . . .

I stopped there because they knew the rest. They deliberated the rest of the afternoon and all evening. The ZANU supporters thought we had clinched the case with the testimony of the bus driver Watson, but I knew it was not that simple. Many of the jurors in a small town like Dover would have great difficulty believing that the state would prosecute people who were not guilty. The jury might believe that perhaps they really were guilty, and only a clever defense had beclouded the issue.

When the jury came in, it was to find Mawere innocent of all charges; they were still debating about Mangazva.

The jury deliberations dragged endlessly into the next day. A reporter for the *Delaware State News* researched Delaware history and discovered that the jury had set a state record for the length of the deliberations.

The crowd that had stayed throughout the trial continued to mill outside the courtroom. I was particularly moved by an elderly black couple who had attended every day of the trial and now were determined to see it all through to the finish. The woman said to a reporter, "I was so proud of the young people who demonstrated every day for the Africans. When I was young there were only trials of black people when no one dared to stand up."

The jury finally came in. They had obviously compromised. Magazva was acquitted of public intoxications, assault and disorderly conduct but found guilty of resisting arrest and offensive touching (this latter charge in Delaware can include grabbing a policeman's arm when he is about to hit you).

I was later told that the jury had compromised merely to be allowed to go home. They acquitted Mangazva of public intoxication and those who originally voted for acquittal figured the other charges would be thrown out on appeal.

But there was no appeal. Mawere and Mangazva believed that Mangazva should appeal, but it would have been an enormously costly project, and no one's mind would have been changed.

Mangazva in my opinion was innocent, and Judge Trader gave him a suspended sentence. He later took over the duties of Mawere in the United Nations.

Tapson Mawere returned to Africa to pursue ZANU's undeniably just program of overthrowing fascism and racism in Rhodesia. It would seem, as I write this, that Tapson is very close to his dream of an independent Zimbabwe.

Epilogue

Many victories have been won; imperialism has its back against the wall; but premature optimism is not warranted. In the major industrial nations of the so-called free world, the domination of finance and monetary manipulation are the major "peaceful" tools for continued control. The International Monetary Fund is a major weapon used by the American Government in causing its comprador agents in the under developed countries to enforce grinding misery on their underlying masses. However, as I write this the children of Sandino, my first hero, are showing that it is too late to expect vast deprived populations to endure their suffering any longer.

The last years of the century may be very bloody, but Leon Trotsky was too pessimistic in writing at the outset of the Second World War "if the world proletariat proves itself in fact incapable of fulfulling the mission conferred upon it by the course of historical development, nothing else remains than to recognize frankly that the Socialist program, founded on the internal contradictions of Capitalist society, has ended as a Utopia."

The forces fighting for a humane future have proved themselves in the past capable of incredible sacrifices in order to defeat the forces of darkness. The struggle of our brothers and sisters in the neo-colonial regions of Africa, Asia, Central and South America will at long last re-arouse the spirit of the working people in the so-called advanced countries. As their own conditions worsen in this last stage of the traditional order, the majorities in the more established countries will have to make a choice between fascism and a social revolution.

Perhaps, it will still be possible in the cases I continue to handle to encourage in a small way the building of a base for a real civilization.

Index

A

Aberle, Kathleen 180
Abraham, Prosecutor 226
Abyssinian Baptist Church 63
Acion Fecundo 4
Aiken, Professor 43
Alexander, Kelly 143
Allen, James 50
Allen, Joseph 82
Allport, Gordon 43
Almeida, Juan 169
Amalgamated Clothing Workers 77
America First Committee 71, 84
Amer. Assoc. of University Professors 79
American Civil Liberties Union 117, 179
Amer. Com. For Puerto Rican Independence 126, 128
American Committee on Africa 222
American Friends Service Com. 109
American League Against War & Fascism 67
American Socialists 119
Anarchists 66, 68, 77
Anti-Semitism 74, 115, 210
Armstrong, Louis 35
Aspinall, Alberta 53
Atlanta, Ga. 50
Augusta, Ga. xii, 34
Axis 70, 76

B

Backer Judge Frederick 16, 17, 19, 21, 22
Bailey, Major 98–101
Baker, Ella 66, 120
Baker, Wallace 5, 6, 14, 17, 19, 29, 33
Baldwin, Roger 126, 128
Bao Dai 198
Barnes, Robert 7, 17, 18, 23, 24, 25, 26, 30, 31
Bates, Daisy 161
Bay of Pigs 170

Bazelon, David 108
Beard, Charles A. xiii, 71
Bellevue Hospital 11, 12
Belzoni 119
Bernstein, Leonard 210
Besse, Prof. 197, 200
Best, Ruth 169, 170
Bilbo, Senator 188
Birns, Judge Harold 211–213
Birnstingl, Dr. Martin 200
"Black Bolshevik" 67
Black, Joe 101
Black Muslims 168, 185, 187
Black Panthers 208–220
Blum, Leon 67
Boggs, Grace 185
Boggs, Jim 185, 186
Bolsheviks xiii, 43, 47
Booker, James 169
Booth, Judge William 227
Boudin, Leonard 122, 176
Braden, Carl & Ann 118–120
Brennan, Jack xiv
Bromley, Ernest 119
Brotherhood of Sleeping Car Porters 87
Broun, Heywood 62
Brown, John 228
Brownell, Herbert 116
Buber, Martin 197
BunCamper, Pierre 47
Burchett, Vessa 199
Burchett, Wilfred 198, 199
Burnham, James 79
Byers, Judge Mortimer, 94, 95, 126, 128

C

C.O.R.E. 108, 162
Cain, Alfred 208, 213, 214
Cain, Melvina 214

Campbell, Judge Marcus 96
Campos, Pedro Albizu 70, 123–140, 167, 175
Cancio, Hiram 138
Capone, Al 38
Carolina Israelite 151
Carter, Joe 78
Castro, Fidel 168, 175
Castro, Pauline 129
Catholic hierarchy 68
Catholic Workers 86
Center, Anna 55–57, 75
Chamberlain, Prime Min. 78
"Charlotte Observer" 150
Chevigny, Paul 208–219
Ciano, 65
Civil Liberties Union 93
Clark, Charles 161
Clark, Gen. Mark 105
Clarke, John Henrik 162, 171
Clarkson, Judge John 150
Clausen, Bernard 44
Clinton Prison 30
Coffin, Wm. Sloane 162
Cohalan, Judge Dennis 116
Collazo, Oscar 127, 128
Colored Merchants Assoc. 61
"Columbia Spectator" 62
Com. of Industrial Organizations 66, 77
Communist Party xiii, 44, 51, 53, 58, 60–71, 75, 112, 121, 208
Condon, Gene Ann 9, 12, 31, 178
Connor, Bull 183, 189
Cooper, Wilbert 222
Coordinating Com. for Southern Relief 162
Cordero, Andres Figueroa 125
Cordero, Attorney Gen'l 129
Cowan, Paul 182
Craig, Phoenicia 10
Craig, William 7, 11, 15, 17–20, 24, 33
Cross, Lonnie 162
Crosswaith, Frank 63
Crouch, Mary
Cruz, Angel 133
Culkin, Judge Gerald 14–16
Current, Gloster 155

D

Dana, Charles 53
Darling, Marilyn 224
Darrow, Clarence 45, 93

Davis, Nathaniel 225
Davis, Ossie 164, 171
Davis, William C. 115
Day, Dorothy 86
Dearlove, J. W. 42
"Decline of the West" 43
"Delaware Spectator" 221
"Delaware State News" 223, 228
DeLuca, Edward 3, 5
DeLeon, Ricardo 208–220
Delgado, Gerardo 137
DeMeneses, Laura 124, 137
Democratic Party 8, 48, 63, 69
Dickerson, Jim 168
Diego, Jose de 126
Dingle, Alan 54
Divine, Father 49, 90
Douglas, Fred 46, 63, 82, 83
Douglass, Frederick 148
Dunbar Community Center 40, 45
Dunbar National Bank 53, 73
Durazzo, Dr. Emma C. 221
Dutt, R. Palme, xiii, 65, 71
Dworsky, David 42, 50

E

ECLC 117, 122, 173, 176, 180
Eastland, Sen. James 177
Egginton, Joyce 148, 155
Eisenhower, Dwight 156
Elaine, Ark. Nassacre 47
"Elegy In a Country Churchyard" 217
End the Draft Com. 190, 196
Engels, Friedrich 67, 68
Epifanovich, Pyotr 62, 63
Episcopal Church. For S. Africa 227
Establishment xiv
Ettinger, Al 115
Europe, Jim 35
Eversley, Miriam 171

F

FBI 118, 173
Fair Play for Cuba Com. 168
Farmer, Fyke 193
Farmer, James 170
"Fascism & Social Revolution" xiii, 65
Felder, Ronald 7, 17, 33
Fellowship of Reconciliation 108–109

Fetchit, Stepin 41
Fifth Amendment 179, 180
'Final solution' 206
Fischer, Dr. 200
Flores, Irving 135
Flynn, Elizabeth Gurley 117
Ford, James 60
Foreman, Clark 171
Foreman, James 165
Fort Dix, 106
Fortunato, William 115
Fosburgh, Lacey 30
Foster, William Z. 44
Foy, Hope 89
Freedom Now Party 183, 184, 187
Fuentes, Burgos 127
Fuller, Jimmy 105

G

Gabrielle, Mrs. 171
Galperin, Leroy 115
Garretson, Mary Louise 113
Garry, Charles 208
Garvey, Marcus 50, 61, 186
Geismar, Anne 180
Geismar, Elizabeth 180
Geismar, Maxwell 180
Gellers, Don 137, 178
Ghandi, Mahatma 86
Gillette, Guy 194, 195
Gilliam, James H., Jr. 222
Glazer, Nathan 108
Goering, Herman 84
Golden, Harry 151
Goodman, Paul 108
Grant, Henry 76
Gray, Thomas 217
Greene, Felix 200, 201, 205, 207
Griffin, Junius 7
Griffin, Martha 146,
Griswold, Deirdre 196, 197
Grove Press 196
"Guardian" 213
Guderian 84

H

HUAC 179
Hall, Frances 86
Hall, Margaret 47
Hall, Pearl 86

Hall, Prof. 38
Hawes, Charles A. 222, 223
Hamm, Daniel 7, 12, 13, 14, 16, 17, 31–33
Hampton, Fred 177
Hanoi xiv, 72
Hansberry, Lorraine 171
Harlem Hospital 6, 7
Harlem Lawyers Assoc. 15
Harris, Herbert 58
Harrison, Mrs. 37, 39, 40, 42
"Harvard Crimson" 182
Hatten, Capt. 101, 102
Hayes, Arthur Garfield 93–96
Haywood, Harry 67
Headley, Byron 61
Hegel xii, xiii, 42, 80
Helfand, Judge Julius 11
Herndon, Angelo 50, 69
Hewlett, Freddie 97
Hicks, Cal 163, 171
Hilferding, Rudolph 71
Himstead, Ralph 37, 38, 42, 46, 52, 7
Hitler, 65, 68, 71, 77, 85, 192
Ho Chi Minh, a00, 204
Hobbes, Thomas 80
Hodges, Gov. Luther 151, 156
Hogan, Frank 23, 30
Holliday sisters 171
Holmes, John H. 125
Holmes, Oliver W. 48
Hooley, Thomas 74
Hoover, Herbert 45, 58
Hopkins, Harry 85
Houser, George 108–111, 222
Howard University 71
Huberman, Leo 180
Hughes, Charles E. 35
Hunter, Prof. Rob't 125
Huntzinger, Col. 99

I

ILGWU 77
Ickes, Harold 65
Independent Negro Com. 180
International Brigade 67, 68, 71
International Control Com. 198
Irving, Nellie 34

J

Jack, Homer 109
Jackson, Juanita 90

Index

Jamaica Forum 61
"Jamaica Gleaner" 84
James, C.L.R. xiii, 80, 81
Jerome, Freddie 180
Jerome, V. J. 180
Jim Crow 110, 119
Johnson, DeVera 87
Johnson, James 53, 54, 57, 73
Johnson, Judge Clarence 150, 152
Johnson, Lyndon 189, 192, 206
Johnston, William 227
Jones, Charles 112, 120
Jones Act 70

K

Kant, Immanuel 42
Kaufman, Mary 9, 12
Kempton, Murray 108
Kennedy, Pres. John 166, 183
King, Martin L. 163, 164, 183, 184
Kingsley, J. D. 42
Kipling, Rudyard xii
Kissing Case 193
Kissinger, Henry 221, 225
Kleiman, Gussie 16, 17, 19
Knickerbocker, Wm. 115
Kochiyama, Mary 188
Krushchev, Nikita 168
Ku Klux Klan 47, 118, 142, 145
Kunstler, Wm. 9, 12, 14, 15, 22, 24, 25, 27, 28, 33, 193
Kuntz, Eddie 60
Ky, Ngyen Van 192

L

LaGuardia, Fiorello 69
Lamont, Barbara 27, 29
Landon, Alf 69
Lawrence, Charles & Margaret 87
Laval, Pierre 78
League of Nations 38, 45
Lebron, Lolita 134
Leff, Judge James 213, 219
Lehman, Myra 36
Lehner, Robert 19–21, 23–25, 28, 29
LeMay, Curtis 205
Lester, Julius 200, 201, 206
Levine, Prof. 49, 52
Lewis, John 183

Liggio, Leonard 196
Lincoln, Abraham 17
Lipscomb 74
Little Fruit Stand Riot 7, 13, 16, 21, 29
Locke, John 80
'London Observer' 148, 149, 155
Long Island Com for Bro. 172
Lorge, Irving 62
Lowell, James R. 228
Luftwaffe 78
Lumbard, Prosecutor 136
Lusky, Louis 120
Lynn, Alexander 135, 177, 139, 167
Lynn, Arnold 41
Lynn, Charlotte 71
Lynn Com. vs. Segregation 100, 103, 105, 108
Lynn, Dorothy 49, 61, 71, 116
Lynn, Gabrielle 167
Lynn, Joseph xii
Lynn, Samuel 71, 99, 100, 114
Lynn, Sophia 41, 49, 54
Lynn, Suzanne Marie 113, 167
Lynn, Winfred 34, 41, 36, 46, 49, 50, 52, 60, 61, 71, 92, 96, 99, 100, 104, 119
Lynn, Yolanda 1a, 135, 167, 176, 199

M

MacArthur, Arthur 58
MacDonald, Dwight 79, 108
Machado 69
Madame X 121
Maddox, Lester 189
Madison Barracks 98
Malcolm X 185, 187
Mallett, Gwen 186
Mallory, Mae 163
Malverne High School 36
Mangazva, Synos 221
Manifest Destiny xii
Marcus, Bernice, 141, 142, 144
Marcus, Sissy 141, 145
Marin, Luis Munoz 130, 134, 139
Marshall, Thurgood 93, 194
Martinia, J. A. 22–25, 28, 29
Marx, Karl xii, 42, 59, 67, 80
Matthews, Christine 40
Mayfield, Julian 162, 163
Mawere, Tapson 221–229
McCarthy, Joe 117, 131
McCarthyism 116

McCall, Sheriff 119
McKinney, Father 60, 61
McLaurin, Ben 87
McLean, Leroy 61
McNatt, Isaac 103
Meany, George 87
'Mein Kampf' 77
Merleau-Ponty, Maurice 79
M'Gabe, Davis 227
Mielke, Thelma 130
Miles, Gen. Nelson 70
'Militant' 188
Miranda, Rafael C. 135
Mistral, Gabriela 125
Mitchell, Att'y Gen'l 209
Mitchell, David 189–194
Mobley, Ora 163, 164, 171
Mohammed, Elijah 188, 189
Moore v. Dempsey 47
Moreno, Yolanda 128, 129, 131
Morgan, Irene 108
Morton, Nelle 112
Moynihan, Daniel 190, 191
Murphy, Commissioner 7
Murray, J. P. 180
Murray, Pauli 66
Mussolini, 65, 67, 68
Muste, A. J. 126, 128

N

NAACP 7, 8, 61, 93,104, 119, 121, 142–166, 209, 222
Nagasaki 105
Napoleon 84, 85
Nasser, Gamul Abdul 168
Nation of Islam 187
'Nation' the, 144, 145
National Lawyers Guild 208
National Negro Congress 69
Nationalists, Puerto Rican 124–140
Negro Renaissance 40, 50
Nelson, Truman 3, 8, 11, 30, 148, 180
Nelson, Wallace 109, 110
Nehru, Jawaharlal 133
Neuburger, Samuel 9, 12
'New International' 79–81
Newton, Isaac 80
Newton, Huey 208
'New Yorker' 182
New York City Bar 73

N. Y. Council to Abolish HUAC 180
New York County Lawyers Assoc. 179
New York Daily News 105
New York Post 62, 145
New York Times 115, 116, 148, 182, 184, 224
New York World 62
Nicaragua 42
Nicholson, Liston 61
Nickerson, Wayne 88, 89
Nietschze, Friedrich 80
Nixon, Richard xiv 210
Noble, Larry 36
Northport V.A. Hospital 101
Nuremberg Judgment 191
Nutter, Vernetta 49

O

Oglethorpe, Chauncey 146, 147
Olivares, Carlos 177
Oppenheimer, Robert 115
Organization of Afro-American Unity 188
Orwell, George xiv
'Othello' 103
Oxford Peace Oath 46

P

POUM 68
Pacifism 46
Page, Tom 67
Paine, Herbert 4
Palisades Amusement Park 114
Paris Commune 67
Parker, Theodore
Peacock, Inspect John 43
Peck, Jim 109
Perez-Marchand, Rafael 125
Perry, Albert 142
Phillips, Gene 53, 54, 82, 108
Phillips, Wendell 148
'Phoenix' 205
Piper, Professor 43
'Pittsburgh Courier' 105
Poitier, Sidney 101
Police power 208
Ponce Massacre 70, 125
Popular Front 65, 69, 71, 73, 77
Populism 120
Poston, Ted 145
Powell, Adam 46, 63, 64, 77, 82, 83, 107, 177, 188, 206

Index

Price, J. Hampton 144–160
Progressive Labor Party 8
Prohibitionists 77
'Projector', the 60
'Puerto Rico: Commonwealth, State of Nation' 124

Q

Quakers 90, 205, 206

R

Radio Free Dixie 179
Randle, Worth 109
Randolph, A. Philip 63, 86, 87
Rapp-Couder Committee 81
Remond, Charles L. 148
Reneks, 219
Republicans xii, xiii, 35, 48
Reunification Hotel 205, 206
Reuther, Walter 183
Reynolds, Ruth 86, 90, 127–140
Rhine, Harry 122
Rice, Mrs. 9
Rice, Robert 7, 12–14, 16, 17, 18, 32, 33
Riddick & Doles, 107
Riggs, E. Francis 124
Riley, Hezekiah 66
Robeson, Paul 67, 103, 104
Robinson, Edward 108
Robinson, W. Spottswood 114
Rockland County 121, 169, 170
Rockville Centre xii, 35, 46, 75, 99
Rockwell, G. L. 188
Roe, Ollie 18, 23, 26, 27, 30
Romerstein, 170
Roodenko, Igal 109
Roosevelt, Eleanor 85, 121, 155, 156
Roosevelt, Franklin D. 58, 59, 66, 69, 70, 85, 92, 104, 121, 155
Roosevelt, Theodore xii, 35
Rosado, Walter 183
Rosario rule 24
Rundstedt, Marshal von 84
Russell, Bertrand 80, 196
Russian Revolution 64, 209
Rustin, Bayard xiv, 86, 87, 109, 112, 113, 170, 183

S

Sacco-Vanzetti case 192
Sandino, 42, 123, 230

Satriano, Vincent 8
Satyagraha 88
Saunders, Rorie 165
Schachtman, Max 79, 80
Schaffer, Don 192
Scotic 75, 76
Scottsboro case 10, 82
Seale, Bobby 298
Seaman, Grace 46
Seawell, Att'y Gen'l Malcolm 151–160
Second Declaration of Havana 178
Selective Service 92, 187
Self-Determination of Black Belt 50
Sena, George 9, 10, 11
Serge, Victor xiii
Seymour, Whitney No., Jr. 179
Shapiro, David 179
Sheppard v. Maxwell 224
Sherman, William T. 100
Sihanouk, Prince Norodom 198
Simpson, Fuzzy 141–160
Simpson, Mrs. 143–145
Smith, Editor Hazel 120
Smith, Ian 225
Smith, J. Holmes 126, 130
SNCC 183, 201
Snyder, E. Cecil 125
Socialist Labor Party 77
Socialist Party xiv, 48, 66, 67, 68, 171
Socialist Workers Party 77, 172, 185
Southern Conference Educational Fund 120
Soviet Union 65, 69
Spanish-American War 70
Spanish Civil War 67, 71, 72
Spauldings, the 143
Spengler, Oswald 43, 53, 50, a03
Spires, Arlene 74
Spitz, George 171
Stafford, Frank 4, 5, 6
Stalingrad 205
Stalin, Joseph 50, 67, 68, 76, 80, 106
Stammites 66
Steagalls, the 165, 166
Steel, Lewis 22, a7, 29, 30
Stecher, Judge Martin 29, 30
Stevens, Judge Harold 15
Stone, Candace (Pan) 42, 48, 53, 93, 171, 181
Strachey, John 60
Sugar, Frank 7
Sugar, Margit 7, 11, 13, 19, 33
'Sunday Worker' 104

Sweezy, Paul 180
Syracuse University 37, 40, 41, 45

T

Tabor, Bob 168
Tagore, Rabindranath 123
Taikheff, Elliott 208
Tannenbaum, Ass't D. A. 31, 32
Taylor, Telford 9
Telesford, Darwin 54
Templin, Ralph 130, 132
'The Black Jacobins' 80
'The Coming Struggle for Power' 60
'The Negro Family'—The Case for National Action
   190
'The People's Voice' 64
'The Southern Negro Stirs' 119
'The Torture of Mothers' 3
Thomas, Norman 45, 66, 71, 100, 126, 128
Thomas, Walter 7, 17, 19, 22, 33
Thomas, Wilbert 209, 214
Thompson, Hanover 141–145
Thompson, Mrs. 143
Thurman, Strom 177
Till, Emmet 155
Tillich, Paul 128
Todd, Aubrey C. 109
Tomlinson, William 54
Torresola, Griselio 127, 128
Trader, Judge Merril 222–230
Tribbett, Gov. Sherman a22
Trinidad Oil Workers Union 68
Trotsky, Leon xiii, 79, 230
Trotskyists 66, 68, 76, 79
Truman, Harry 105, 106, 114, 127, 128, 129
Tucker, Bishop 122
Tukhashevsky, Marshal 84

U

United Nations 196
U. S. v. Terminiello 131
Universal Negro Improvement Assoc. 50
Upshure, Anne 54
Upshure, Theodore 54
Urban League 209

V

Valera, Gen. 127
Valle, Hernandez 133

Van den Heuvel, William 30
Varadero Beach 167
Vaughn, Ray 46
Veblen, Thorstein xiii
Vegetarians 77
Vieques 127
Voronov 205

W

WOR 159
WPA xiv, 58, 59, 72, 74, 75
Wade, Andrew 118
Wagner, Mayor Robert 3
War Crimes Commission 196, 197, 200
Ward, Harry F. 77
'Washington Post' 224
Watson, James 227
Weber, Max 60
Wechsler, James 62
Wehrmacht 78, 84
Weiss 65
Weissman, George 144
Welch, Eddie 66, 67
West, Don 120
West, Irene 36
West, Jerome 208–220
White Citizens Councils 181
White, Walter 85
Wilkins, Roy, 143, 159
Williams, Byron 124, 125
Williams, Robert 142–169
Willis, Edwin 180–182
Willis, Mary 211
Wilson, Woodrow 35
Winship. Blanton 125
Winston, Henry 168
Wolf, Major 98, 99
Woods, Love 168
World War I xiii, 106, 123
World War II xiv, 38, 118, 230
Worker Education Project 66
Workers Defence League 109
Workers Party 80, 81
Worrell, Jim 101
Worthy, William 171, 175, 176, 183
Wright, Ellen 196
Wright, Nathan 109
Wright, Richard 197
Wulf, Melvin 179

Y

Young Com. League xiii, xiv, 43, 45, 50, 53, 71
Youth vs. War & Fascism 196

Z

ZANU 221
Zollinger, Bill 122